The BRAND MANAGEMENT Checklist

proven tools and techniques for creating winning brands

BRAD VANAUKEN

KOGAN
PAGE

First published in 2002

Kogan Page Limited
120 Pentonville Road
London N1 9JN

British Library Cataloguing in Publication Data

A CIP record for this book is available from the British Library

ISBN 0 7494 3699 9

Typeset by Saxon Graphics Ltd, Derby
Printed and bound in Great Britain

311081

Contents

SECTION 3 BUILDING THE BRAND

SECTION 4   LEVERAGING THE BRAND

SECTION 5   BRAND METRICS

SECTION 6   OTHER BRAND MANAGEMENT CONSIDERATIONS

SECTION 7   BRAND MANAGEMENT: A SUMMARY

the right brand benefits 277; The importance of superior products and services to strong brands 279; Create a total brand experience for your customers 279; The future of brands: co-creating products, services and experiences with customers 279; Celebration of the brand manager – it is an underrated, difficult, but intrinsically rewarding job 280; Waxing philosophical: brand management at its best 280

Foreword

A few years back, the topic of branding began to surface on the radar screens of senior executives. Managers everywhere began to grow in their appreciation for brands as they began to recognize the impact the brand has on overall business performance. Brands became recognized and promoted as assets for the corporation, and the language of branding became required vernacular for anyone involved in business.

With this recognition of the importance of the brand came a flurry of industry conferences, published white papers, academic books, and business articles on the subject. Everywhere you turned, it seemed that someone was talking about branding. It was in this environment that I first met Brad. We were both working inside major corporations and tasked with the complex challenge of managing our brands in dynamic business environments. While both of us found the plethora of material written on the subject intriguing, we agreed that much of it only began to scratch the surface in addressing the broad range of issues we were facing in managing our brands.

There can be little argument that strong brands enable organizations to prosper. But how do you get there? After all, strong brands do not just happen. Rather, they result when a series of cross-organizational fundamentals, designed against a common strategy, come together in alignment and are delivered through every business process and point of contact the organization has with its customers. Successfully managing a brand goes beyond understanding the fundamentals of the branding process – it also requires formally applying and establishing them within the organization.

In practice, brand management involves solving complex issues. How do you go about obtaining the kind of information that will allow you to position your brand in the marketplace? How do you build a unique relationship with your customer when competition is fierce? How do you communicate and translate your strategy consistently throughout the range of interactions your customers will have with your brand? How do you stand out with your brand in the market when you are working with limited resources? And how do you get every part of the organization to live the promise of the brand? These are the questions and challenges brand managers face in their day-to-day responsibilities. And it is for this reason that *The Brand Management Checklist* is so important.

If you are a brand and marketing professional chartered with managing brands inside your organization, *The Brand Management Checklist* is an essential resource for you. Based on extensive research and Brad's first-hand experience, *The Brand Management Checklist* is a comprehensive guide unlike any other on the market today. It walks you through the complex range of topics facing brand managers today and is organized in an easy-to-understand, quick reference style that will prove useful to return to time and again. It is ideal for practitioners looking to understand the various components involved in the brand management process, and especially tailored to those looking to directly apply what they have learnt.

The robust set of tools incorporated throughout the book will prove immediately useful. The comprehensive checklists included at the conclusion of each chapter help you assess your own organization's brand health and help you directly apply what you have learnt throughout the chapter to your own brand building challenges. Importantly, the checklists also enable you to prioritize elements that may need immediate attention and will subsequently help guide you in both short and long-term decision making.

Brad provides a comprehensive overview of the brand management process. This overview, unique in its comprehensive design, helps articulate how the various components of branding come together and work as part of an overall system. Understanding this system is critical for those charged with managing brands within organizations, because it helps outline the linkages and processes which must be developed to establish and maintain brand management as a discipline within an organization.

If you are chartered to increase the value of your brand, I know you will find *The Brand Management Checklist* an important companion in your quest. I am confident it will prove to be an essential reference tool for you, and one that you will return to time and again. Read it. Write in it. Keep it on your desk. And most importantly, apply what you learn to your own brand building activities and watch the value of your brand and business bottom line increase.

Amy Kelm
Worldwide Consumer Marketing Manager
Hewlett-Packard

About the author

Brad VanAuken, President and founder of BrandForward, Inc, has over 20 years' experience as a marketing manager. BrandForward provides the following consulting services: brand strategy formulation, brand positioning, brand research, brand equity measurement, brand building on the World Wide Web, internal brand building, brand extension and brand education and training. Previously, Brad was vice president of marketing at Element K (one of the world's leading e-learning companies). He built Element K's marketing function and brand, propelling the brand from relative obscurity in a highly fragmented market to industry leadership in less than 18 months. Prior to that, he was the director of brand management & marketing at Hallmark Cards where he was responsible for the marketplace positioning of all North American brands. During his tenure, Hallmark market share increased by four points, Hallmark rose in the EquiTrend national quality brand ranking from 7th to 4th and Hallmark received the Brand Management of the Year award from Sales and Marketing Executives International. Prior to joining Hallmark, he worked for Arthur Andersen & Co consulting to the advertising industry.

Brad graduated from Rensselaer Polytechnic Institute with a BS in Management and Harvard Business School with an MBA. He received the (Kansas City) Top 25 UP AND COMERS award in 1997 and is listed in *Who's Who in the World*.

Brad is a well-known and sought after expert on brand management and marketing. He has spoken to groups such as The Conference Board, American Marketing Association, Institute for International Research (IIR), Stanford University, Vanderbilt University, The Buffalo Ad Club, and Southwestern Bell Yellow Pages. He has been the American Management Association's featured speaker on measuring corporate brand value. He was a member of The Conference Board's working group on Managing the Corporate Brand and APQC's Brand Building & Communication Benchmarking Study sponsor group. He chaired the IIR Brand Masters conference and the IQPC conference on Internal Brand Building. He is a founding member of the World Class Branding Association and is on The Advertising Council of Rochester's board of directors.

BrandForward's clients have included AAA, Allstate Insurance, Aris Vision Institute, Black & Veatch, Bush Brothers, California Casualty, CBC/Radio-Canada, Hallmark Cards, Kaiser Permanente, Motion Engineering, Mutual of Omaha, Nationwide Insurance, Potomac Electric Power Company, Royal Appliance (Dirt Devil), The Ivy League Magazine Network, The Marley Cooling Tower Company, The Nature Conservancy, Vectren and Xerox Corporation.

Acknowledgements

As I have discovered, while writing a book is a somewhat daunting task, it is not an entirely solitary task. I am indebted to the following people for contributing to the success of this book: Lance D'Amico, Julianne Hanes, Jeff Kuzmich, Lance Teitsworth and Dan Vandenberg. I am particularly grateful to Amy Kelm for agreeing to write the Foreword and to Susan Stim for her invaluable help in editing the book.

Some sections of this book have previously been published, and I am grateful for the permission of the copyright holders for them to be reprinted here: versions of Chapter 11, 'Brand building on the Internet,' as 'Branding.com: building and leveraging brands online,' in The Advertiser, Oct/Nov 2000, pp 70–76 (copyright Association of National Advertisers) and as 'Branding.com:brand building on the internet,' in *Admap*, issue 421 (October 2001) pp 21–25 (copyright World Advertising Research Center); and Chapter 12, 'Developing a brand-building organization,' as 'Developing the brand building organisation,' in *Journal of Brand Management*, **7** (4) (March 2001) pp 281–90 (copyright Henry Stewart Publications).

Introduction

The brand is increasingly becoming the key source of differentiation that guides customer purchase choice. It is the focal point around which an organization defines how it will uniquely deliver value to the customer for a profit – effectively embodying the 'heart and soul' of that organization. The brand's promise is delivered through its products, services, and consumer communication – the total customer relationship and experience. If the brand is well conceived and consistently delivered through all business processes and customer contacts, the organization will grow and prosper.

Not too long ago, marketers at consumer product companies seemed to be the only ones interested in talking about brand management and branding. But these days, all kinds of organizations are recognizing the importance of branding. In the past few years, museums, universities, restaurants, churches, and individuals have approached me to help them build their brands. And now, it seems as though even the average person on the street is talking about brands.

So why has this marketing discipline become so popular? In an age of increasing product commoditization and choice, the brand is an easy way for people to break through the clutter. It helps them simplify certain choices in their lives. And brands are increasingly fulfilling people's needs for affiliation and identification – needs that traditional institutions are struggling to deliver as well as they used to.

Senior management interest in brands has soared for a variety of reasons:

- Studies have shown that more and more categories are moving toward commoditization as companies: first, use increasingly sophisticated customer research to understand and address customer needs; and second, are able to quickly determine and emulate the best practices of their competitors. A strong brand can help combat category commoditization and the resulting downward pressures on price.

- To shift some leverage back to the manufacturer from the retailer. (This is a relationship the manufacturer can own with the consumer.)
- Brands provide a flexible platform for growth (beyond current categories).
- Recent deregulation in several industries (notably the utilities) has resulted in a need for differentiation.
- Increased competition.
- The emergence of the Internet.

Branding also becomes a critical issue for businesses that are spun off from the parent company (such as AT&T's Bell Labs, now Lucent Technologies), and as more and more companies merge or acquire one another. The brand identity of the new combined enterprise becomes a critical decision.

Organizations have discovered that brands are perhaps their most important assets (along with their people) for a number of reasons. There is increasing evidence and consensus that strong brands deliver the following benefits to organizations:

- increased revenues and market share;
- decreased price sensitivity;
- increased customer loyalty;
- additional leverage with retailers (for manufacturers);
- increased profitability;
- increased stock price and shareholder value;
- increased clarity of vision;
- increased ability to mobilize an organization's people and focus its activities;
- increased ability to expand into new product and service categories;
- increased ability to attract and retain high quality employees.

If brand management is new to you or your organization, you most likely need a quick but comprehensive overview of the key elements necessary for successful brand building. (I certainly would have found this very helpful a few years ago when I assumed the role of Director of Brand Management and Marketing for Hallmark Cards.) So, with this in mind, I have taken what I have learnt from a wide variety of sources: books, seminars, consultants, industry benchmarking studies, my own consulting on this subject, and most importantly, hands-on experience establishing brand management functions and brand building cultures at Hallmark Cards and at Element K, a leading online learning company.

I wrote this book to be a thorough but pithy quick reference guide to all of the most important aspects of brand management and marketing. I have included every concept, template, formula, worksheet, research finding, 'rule of thumb', checklist and assessment tool that I have found to be useful in building strong brands throughout my 20 years as a marketing practitioner. Feel free to read the book a chapter at a time or to 'zero in' on the topics that are of greatest interest to you.

For most topics, I include a brand management checklist at the end of the chapter. Use this checklist to identify the areas where your brand practices are strong and where they may be weak. Also use it to identify brand management activities and approaches that are new to you. The checklist takes the form of questions. The more questions to which you can answer 'yes', the better you are doing. After answering all of the questions, it should be obvious which areas of brand practice require your attention. If you have answered 'no' to a question, it should be clear what the associated action step should be. If it is not clear, you should at least be able to identify the general area in which you need help and the type of resources that may be of help to you. My consulting firm, BrandForward Inc. (www.BrandForward.com) also offers workshops to help you develop action plans from this checklist.

In many chapters, I have include online resource sections to help you further explore topics in much greater detail than I can cover in this book. I also provide 'Did you know?' boxed-out sections throughout the book, featuring interesting facts, rules of thumb, and other handy information you may find useful as you manage your brand.

Did you know...?

- In December of 1993, Charles Cobb purchased the PanAm trademark for $1.32 billion.

- Disney paid more than five times book value for Capital Cities/ABC (Shultz and Anders Gronstedt, 1997).

- In 1988, Phillip Morris Co. acquired Kraft Foods for $12.9 billion, $11.6 billion over book value.

BOOK OVERVIEW

The book's first section is an introduction to brand management, and it assumes no prior knowledge of this subject. I begin with a story that communicates the importance of brand management in a simple but compelling way. The story helps people 'internalize' the importance of brand management by asking them to visualize a situation in which a very close friend behaves in an unacceptable way. It then asks for their reactions, including the feelings the friend's behaviour evokes. I then retell the story with one twist: the person who behaves badly is a complete stranger. This story reinforces *the brand's essential role in creating emotional connections and building relationships,* and I have found it to be a very effective introduction to the essence of brands and brand management.

Next, in order to establish a common working vocabulary (something brand managers must do within their organizations), I define a number of *brand-related terms* as a quick reference.

The introduction section ends with an *overview of the brand management process*, to help put the rest of the book in perspective. Many marketing practitioners have unsuccessfully searched for this overview and the context it provides. Most experts focus on brand positioning, brand naming, brand identity, brand equity research or other brand management specialities, but not the entire process. My clients find this visual and verbal overview to be very helpful. The remainder of the book roughly follows this brand management process.

In the next section, I cover brand design. Brand management must start here, with a thorough *understanding of the target consumer*. Do the brand marketers have a profound understanding of the consumer? Do they understand the consumer's benefit structure (including functional, emotional, experiential, self-expressive, cost-of-entry, and differentiating benefits) and how it varies by consumer segment? Do they know how to acquire and analyze this information?

Before marketers can design and position the brand, they must have not only a profound understanding of the consumer, but also a *thorough knowledge of the competitive set*. The best benefit for a brand to deliver is one that is very important to the consumer, for which your organization has unique capabilities, and that competitors are not adequately addressing.

I then get into the 'meat' of *brand design*: defining the brand essence, promise, personality and positioning. Six components of brand design are discussed: target consumer, frame of reference, brand essence, brand promise, brand personality and brand positioning. The chapter includes templates and exercises to develop each of these brand design components and also features three brand positioning case studies.

The final chapter in this section covers *brand identity standards and systems*, the codification of the brand design. This chapter addresses the key practical considerations when designing or revamping brand identity standards and system, covers brand naming and the importance of colour in brand identity development, and also highlights 'tools' that can aid in creating brand identity consistency throughout the enterprise. It concludes with a comprehensive brand identity worksheet.

The next section focuses on building the brand, and it begins by showing the reader how to create brand insistence. This chapter gets to the heart of brand building. It presents BrandForward's model for *creating consumer brand insistence* in detail. This model is based on extensive research across multiple product and service categories, and it demonstrates that five common elements drive consumers to insist upon a particular brand: awareness, accessibility, value, relevant differentiation, and emotional connection. This chapter focuses on different brands to emphasize the importance of each driver (for instance, Coca-Cola: the power of accessibility, McDonald's: the importance of consistent icon repetition, Harley-Davidson: the power of emotional connection building). The chapter concludes with a case study on managing brand equity.

In the *'Brand advertising'* chapter, I cover the basics of translating a chosen brand strategy and position into effective advertising. This chapter includes choosing an advertising agency and development of the agency brief. It also includes advertising effectiveness evaluations (for print, radio, television, outdoor and overall), advertising 'rules of thumb', an overview of advertising research, a quick advertising assessment tool and a comprehensive listing of online advertising resources.

Next, I provide brief examples of over 60 different types of *non-traditional brand marketing techniques which work*, including those applicable for small businesses and business-to-business organizations. The categories include membership organizations, larger than life brand owners, ingredient branding, museums and factory tours, and flagship stores. This chapter also features a list of considerations in getting the news media to cover your story. I also briefly touch upon customer relationship management (CRM) and creative problem solving and ideation techniques.

I devote an entire chapter to *brand building on the Internet*. This chapter compares and contrasts 'dirt world' and cyberspace brand building. It presents 30 techniques that effectively build brands online. Specific topics include creating a brand-building Web site, community building techniques, online advertising and promotion, search engine and directory placement, creating effective banner ads, leveraging online newsletters, building a successful online store, and online brand marketing resources.

In this chapter, I also feature an overview of the results of *BrandForward's acclaimed Cyberbranding 2000 Study*. This study, based on a comprehensive survey of over 1,500 online shoppers, addresses the questions most often asked by marketing executives about building and leveraging brands on the Internet. It identifies major implications for pure Internet and 'brick and mortar' brands.

I then focus on what may be the most important and difficult component of brand management within a large enterprise – the non-marketing aspects of brand building: *developing the brand-building organization*. This is a topic most academicians, consultants and other non-practitioners nearly always overlook. This topic answers the all-important questions of, 'How can we make the brand promise real?' 'How can we get our organization to deliver against the promise?' and 'How can we align all that we do with the brand's positioning?' In this chapter, I share specific tactics that people in a wide variety of organizations have found to be helpful in addressing the most prevalent internal brand building issues.

In my *'Integrated brand marketing'* chapter, I outline all the components that must be integrated to deliver consistently against the brand promise. I cover traditional marketing elements such as product, packaging, pricing, distribution, advertising, promotion and publicity. I also cover human resource and organization design components which must be aligned in support of the brand's promise, and an overview of the most important integrative mechanisms.

Brands are more than names and logos that are applied to products and services. They are the source of integrated consumer experiences. The next chapter addresses how to create those experiences by featuring several examples of situations in which the *total brand experience* has been created. It also provides a simple list of questions to help you optimize your total brand experience. Finally, the chapter provides an overview of effective crisis management, or what to do when the brand experience goes awry.

The next section covers the 'R' in brand 'ROI': leveraging the brand for increased revenues and profits. I focus on two ways of doing this, through *brand extension and leveraging the brand globally*. In the 'Brand extension' chapter, I discuss ways to leverage a brand's equity and prolong its life by extending the brand into new product and service categories. I also touch upon the most likely brand extension pitfalls and how to avoid them. The global branding chapter begins by highlighting the advantages of global branding, and then discusses the most important considerations in building global brands.

The next section addresses *brand metrics*. Most organizations conduct ongoing market (consumer and competitor) research to help them position and reposition their brands. Organizations should also monitor and measure their brands' equities. Some organizations also measure the effectiveness of specific marketing programs. This chapter covers the spectrum of *brand research* (from logo recognition and recall to brand extension), emphasizing in-depth qualitative techniques that lead to a better understanding of consumer needs.

How can you manage what you have not measured? This chapter provides a detailed look at brand equity measurement. It is based on BrandForward's brand insistence model, which incorporates the latest thinking on *brand equity measurement*. The model includes the five brand equity drivers covered in Chapter 8 and measures of usage, preference, consideration set ranking, loyalty and vitality.

The next section covers two miscellaneous brand management topics: the *relationship of brand management issues to organization age and size*, and *legal issues in brand management*. Here the book looks at how older, larger companies differ from younger, smaller companies on the following dimensions and how those differences affect the brand management issues they are likely to encounter: leadership, size, business scope, brand structure, organization infrastructure, corporate culture, marketplace, decision making, financial resources, primary marketing method, brand identity, brand awareness and esteem and brand differentiation.

The chapter on 'Legal issues in brand management' focuses on the most important concepts marketing managers should understand about trademark law and protection. It also covers trade dress, trade secrets, false or deceptive advertising and intellectual property issues on the Internet. It concludes with a listing of online resources for legal issues in brand management.

The final section serves as a *brand management summary*. It includes a chapter that outlines the 40 most common brand problems organizations encounter in managing, building and leveraging their brands. It briefly analyzes each problem and offers practical suggestions on how to address the problem. These real life problems are based on the experience of marketing practitioners in a variety of organizations.

Discover the 70 plus most important considerations in managing, building and leveraging strong brands in the chapter on 'Keys to success in brand building'. And, in my 'Brand management and marketing resources' chapter, check out a list of online brand management and marketing resources not covered in other chapters, including URLs for a wide variety of brand management and marketing articles and publications.

The final chapter explains the value of a *brand audit*. Through a brand audit, an organization can assess the strengths, weaknesses, opportunities and threats of its brands and its brand management practices. In this chapter, I outline the components of a brand audit, offer suggestions on what to look for when selecting an outside brand auditor, and feature a quick (six question) brand health assessment.

One of the book's two appendices features *references and further readings*. The reference section cites over 150 books, papers and articles that I referenced to write this book – some of the best-written documents available on various aspects of brand management.

Finally, congratulate yourself on how much you now know about brand management with my short and interesting *brand management quiz*. It touches upon some key brand management and marketing concepts, including brand differentiation, brand loyalty and ingredient branding.

Section 1

Introduction to brand management

1

A brand is a friend

People often ask me, 'What is brand equity?' There are many ways to answer this. Some would say it is everything associated with the brand that adds to or subtracts from the value it provides to a product or service. Others would emphasize the financial value of the brand asset. Still others stress the consumer loyalty or price premium generated by brand equity. Some even talk about the permission and flexibility a brand gives an organization to extend into new product and service categories. While all of these are very important parts of brand equity, I think the following story best illustrates what brand equity is.

Imagine you are having lunch with a long-time and very good friend. Several times throughout the lunch, she makes disparaging and sarcastic remarks that make you feel bad. You think to yourself, 'This just isn't like her. She must be having a bad day.' You meet with her again a week or two later, and again she acts in a negative and bad-tempered way. You think to yourself, 'Something must be going on in her life that she's really struggling with. Maybe she is having difficulties with her job or her health or her marriage or her children.' You may even ask her if everything is all right. She snaps back, 'Of course it is.'

Your interaction with her continues in this vein over the next couple of months. You continue to try to be supportive, but she is definitely getting on your nerves. After many meetings and much interaction, you finally decide that she is a changed person and someone with whom you prefer to spend less and less time. You may get to this point after a few months, or perhaps even after a year or more. She does not change, and eventually the relationship peters out.

Now consider for a moment that the person you first had lunch with was the same person as before, with one exception: she was a total stranger to you. You had not met her previously and she was not your dear friend. I would guess that after enduring many caustic comments and being insulted a few times at that lunch, your first impression would not be very positive. In fact, you would probably be inclined not to get together with that person again. You would probably walk away from that lunch thinking, 'What a miserable person. I hope I don't run into her again.'

In both of these scenarios it is the same person behaving the same way in the same situation. Yet in the first scenario, you are very quick to forgive the behaviour. In fact, you feel a lot of concern towards her. In the second scenario, you cannot wait for the lunch to be over and you hope never to see her again.

In the first scenario, the person was a long-time good friend. She had a lot of equity with you. In the second scenario, she had no equity at all. You see, if people or brands have a lot of equity – that is, if you know, like and trust them – you will 'cut them a lot of slack' even if they repeatedly fail to meet your expectations. If a person, product, service or organization has no equity with you, no emotional connection and no trust, then you are much less inclined to forgive unmet expectations.

Brand equity creates a relationship and a strong bond which grows over time. It is often so strong that it compensates for performance flaws: an out-of-stock situation, poor customer service, a product that falls apart, inconvenient store hours, a higher-than-average-price, and so on. In the end, you want to deliver good quality and good value, innovation, relevant differentiation, convenience and accessibility with your brand. However, we must never forget that building brand equity is like building a close friendship. It requires a consistent relationship over time, trust, and an emotional connection.

Robert T. Blanchard of Procter & Gamble had this to say about brands in his 'Parting Essay', dated July 1999:

A brand is the personification of a product, service or even entire company. Like any person, a brand has a physical 'body': in P&G's case, the products and/or services it provides. Also, like a person, a brand has a name, a personality, character, and a reputation. Like a person, you can respect, like, and even love a brand. You can think of it as a deep personal friend, or merely an acquaintance. You can view it as dependable or undependable; principled or opportunistic; caring or capricious. Just as you like to be around certain people and not others, so also do you like to be with certain brands and not others. Also, like a person, a brand must mature and change its product over time. But its character, and core beliefs shouldn't change. Neither should its fundamental personality and outlook on life. People have character… so do brands. A person's character flows from his or her integrity: the ability to deliver under pressure, the willingness to do what is right rather than what is expedient. You judge a person's character by his/her past performance and the way he/she thinks and acts in both good times, and especially bad. The same is true of brands.

Did you know...?

- Familiarity (exposure and/or use) leads to liking.[1]

- Declining brands tend to lose buyers while the brands' loyalty and purchase rates stay stable among remaining buyers.[2]

- In most product categories, price is the primary purchase incentive for no more than 15 per cent to 35 per cent of all customers.[3]

NOTES

1   Source: Ehrenberg, Andrew, Neil Barnard and John Scriven, Differentation or Salience, *Journal of Advertising Research*, November/December 1997, p9.
2   Source: Andrew Ehrenberg, Description and prescription, *Journal of Advertising Research*, November/December 1997.
3   Source: Clancy, Kevin J, At what profit price?, *Brandweek*, vol 38, issue 25, June 23, 1997, pp24–28.

2

Understanding the language of branding

It is important to establish a common brand management vocabulary in your organization. Establishing this common vocabulary will ensure that people can communicate with fewer misunderstandings. More importantly, it will help communicate and reinforce key brand management principles.

I worked with one organization in which different managers used different terms to describe positioning the brand. Terms ranged from 'essence' and 'promise' to 'position' and 'unique value proposition'. This caused great confusion. I worked with another organization that struggled with the difference between master brand, family brand, parent brand, umbrella brand, corporate brand, brand, sub-brand, endorsed brand, product brand, and so on. The aim is to agree to one set of terms and to simplify the brand architecture.

Brand

The American Marketing Association describes a brand as a 'name, term, sign, symbol or design, or a combination of them intended to identify the goods and services of one seller or group of sellers and to differentiate them from those of competition'. More importantly, a brand is the source of a promise to the consumer. It promises relevant differentiated benefits. Everything an organization does should be focused on enhancing delivery against its brand's promise.

Combining a few different definitions, a brand is the name and symbols that identify:

- The source of a relationship with the consumer.
- The source of a promise to the consumer.
- The unique source of products and services.
- In their book _The 22 Immutable Laws of Branding,_ brand management experts Al Ries and Laura Ries (1998) offer another definition for brand: 'What's a brand? A singular idea or concept that you own inside the mind of the prospect.'
- The sum total of each customer's experience with your organization.

Brand essence

This is the heart and soul of a brand – a brand's fundamental nature or quality. Usually stated in two to three words, a brand's essence is the one constant across product categories and throughout the world. Some examples are: 'Nike: Genuine Athletic Performance', 'Hallmark: Caring Shared', 'Disney: Fun Family Entertainment' or 'Disneyworld, Magical Fun', 'The Nature Conservancy: Saving Great Places'. (Typically, it is rare for an organization's brand essence and slogan to be the same. For instance, Nike's essence – 'genuine athletic performance' – was translated to the following two slogans: 'Just do it!' and 'I can'. But 'saving great places' happens to be the Nature Conservancy's brand essence and its slogan.)

Kevin Keller, brand expert and author of the popular brand book, _Strategic Brand Management_ (1998), has coined a term 'brand mantra', which is very closely related to brand essence. The 'mantra' concept reinforces the role of brand essence in internal communication. Kevin says the brand mantra should: 'define the category of business for the brand and set brand boundaries. It should also clarify what is unique about the brand. It should be memorable. As a result it should be short, crisp and vivid in meaning. Ideally, the brand mantra would also stake out ground that is personally meaningful and relevant to as many employees as possible.'

Brand promise

To be successfully positioned in the marketplace, a brand must promise differentiated benefits that are relevant and compelling to the consumer. The benefits can be functional, experiential, emotional or self-expressive. A brand promise is often stated as: _Only [brand name] delivers [benefit] in [product or service category]._ Sometimes, with corporate brands, it is stated as: _[Brand name] is the (trusted/quality/innovative) leader in [benefit] in the [product or service category]._ It is important to develop compelling proof points in support of the brand promise.

The brand promise is one of the most important brand concepts. A brand promise must:

- address important consumer needs;
- leverage your organization's strengths;
- give you a competitive advantage through differentiation;
- inspire, energize and mobilize your people;
- drive every organizational decision, system, action and process;
- manifest itself in your organization's products and services.

As Kristin Zhivago, respected marketing consultant and editor of the *Marketing Technology* newsletter, puts it in the July/August 1994 double issue of her newsletter:

> The simple truth about branding – a brand is not an icon, a slogan, or a mission statement. It is a promise – a promise your company can keep. First you find out, using research, what promises your customers want companies like yours to make and keep, using the products, processes and people in your company. Then you look at your competition and decide which promise would give you the best competitive advantage. This is the promise you make and keep in every marketing activity, every action, every corporate decision, every customer interaction. You promote it internally and externally. The promise drives budgets and stops arguments. If everyone in the company knows what the promise is, and knows that they will be rewarded or punished depending on the personal commitment to the promise, politics and personal turf issues start to disappear.

Visually, the brand promise should drive each of the elements shown in Figure 2.1.

Brand positioning

This is the way the brand is perceived within a given competitive set in the consumer's mind. Ideally, it is a function of the brand's promise and how the brand compares with other choices with regard to quality, innovation, perceived leadership, value, prestige, trust, safety, reliability, performance, convenience, concern for customers, social responsibility, technological superiority and so on. One could argue that the brand essence and promise are also a part of the brand positioning. Given that, brand positioning is very similar to what I refer to as brand design in Chapter 3.

Brand personality

This refers to adjectives that describe the brand (such as fun, kind, sexy, safe, sincere, sophisticated, cheerful, old fashioned, reliable, progressive). How consumers perceive a

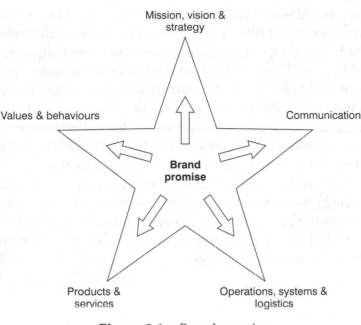

Figure 2.1 *Brand promise*

brand's personality is often discovered through qualitative research, by asking people to describe the brand as if it were a person or an animal.

Brand associations

This refers to anything a consumer associates with the brand in his or her mind. As David Aaker, 'guru' of brand management, points out, these associations could be organizational, product related, symbolic or personified. If there is a strong brand connection with a specific retail outlet, the associations could also be based on the retail experience.

Brand equity

This is the commercial value of all associations and expectations (positive and negative) that people have of an organization and its products and services due to all experiences of, communications with, and perceptions of the brand over time. This value can be measured in several ways: as the economic value of the brand asset itself, the price premium (to the end consumer or the trade) that the brand commands, the long-term consumer loyalty the brand evokes, or the market share gains it results in, among many others. From an economist's perspective, brand equity is the power of the brand to shift the consumer demand curve of a product or service (to achieve a price premium or a market share gain).

To use a metaphor, brand equity is like a pond. People may not know how long the pond has been around or when it first filled with water, but they know that it supports life, from fish and frogs to ducks and deer. It may also be a source of recreation, irrigation and possibly even human drinking water. Clearly it is a valuable resource. But many people take the pond for granted. It seems as if nothing can diminish its supply of water, but yet we sometimes notice that it rises with the spring rains or lowers after a long draught or excessive overuse for irrigation. Brand equity is a reservoir of goodwill. Brand-building activities consistently pursued over time will ensure that the reservoir remains full, while neglecting those activities or taking actions that might deplete those reserves will reduce the reservoir, imperceptibly at first, but soon all too noticeably until it is too late and all that is left is mud.

This illustrates one of the most difficult problems in brand management. While brand equity is critically important to a company's success, because of its reservoir-like nature, it is often taken for granted, overly drawn upon, and not adequately replenished, especially in times of crisis and to meet short-term needs.

Brand image

This is the totality of perceptions resulting from all experience with and knowledge of the brand. Brand image is how consumers perceive the brand.

Brand identity

This refers to a combination of visual, auditory, and other sensory components that create recognition, represent the brand promise, provide differentiation, create communications synergy, and are proprietary.[1] Some define brand identity more broadly to include almost everything in a brand's design: essence, promise, personality and positioning. The more specific definition used in this book reflects the most common usage of the term, especially by firms focused on the creation of brand identity standards and systems.

Names and nomenclature, logotypes, symbols and other graphic devices, distinctive shapes and colours, brand voice and visual style, sounds, jingles and other mnemonic devices, typography, theme lines or slogans, and characters that are uniquely associated with a brand are all components of a brand's identity.[2] Textures, scents, flavours, and other sensory elements can also be components of a brand's identity.

Brand architecture (or brand structure)

Think of this as a brand's family tree or its hierarchy. It is how an organization organizes the various named entities within its portfolio. Ideally, the brand architecture is simple with no more than two levels: brand and sub-brands. In fact, brand/sub-brand is the type of architecture most often used. It takes many forms, mostly based upon the type of name used for the sub-brands. Some organizations add a third level: named products. But any more than two levels can be confusing.

The four general types of architecture are:

- master brand;
- brand/sub-brand;
- endorsed brand;
- separate (stand-alone or independent) brands.

Brand architecture addresses the following:

- number of separately named entities;
- criteria for becoming a separately named entity;
- levels of relationships between separately named entities;
- naming and other brand identity conventions for each level;
- the nature of the relationships between the named entities at different levels.

Trade dress

This describes the aesthetic elements that provide legal protection for a brand's identity.

Brand portfolio

This is the mix of brands and sub-brands owned by an organization. This portfolio should be actively managed to ensure effective, efficient brand management.

Corporate brand

This is the brand bearing the company name. It is always the highest in a brand hierarchy.

Master brand

This is the dominant, highest level brand in a brand hierarchy. Corporate brands are master brands. Parent brands may or may not be master brands.

Parent brand

This is a brand that is extended into more than one product category. It may or may not be the same as the corporate brand. Parent brands offer the following advantages:

- less expensive new product launches;
- trust/assurance;
- marketing economies of scale.

Sub-brand

This is a new brand that is combined with a parent or corporate brand in the brand identity system. The sub-brand can make the parent brand more vital and relevant to a new consumer segment or within a new product category.

Endorsed brand

This is the primary name the consumer is intended to use to refer to a product. It is a brand that is endorsed by the parent or corporate brand in the brand identity system. The parent brand is also identified with the product; however, the endorsed brand is given much greater visual weight than the parent brand. In this situation, the corporate or parent brand lends credibility or assurance to the endorsed brand without overpowering it with its own associations.

Brand extension

This refers to the introduction of an existing brand into a new product category or market segment. If this is done by combining the existing brand with a new brand, the new brand is called a sub-brand. If executed properly, brand extensions can broaden and clarify the meaning of the brand. If executed improperly, they can dilute or confuse the meaning of the brand.

Marketing plan

A marketing plan is a request for funds in return for a promised level of incremental revenues, unit sales, market share or profits.[3] One can develop marketing plans for products, services, market segments or brands. The critical components of a marketing plan include the following:

- Summary.
- Objectives (attract new consumers, create new uses, increase share of requirements, incentivize a trial, encourage repeat purchase, encourage add-on purchase, increase awareness, increase loyalty, change value perception, increase emotional bond, extend into new product and service categories, etc).
- Situation analysis:
  - market analysis;
  - competitive context;
  - customer profile (segments, needs, attitudes, behaviours, insights, etc).
- Strategies and tactics (touching upon all key marketing components that will be used: product, packaging, pricing, distribution, advertising, publicity, sales promotion, selling, etc). Be specific.

- Operations considerations (impact on plant capacity, need for new assets, etc).
- Financial projections:
    - pro forma profit and loss statements, balance sheets, cash flows, etc;
    - including funds required to execute plan.
- Supporting customer research (qualitative research, concept testing, volumetric modelling, market test results, etc).
- Risks and contingency plans.

Brand plan

Similar to a marketing plan, a brand plan's objectives focus primarily on changing or improving brand equity components, like those listed below. Increased market share is a frequently specified brand objective:

- brand awareness;
- brand accessibility;
- brand value;
- brand relevant differentiation;
- brand emotional connection;
- brand vitality;
- brand loyalty;
- brand personality;
- other brand associations.

Did you know…?

Advertising rules of thumb:

The cost of airing ineffective commercials is very large compared to the cost of copy testing, [… so] test all copy before airing it [… and] when it comes to ineffective advertising… cancel the media schedule [and] wait until you have an effective commercial.

Continuity pays off. You will do best to advertise steadily to changing audiences (versus bunching your media placement into flights).[4]

NOTES

1   Definition courtesy of Lister Butler Consulting of New York.
2   Courtesy of Lister Butler Consulting of New York.
3   Source: *What are the Key Issues to be Covered in My Marketing Plan* [Online] www.uwa.com/marketing/consultants/mrktplan.htm 8/7/01
4   Source: from a research analysis of data on exposure of frequency compiled for the Coalition for Brand Equity, cited by Kenneth A. Longman of Longman-Moran Analytics, Inc. in If Not Effective Frequency, Then What?, *Journal of Advertising Research*, July/August 1997, pp 44–50.

3

The brand management process: an overview

The brand management process starts with a deep understanding of consumers and competitors. You will need to fully understand the consumer benefit structure by segment, including which benefits are cost-of-entry and which are differentiating. In-depth qualitative consumer research will help uncover this information. You will also need to know which benefits each competitor delivers in consumers' minds. Ultimately, you will need to know which benefits are important, personally relevant, unique and differentiating, purchase motivating, and appropriate for your brand. Consumer benefits can be functional, emotional, experiential or self-expressive.

Once you know this, you can begin to design your brand. Start by defining the target consumer. Next, define your brand's essence. In designing your brand's promise, you must choose the differentiating benefits your brand will own. You must also decide what personality you want your brand to have. Finally, define your brand's competitive frame of reference and map out how your brand is positioned against competitors. Although this may sound like a linear process, it is actually iterative and even organic. In the end, though, you will have determined each of the elements of your brand's design.

Figure 3.1 provides an overview of the brand management process.

Once the brand is designed, this design must drive all of your consumer communication, all your other marketing elements, and your organization's design, particularly the company culture and what Michael Porter, Harvard Business School professor and

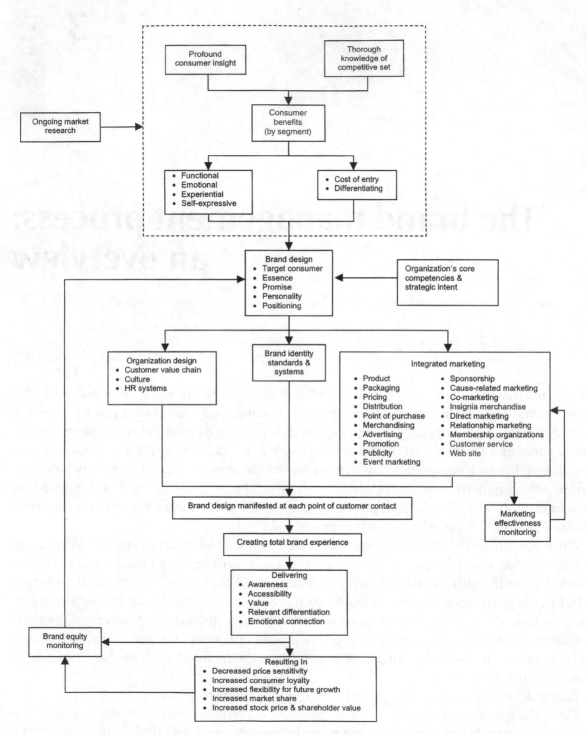

Figure 3.1 *The brand management process*

thought leader, calls the 'customer value chain'. ('Value chain' is the concept that each activity an organization undertakes should lead to added value to its target consumers. If it does not, it should be re-evaluated and possibly eliminated.)

The brand design should be directly translated into and supported by the brand identity standards and systems. This ensures that the brand design is realized at each point of contact with the consumer, resulting in a total brand experience. If done right, a brand and the experience it delivers transcends the brand's products and services. In essence, you are selling the brand experience more than anything else. All of this should deliver awareness, relevant differentiation, value, accessibility and emotional connection, the key components in creating brand insistence.

Ultimately, strong brand equity should result in the ability to change price premiums, decreased price sensitivity, increased consumer loyalty, increased flexibility for future growth, increased market share and increased shareholder value.

There are many types of research that aid in the brand management process. Some are ongoing, while others are only conducted periodically or as needed. Ongoing research includes brand equity, marketing effectiveness and competitive monitoring, among other categories of research.

Brand equity monitoring should highlight changes in consumers' attitudes, preferences and behaviour regarding your brand. It should also perform a diagnostic role, providing insights into why those changes are occurring.

Marketing effectiveness monitoring takes many forms, from simple advertising copy testing to using an ongoing system to identify the relative effectiveness of each element in your marketing mix, including estimates of return on marketing investment. It can be even more detailed, including analysis of effectiveness against different marketing objectives such as customer retention, share of requirements, category buying rate, in-store capture and conversion rates.

Competitive monitoring can take many forms, from diary panel studies and market tours to product preference testing and POS (point of sale) data analysis – chain specific data or from ACNielsen (Scan Track) or IRI (DataServer, FasTrac, and InfoScan).

One-time or periodic research includes attitude and usage studies, in-depth qualitative consumer research, focus groups, conjoint analysis, Perception Analyzer testing, recognition and recall tests, concept testing, benefit testing and test markets.

A brand is an asset, and to provide strong shareholder value, assets must be leveraged. Brand extension is the primary way of doing that. Brand extension can be a powerful way to optimize the performance of your brand, but it can also be a complicated endeavour. Instead of including this part of the brand management process on the diagram, I will address the benefits and risks of brand extension in chapter 15.

─────────── **Did you know...?** ───────────

There is a direct correlation between advertising spending, brand awareness, and market share (given that the brand's distribution is equal to that of other brands in the category and consumers like the brand's point of difference). In fact, James Gregory and the Corporate Branding Partnership (and others) have linked advertising spending with increases in sales, earnings, market share and stock price.

A brand's perceived quality increases with increases in advertising impressions, regardless of message.

Section 2

Designing the brand

4

Understanding the customer

Organizations exist for one purpose: to meet human needs. Thriving organizations do that exceedingly well. Venerated organizations have managed to meet evolving human needs over a long period of time. All of an organization's revenues and profits result from one thing: customers who are willing to pay money for products and services that meet their needs. Any brand management initiative, any marketing initiative, and indeed any business or organizational initiative must start with a solid understanding of the customer.

DEFINING THE TARGET CUSTOMER

Focus is an important part of a brand's success. Brands focus on a target customer, and often narrow their focus to a particular customer need segment. As mentioned in the previous section, customer targeting is the first step in brand design. Everything else emanates from that. So let us start with how to identify your brand's target customers.

Look for customers that meet the following criteria:

- They have an important need and your brand meets that need.
- Your brand has the potential to be preferred by them.
- There is something about your brand that they admire.
- They have the potential to provide your organization with ample revenues and profits over the long run.

● Your organization can grow by building a long-term relationship with and increasingly fulfilling the evolving needs of these customers.

At a minimum, you should identify and understand the following target customer attributes:

● demographics;
● lifestyle;
● needs/desires;
● hopes/aspirations;
● fears/concerns;
● product purchase behaviour;
● product usage behaviour.

TECHNIQUES TO BETTER UNDERSTAND THE CUSTOMER

Understanding your customer is a never-ending process. Here are some simple ways to do so:

● Conduct ongoing customer research, from focus groups and depth interviews to anthropological and quantitative research techniques (see chapter 17 on brand research).
● Carry out customer satisfaction surveys.
● Maintain and monitor customer service/support mechanisms (help lines, e-mail support, etc).
● Establish and monitor online discussion boards and chat rooms devoted to different customer groups/segments.
● Establish and consult with customer advisory boards.
● Establish customer membership organizations. Participate in and monitor their events. (Harley-Davidson executives are masters at this. They attend – and ride in – HOG rallies, talk with their customers at those rallies, observe new product accessories and debrief every HOG rally back at the office for new product ideas and other action items.)
● Key executives/managers should participate in sales calls.
● Key executives/managers should occasionally rotate through front-line customer service positions.
● Hire employees who are also passionate customers. (There is one danger with this approach. Even if you are a passionate brand customer, don't assume that all other customers are just like you.)

For most businesses, environmental scanning can also be very helpful in staying abreast of the latest customer, industry and societal trends. 'Environmental scanning' is a fancy term for the following process:

● reading a broad cross-section of books and publications of relevance to your business;
● monitoring any other relevant media;
● keeping very close track of the emerging trends by counting the number of times certain ideas, needs or concepts are referenced;
● seeking to better understand emerging ideas, needs or concepts – those that are steadily increasing in frequency and intensity.

MARKET SEGMENTATION

Market segmentation is often necessary to meet the needs of different customer groups effectively. Different segments will value different aspects of your products, services and brands differently. You should have a good understanding of the following dimensions of each market segment:

● its overall size and its growth rate;
● its price sensitivity;
● the benefits that are most and least important to it;
● how well it is served by existing products and brands;
● how brand loyal it is;
● how it selects and purchases the product;
● how accessible it is;
● the distribution methods it prefers;
● how it uses the product;
● its product usage/replacement rate;
● its longevity and projected evolution over time.

Markets can be segmented in the following ways:

● Product usage segmentation.
● Purchase behaviour segmentation. (In many industries, four groups that often emerge to one degree or another are: 1) brand loyal consumers; 2) convenience driven consumers; 3) price driven consumers, and 4) consumers that enjoy seeking out new brands and products within the category.)
● Benefit segmentation.

- Price segmentation. Price segmentation will yield higher overall revenues and profits if designed properly. Airlines have made a science out of price segmentation. First class travellers pay more. Business travellers with tight schedules will be less price sensitive. Tourists with fixed budgets, flexible schedules and a long planning horizon will look for lower fares. Some people will only travel taking advantage of last minute seat-filling bargain prices. Other last minute travellers have no choice and behaviourally (but probably not attitudinally) are virtually price insensitive. Seats are less expensive on slower days (Saturdays, December 25, etc).
- Lifestage segmentation. (Consult: Stanford Research Institute's VALS(™) 2 (values and lifestyles) at www.sri.com, Yankelovich MONITOR(r) at www.yankelovich.com, and the University of Michigan's LOV (list of values).)
- Cohort group segmentation (people who were born at approximately the same time and who have experienced the same events at the same lifestages).
- Psychographic segmentation.
- Geographic segmentation
- Geodemographic segmentation. (Consult: Claritas' PRISM and MicroVision at www.velocity.claritas.com and CACI's ACORN(r), www.demographics.caci.com.)

As the list above illustrates, consumers can be segmented on many dimensions. The trick is to arrive at a segmentation scheme that relates to differences in purchase motivations and behaviours. Different brands are designed to appeal to different needs with unique points of difference. It is important to understand the consumers to whom your brand will mean the most and who will have the highest likelihood of responding to your brand messages.

BUSINESS-TO-BUSINESS CUSTOMERS

For B2B (business-to-business) organizations, understanding the purchase decision-making process is usually more complicated. Decisions are often made by teams or committees comprised of people from different functions. Some people initiate the purchase order or RFP (request for proposal). Other people are gatekeepers, influencers, decision makers, purchasers and users. Each has a different role in the process at a different point in the process. They often focus on different product, service and brand attributes, and respond to different types of appeals. Finally, they usually rely upon different sources for their information. An astute B2B marketer should understand how best to get to each of these individuals, what angle to emphasize in the communication and in what verbal style.

For instance, in a corporation considering e-learning (online learning) solutions, the CLO (Chief Learning Officer) may be the primary decision maker for enterprise-wide solutions; however, many others are typically a part of the process:

- The CFO (Chief Financial Officer) may have suggested that e-learning be investigated as a cost saving measure and may have final approval of the purchase.
- General managers whose employees will be beneficiaries of the training will have their own point of view.
- The CIO (Chief Information Officer) may have an opinion regarding the technology training components of the solution.
- The HR vice president may want to know how this fits into the organization's overall approach to human capital management.
- There may even be a group of end users set up to evaluate each of the alternatives considered.
- Lawyers may provide their opinion on aspects of the deal.
- Depending on the organization, the list of stakeholders in the decision-making process may go on and on.

A marketer will have to decide which audiences are the most important, how many different types of communications are necessary and how much the brand needs to be built with each stakeholder. As resources are always finite, decisions on reach versus frequency for each audience will be necessary.

In B2B situations, once one decision maker has been identified through research, it is very useful to ask that person, 'Who else in your organization is involved in the decision making process?'

B2B purchaser motivations

These purchaser motivations are usually present in B2B buying situations:

- price;
- perceived quality;
- technical specifications;
- warranties;
- other service or post-sale support;
- financial stability of the seller;
- buyer's past experience;
- organizational policies;
- fear of making a mistake;
- friendship;
- seller's interest in buyer's business;
- persuasiveness of seller.[1]

Business markets can often be segmented by Standard Industrial Classification (SIC) code. Various publications and other sources provide information by SIC code: *US Industrial Outlook, US Census of Manufacturers*, Dunns Marketing Services, and mail houses, among others.

In organizations with a wide variety of products and services serving multiple markets, business units are often formed around different customer groups. Another approach to serving different markets is to create the segment marketing manager role. Segment marketing managers become experts in their assigned markets through primary and secondary research, and develop (and execute) integrated marketing plans (including product requirements) for their assigned markets. These people often interact in a matrix fashion with the product managers.

THE POWER OF FOCUS

The power of brands lies in focus. Very few, if any, brands can be all things to all people within a product or service category. That is why segmentation is important. Ideally, a brand or sub-brand focuses only on the customer segment that it can best serve. It becomes an expert provider of products and services to that segment. I am a firm believer that in today's business environment, the most robust brands will be those that:

- focus on one customer group;
- become intimate with that group;
- strive to meet more and more needs of that group;
- co-create products and services with the group;
- epitomize what that group stands for.

While we most often think of brands targeting specific customer groups, different brands can also target different needs for the same people. For instance, different needs are driving your purchase decision in each of the following situations, and you are very likely to consider a different set of restaurants (or brands) for each:

- catching a quick bite to eat on your way to work in the morning;
- taking your children out to eat;
- celebrating a special occasion with a loved one;
- staying on your diet and losing weight.

TECHNIQUES TO RETAIN CUSTOMERS

The 'lifetime value of the customer' concept is based on the fact that it is much more cost effective to keep a good customer than to attract a new one. For large ticket items (automobiles) or items that require frequent purchase over time (breakfast cereals), the lifetime value of a customer can be very high. So encourage young customers to buy your products and services. This will help your business to remain healthy over time and to create a longer lifetime value of the customer.

Techniques for keeping good consumers include the following:

- database marketing;
- special services;
- product customization;
- personal touches;
- legendary service;
- communication that reinforces previously made purchases (especially to overcome post purchase anxiety and doubts for large ticket items);
- programmes that reward loyalty and heavy brand consumption;
- avoiding programmes that encourage brand switching.

Did you know...?

Customers share bad brand experiences with approximately twice as many people as they do good brand experiences.

NOTES

1   Source: Gabriel M Gelb, *The Nuts and Bolts of Business-to-Business Marketing Research*, Gelb Consulting Group, Inc. [Online] CRM University Learning Center (http://www.techmar.com/ubusmktresearchbma.asp), accessed 25/9/01.

Table 4.1 *Brand management checklist: understanding the customer*

	Yes	No
Do you conduct customer research frequently?		
Do you use in-depth, qualitative consumer research techniques (such as laddering, hidden-issue questioning and symbolic analysis) to better understand your consumers' needs and motivations as they relate to your brand?		
Do you know who your customers most frequently rely upon to gather information about your products and services? Do you know which of these sources 'carry the most weight' with them?		
Do you know the process customers use to select and purchase products and services in the product/service categories your brand serves?		
Do you know how people are using your products and services?		
Do you fully understand how consumers experience your product or service when using it? Do you know what emotions it evokes? Do you know how it makes them feel? Are you aware of all the sensory components of its use? Does it stimulate their thinking? Do you know what comes to their minds when using it?		
Do you know what problems people encounter when they use your products and services?		
Have you experienced your brand side-by-side with your consumers?		
Do you keep track of household participation, units per household and average price (as components of category dollar sale growth)?		
Do you know what drives brand preference and insistence within your categories?		
Do you know what other brands your customers considered before they bought your brand? Do you know what it was about your brand that caused them to choose it?		
Do you know all the reasons why customers switch from your brand to other brands?		
When your product or service is not available (out of stock or not carried) in a certain store, do you know what portion of your brand's consumers switch brands, switch stores, or postpone their purchases?		
Do you know what consumers infer about your brand?		
Do you know how involved consumers are with your brand? Do consumers have an opinion about your brand?		

Table 4.1 *continued*

	Yes	No
Are consumers willing to defend your brand against naysayers?		
Do you have a thorough understanding of how the market for your brand's product and services is segmented? Do you know which segments your brand best serves? Do you know which segments are likely to provide the most long-term business potential for your brand?		
Do you know which customers are the most valuable to your organization?		
For business-to-business organizations: do you understand the customer organization's decision-making process? Do you know how to reach the decision makers?		
Have you calculated the 'lifetime value' of your customers? Have you done the same by consumer segment?		
Have you identified a specific set of simple questions that separate your customers into different customer need segments?		
Is your brand attractive to younger consumers? Does the average age of your brand's consumer remain constant instead of creeping up over time?		
Do you frequently monitor what people are saying about your brand in chat rooms, discussion groups and other online forums?		
Do you know how people talk about your products and services when they recommend them to others?		
Do you invite customers and potential customers to provide input to new product development?		
Do your organization's systems and databases have a unified view of who your customers are?		
Does your organization have a CRM (customer relationship management) system? Is everything driven off of one relational database?		
Does your organization capture, learn from, and evolve based on consumer complaints? Are there mechanisms in place to ensure that happens?		
Do you share customer information broadly throughout the organization? Do you post customer research and insights on an intranet or extranet site for employees?		

5

Understanding the competition

When a company positions its brand in a customer's mind, it is positioning that brand against other brands. It is critical to understand the strengths, weaknesses, opportunities and threats of each of those competitors along with the industry structure itself. (In fact, wise organizations dedicate a person to understanding the competition.)

This knowledge about your competition is necessary because you want to uniquely 'own' an important benefit in your customer's mind. Ideally, this benefit is one your competitors have not addressed and cannot easily address in the future. Better yet, the benefit you 'own' should be one that takes advantage of your competitors' 'Achilles heels'.

At a minimum, you will want to collect the following information on each of your key competitors:

- key business objectives, goals and strategies;
- sales, sales growth, profitability, market share and other key financial measures;
- brand equity, including brand awareness, usage, preference, relevant differentiation, quality, value, accessibility, vitality, personality, key associations, emotional connection and loyalty;
- product and service offerings;
- pricing and distribution;
- major customers;
- corporate culture;
- organization charts;

- sales organization and compensation;
- share of voice/marketing budget/advertising spend.

SOURCES OF COMPETITIVE INFORMATION

The following are sources of competitive information:

- competitor Web sites;
- press releases (there are free online services that can send you daily e-mail messages with press releases on industries and topics of interest to you);
- industry analyst reports;
- financial analyst reports;
- news clipping services;
- FIND/SVP (consulting and research services) and other similar services;
- Harte-Hanks (www.harte-hanks.com), Hoovers (www.hoovers.com), OneSource (www.onesource.com) and other company databases;
- online database searching services, such as FirstSearch, ProQuest and Lexis-Nexis Academic Universe;
- services that track advertising spending;
- online chat rooms, bulletin boards and discussion groups;
- trade magazines;
- trade shows;
- competitor direct mail campaigns (add a friend or relative to their lists);
- your field sales force; responding to the information they send encourages them to send more;
- ex-employees from those firms (may be under your employ now, or from job search databases);
- current customers (many will pass on competitive communications they receive);
- primary and secondary research (qualitative and quantitative, including brand equity studies); make sure to investigate syndicated studies;
- self-purchase and use of their products (become one of their customers): your management team should buy and use competitive products, an excellent way to better understand your competitors' customer experiences;
- market tours: if in retail, visit stores that carry your competitors' products and talk with the sales associates about their products and services and what the companies are like to work with;
- competitive intelligence firms.

Co-opetition

This competitive strategy recognizes the value of viewing the marketplace not as a 'zero sum game' in which your gain is always someone else's loss, but rather as a place in which value can be created by discovering mutually beneficial relationships with other organizations that would traditionally have been considered competitors. This approach recognizes that organizations become stronger the more value-generating relationships that they forge. We believe in and extensively practise this approach at Element K.

- We provide our content/courses to learning management system vendors.
- We offer our Learning Management System to organizations that want to host other companies' content.
- We actually private label our entire e-learning solution to organizations that want to compete with Element K in the e-learning space.
- We provide referrals to online degree granting schools in return to their referrals to us for continuing education.

The list could go on and on. Suffice it to say that most of our competitors are also our business partners in one way or another. This approach offers numerous advantages for the company that pursues it:

- value-added exchange of information (latest product/service features, competitive information, industry trends, etc);
- a cooperative relationship with your competitors;
- more business referrals;
- the ability to provide products and services and gain business that would have been difficult to accomplish alone;
- more exposure to more deal flows;
- a greater exposure of your brand in the marketplace (leading to greater brand awareness);
- the ability to focus on building your organization's unique core competencies.

For more information on the concept of co-opetition consult the following:

Adam M Brandenburger, Barry J Nalebuff, and Ada Brandenberger, *Co-opetition*
James Moore, *The Death of Competition*

Table 5.1 *Brand management checklist: understanding the competition*

	Yes	No
Have you identified your brand's primary competitors for each market segment in which your brand operates?		
Have you conducted a careful analysis of each of your competitors' strengths, weaknesses, opportunities and threats? Do you know where your competitors are most vulnerable?		
Do you thoroughly understand each of your competitors' brand equities?		
Do you know how loyal your competitors' customers are? Do you know which of their customers are less loyal than others? Do you know why?		
Is there someone responsible for competitive intelligence in your organization?		
Does your management team buy and use competitive products?		
Does someone in your organization track competitor news and announcements on a daily basis?		
Do you share competitive information broadly throughout the organization?		

6

Brand design

If a brand is the personification of an organization or that organization's products and services, it must have a personality and an identity. There are three major components of brand design on which you must focus once you have identified the target customer: 1) brand essence; 2) brand promise; and 3) brand personality. Let's begin with brand essence.

BRAND ESSENCE

Brand essence is the timeless quality that the brand possesses. It is a brand's 'heart and soul'. The essence is usually articulated in the following three-word format: *adjective, adjective, noun*. For instance Nike's essence is 'genuine athletic performance', while Disney's is 'fun family entertainment'.

Brand essence exercise

When I conduct brand positioning workshops for organizations, I always warm the participants up with an exercise that demonstrates what brand essence is. I divide the group into teams of three to four people. Each team is given five minutes to define the essence of a well-known personality. (Some people I frequently use are: Madonna, Arnold Schwarzenegger, Bill Clinton, Hillary Clinton, Marilyn Manson, Abraham Lincoln, Albert Einstein, Adolf Hitler, Mother Theresa, Wolfgang Amadeus Mozart and Nelson Mandela.) While there is much discussion and debate, most groups are able to agree to an essence within five minutes.

The essences are always distinct for each personality assigned. (Well, almost always. In one workshop I conducted, one group defined Madonna's essence as 'audacious sexual chameleon'. The next group, who was assigned Bill Clinton, indicated that they had arrived at the same essence for him. They must have been copying the adjacent group's notes!)

Most of the essences that teams craft 'ring true' with the larger group of participants in a given workshop and are fairly consistent across workshops in different organizations. The exercise reinforces the power of having a strong and well known essence and personality.

Occasionally, brand essences take a slightly different form. Hallmark's essence is 'caring shared', the Nature Conservancy's is 'saving great places' and Ritz Carlton's is 'ladies and gentlemen serving ladies and gentlemen'.

Table 6.1 defines what a brand essence is and what it is not.

Table 6.1 *Brand essence*

A brand essence is...	A brand essence is not...
The 'heart and soul' of the brand.	A name.
Elegant in its economy of words. Take one word away and it loses its meaning.	An advertising theme, line or slogan (the Nature Conservancy's essence being a notable exception).
Constant, timeless and enduring. It will not change over time, across geographies or in different situations.	A brand promise.
Aspirational, yet concrete enough to be meaningful and useful. (For instance, Hallmark's essence is 'caring shared', not 'greeting cards' (a product category description that lacks the aspirational quality), or 'enriching people's lives' (aspirational but not concrete enough to be useful).)	
Extendable.	A product or service (category) description.

BRAND PROMISE

The brand promise is the most important part of a brand's design. A brand must promise a relevant, compelling and differentiated benefit to the target customer. (People often confuse benefits with attributes and features. The brand must promise a benefit, not an attribute or feature.) The benefit may be functional, emotional, experiential, or self-expressive (Who am I? What do I value? What are my convictions? With whom do I associate? To what do I aspire?). Non-functional benefits are the most desirable, however, as they appeal to people on a visceral level and are the least vulnerable to competitive copying. The benefit must focus on points of difference, not points of parity. The ideal benefit to claim has the following three qualities: 1) it is extremely important to the target consumer; 2) your organization is uniquely suited to delivering it; and 3) competitors are not currently addressing it (nor is it easy for them to address it in the future).

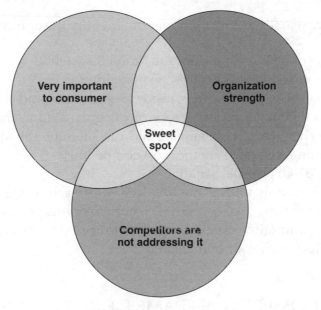

Figure 6.1   *Brand promise*

In their book, *Creating Brand Loyalty: The management of power positioning and really great advertising*, Richard D Czerniawski and Michael W Maloney indicate that the most powerful benefits tap into people's deeply held beliefs, exploit your competitors' vulnerabilities or overcome previous concerns people had about your brand, its product/service category, or its usage (p161).

Competitive copying

The easiest thing for a competitor to copy is a price reduction or discount. Almost as easy to copy are advertised (or otherwise communicated) product and service features. The least easy to copy are consumer benefits that are based on proprietary consumer research or behind-the-scene systems, logistics, or customer service training. For instance, if front line service employees are trained to internalize the brand promise and are empowered to deliver it in whatever way makes sense given the situation, that is much less easy for a competitor to observe and copy. The way a company interacts with different consumers differently through database marketing is also less visible (and often highly effective).

At BrandForward, we usually follow these steps to identify the optimal brand benefit:

- Conduct a review of previous product and brand research.
- Use qualitative research (focus groups, one-one interviews, etc) to better understand the target customer's attitudes, values, needs, desires, fears and concerns, especially as they relate to your brand's product/service category. Within this research step, we usually develop short benefit statements and run them by the target customer iteratively to get a feeling for which are the most compelling.
- Compile a list of 20–40 possible benefits.
- Conduct research that quantifies the importance of each of the possible benefits to your target customer, together with that customer's perceptions of how your brand and each of its competitors deliver against those benefits (to identify the most important benefits which your brand could 'own').

COMPETITIVE FRAME OF REFERENCE

Often, exploring different competitive frames of reference will help you choose the most powerful brand benefit. Here are some questions to help you determine your brand's optimal frame of reference:

- Within which product/service category does our brand operate?
- Within which product and service categories do our customers give us 'permission' to operate today? Do they give us more permission than we give ourselves?
- Does our brand stand for something broader than its products and services? Does that give it permission to enter new product and service categories?
- What compromises do we make with our customers that we take for granted but that might cause our customers to pursue alternative solutions to meet their needs?
- What could another company give our customers that would cause them to become disloyal to our brand?

- Could another brand within our category credibly insert its name into our brand's promise / positioning statement?
- What are the most likely substitute products for our product?
- What could neutralize our point of difference?
- What could make our point of difference obsolete?
- What could 'kill' our category?

Consider the various frames of reference from which Coca-Cola could choose (from most narrow to most broad) (see Table 6.2).

Table 6.2 *Coca-Cola*

Frame of reference	Potential competitors	Potential point of difference
Cola	Pepsi, RC Cola	?
Carbonated beverage (soda pop)	7 Up, Dr. Pepper	?
Soft drink	Crystal Light, Gatorade	?
Non-alcoholic beverage	Chocolate milk, root beer float	?
Beverage	Wine, beer	?
Liquid refreshment	Water, bottled water	?
Psychological refreshment	A walk in the woods, yoga, a swim	?

Consider the various frames of reference from which Hallmark could choose (again, from most narrow to most broad).

Table 6.3 *Hallmark*

Frame of reference	Potential product categories
Greeting cards	Greeting cards
Social expression products	Note cards, invitations, electronic greetings, enhanced e-mail
Caring and sharing	Flowers, candy, gift baskets, romantic cruises, family portraits, family scrapbooks, children's books, children's educational activities, family games, massage oil
Community building	Interpersonal relationship workshops, marriage enrichment courses, planned communities

And, interestingly, Cirque du Soleil did not define its competition as 'other circuses', but rather as 'every other show in town'.[1]

Find out how choosing alternative frames of reference will alter competitive sets, products and services and points of difference. Broadening your brand's frame of reference can help you:

- identify a strong point of difference within your current narrower frame of reference (for instance, Pepsi chose to 'own' psychological refreshment as a point of difference over Coca-Cola);
- identify logical avenues for brand growth;
- identify potential substitute products and other competitive threats.

For the sake of simplicity and focus, I state a brand's promise as follows:

Only [brand] delivers [relevant differentiated benefit] to [target customer].

Use of the word 'only' is very important. It forces you to choose a benefit that only your brand can deliver. Occasionally, clients will ask why they cannot craft the brand promise as, '[Brand] is the best at delivering [relevant differentiated benefit] to [target customer]'. The problem with this approach is that being the best may not change a customer's purchase behaviour if other brands deliver against the chosen benefit to a sufficient degree.

Others may also use a form that incorporates the frame of reference, such as, 'Only [brand] delivers [relevant differentiated benefit] to [target customer] within the [product/service category]'. While I find that the frame of reference exercise can be helpful in identifying potentially powerful differentiated benefits, I do not think that incorporating it into the brand promise itself is helpful.

The following are brand promises that well-known brands seem to make:

- Only Volvo delivers assurance of the safest ride to parents who are concerned about their children's well-being.
- Only Harley-Davidson delivers the fantasy of complete freedom on the road and the comradeship of kindred spirits to avid cyclists.
- Only the Nature Conservancy has the expertise and resources to work in creative partnership with local communities in the United States and internationally with exceptional range and agility to conserve the most important places for future generations.
- Only the Boy Scouts instils values in boys, resulting in a more successful adulthood on a massive nationwide scale through a proven fun programme.

A brand promise must be (and should be tested to be):

- understandable;
- believable;

- unique/differentiating;
- compelling;
- admirable or endearing.

Once crafted and agreed to, the brand promise should be delivered at each point of contact with the consumer. So everyone in your organization should know your brand's promise.

BRAND PERSONALITY

Each brand should choose an intended personality based upon the brand's aspirations and its customers' current perceptions of the brand. The personality is usually communicated in seven to nine adjectives describing the brand as if it was a person. A brand's personality and values are often a function of the following:

- the personality and values of the organization's founder (assuming he or she had a strong personality and values);
- the personality and values of the organization's current leader (again, assuming he or she has a strong personality and values);
- the personality and values of the organization's most zealous customers/members/clients;
- the brand's carefully crafted design/positioning (explained in this section);
- some combination of the above.

While personality attributes will vary considerably by product category and brand, in general, strong brands possess the following personality attributes:

- trustworthy;
- authentic;
- reliable ('I can always count on [brand]!');
- admirable;
- appealing;
- honest;
- stands for something (specifically, something important to the customer);
- likable;
- popular;
- unique;
- believable;
- relevant;
- delivers high quality, well performing products and services;

● ze-oriented;
● innovative.

Employees are also an important factor in communicating the brand's personality in organizations in which the organizational brand is used. This is why companies are increasingly recruiting, training and managing their employees to manifest their brands' promises.

REPOSITIONING A BRAND

Brand repositioning is necessary when one or more of the following conditions exist:

● Your brand has a bad, confusing or nonexistent image.
● The primary benefit your brand 'owns' has evolved from a differentiating benefit to a cost-of-entry benefit.
● Your organization is significantly altering its strategic direction.
● Your organization is entering new businesses and the current positioning is no longer appropriate.
● Competition has usurped your brand's position or rendered it ineffectual.
● Your organization has acquired a very powerful proprietary advantage that must be worked into the brand positioning.
● Corporate culture renewal dictates at least a revision of the brand personality.
● You are broadening your brand to appeal to additional consumers or consumer need segments for whom the current brand positioning won't work. (This should be a 'red flag'. This action could dilute the brand's meaning, make the brand less appealing to current customers, or even alienate current customers.)

You follow the same steps and address the same brand design components when repositioning a brand as you do when first designing the brand. But brand repositioning is more difficult than initially positioning a brand because you must first help the customer 'unlearn' the current brand positioning (easier said than done). Three actions can aid in this process: 1) carefully crafted communication; 2) new products, packaging, and so on that emphasize the new positioning; and 3) associations with other brands (co-branding, co-marketing, ingredient branding, strategic alliances, etc) that reinforce the new brand positioning.

You should not rely upon an advertising agency, a brand consulting company, or your marketing department to craft your corporate or organizational brand's design. This exercise is so critical to your organization's success that your organization's leadership team and its marketing/brand management leaders should develop it, preferably with the help and facilitation of an outside brand-positioning expert.

Brand positioning workshop

Frequently, the brand design is not embraced by the organization because the leadership team was not actively involved in the process at every step along the way. Typically, outside experts will design the brand based upon separate interviews with key stakeholders. This input does not allow for disagreement, debate, discussion, or consensus building among the stakeholders. For this reason, BrandForward offers what have proved to be highly successful intensive brand positioning workshops for organizations. These are highly facilitated, very well prepared sessions in which all the key stakeholders (typically organization leaders and marketing executives) are 'locked in a room' until they reach a consensus on all of the key elements of brand design: the target customer and the brand essence, promise and personality.

We ask key stakeholders (and ad agency personnel, front-line employees, salespeople, customer service reps and marketing researchers with first hand knowledge of your customer's perceptions) the questions in Figure 6.2 in preparation for the brand-positioning workshop.

What does your brand stand for in its customers' minds?

_____

_____

Do you know what your customers would miss most if your brand ceased to exist?

_____

_____

What are your brand's most important benefits to its customers?

_____

_____

How is your brand unique to its customers?

_____

_____

What value does your brand deliver to its customers that they cannot deliver to themselves?

_____

_____

Identify the one word your brand owns in its customers' minds.

_____

What do you often hear repeated about your brand? What are its myths (these may be true or not)?

_____

Does your brand embody certain beliefs, values, attitudes and behaviours that evoke widespread admiration and devotion? What are they?

_____

_____

How is your brand perceived differently by different customer groups?

_____

_____

_____

If its customers were to describe your brand as an animal, what animal would they choose and why?

_____

_____

_____

What is your vision or dream for your brand? What would you like it to become well into the future?

_____

_____

_____

What are the most likely new products and services that your brand could offer to fuel its business growth?

_____

_____

What do other companies in your industry do that you would never do?

_____

_____

What do you do that your competitors would never do?

_____

_____

What is the biggest concern your customers have about your brand?

_____

_____

Describe your organization's culture.

_____

_____

Write down the first two or three words that come to mind associated with each of the following organizations:

Competitor A			
Competitor B			
Competitor C			
Etc			
Your organization			

What type of customer is most likely to benefit from your brand's products and services?

_____

_____

What other types of customers are likely to benefit from your brand's products and services?

_____

_____

Who is not a customer that you most wish would become one?

_____

_____

Please complete this sentence:

Only our brand can deliver_____(key benefits) to _____
(target audience).

Use only two to three words to capture the essence of your brand: _____.
(Examples: Disney: fun family entertainment, Hallmark: caring shared, Nike: genuine athletic performance.)

Figure 6.2 *Brand positioning workshop: pre-session worksheet*

BRAND POSITIONING CASE STUDIES

Element K

I became the Vice President of Marketing at Element K, a leading e-learning company, in September of 2000. Earlier that year, US Equity Partners acquired ZD Education from Ziff-Davis and renamed it Element K. Element K has four business units: Element K Online (e-learning), Element K Courseware (computer training courseware publishing), Element K Journals (journal publishing) and Element K Learning Center (Rochester, NY-based computer training centre).

When I joined Element K, there was virtually no awareness of the brand by our target customers, corporate chief learning officers. And we intended to take the company public after the turbulent market of late 2000 stabilized. My objective was simple: to quickly and aggressively build brand awareness and differentiation to make Element K the number one preferred e-learning brand.

The e-learning market is an increasingly crowded space with hundreds of relatively new companies vying for a greater share of the market and industry leadership. Merrill Lynch estimated the e-learning market at $3.5 billion in 2001, and forecasts growth to more than $25 billion in 2003. According to International Data Corporation (IDC), the US corporate market for online learning alone is projected to grow from $2.2 billion to $11.4 billion by 2003.

This growth is fuelled by the many advantages that e-learning offers compared with traditional classroom training:

- great flexibility in where and when to train;
- e-learning is especially effective for decentralized organizations with geographically dispersed workforces;
- you can train an unlimited number of employees;
- training is 'on demand', decreasing cycle time significantly;
- all for a fraction of the cost of classroom training.

Element K's e-learning solution is fully hosted on the Internet. We had large upfront fixed costs associated with developing our instructional design methodology, 800+ online courses and a robust LMS (learning management system). But our variable costs are very low: providing access to our e-learning solution is as simple as giving someone an ID for access to the site. The cost of adding servers is almost the only variable cost (that is, cost that increases with increased usage/volume). For this reason, we increasingly focused on delivering enterprise-wide solutions to Fortune 1000 companies and similarly large organizations, in which the number of users was substantial with each sales agreement. Simply put, our business model favours large numbers of students.

Most of the companies vying for business in this segment of the e-learning space directed one of the following messages at corporate officers (CIOs, CFOs, etc (assuming they had any semblance of consistent messaging):

- We offer a complete, integrated solution.
- Our e-learning can improve your organization's performance. It produces good business results.
- High profile clients are very pleased with our solution.

Every company seemed to be saying the same things and there was way too much clutter to break through. We embarked on qualitative and quantitative research to identify the key decision makers and the most powerful differentiating benefit for Element K to own. In our qualitative research (one-on-one interviews and mini-groups) we found that the primary decision maker is the senior-most executive with enterprise-wide training responsibility, often bearing the title of CLO (chief learning officer). In this research, we also explored people's needs, desires, fears, concerns and other perceptions regarding training in general and e-learning in particular. From that, we developed 33 different brand benefit statements, which we reviewed with people towards the end of each session. We added, eliminated and revised statements with each round of feedback. In the process, we gained a major insight, which led to Element K's brand positioning: people had an underlying concern that despite all of its potential advantages, e-learning lacked the human touch. In particular they were concerned that, with e-learning:

- you lose the personal attention that only an instructor can deliver;
- it is harder to ask questions;
- feedback is not possible;
- students may feel isolated;
- you lose peer-to-peer learning;
- there is no peer pressure to attend or complete the course;
- there is not enough personal attention available.

Based upon insights from the qualitative research, we developed quantitative research to measure the importance of a wide variety of brand benefits to the target customer. This research also quantified each brand's perceived delivery against each benefit. In this way, we were able to identify the most important benefits and the benefits for which Element K had the biggest relative (and absolute) advantage.

While several benefits were higher in importance, all of them were benefits that would quickly become 'cost of entry' benefits (such as affordable price, quality content and ease of use). E-learning with the human touch was validated to be important, but more importantly, it provided Element K with the biggest advantage. While two-thirds of the respondents believed that Element K integrates the human element into e-learning, only one-third and one-quarter respectively believed Element K's two primary competitors did this.

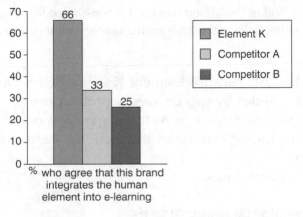

Figure 6.3 *E-learning brand positioning*

This benefit was particularly powerful for Element K to 'own' for the following reasons:

- It addressed one of the major fears about e-learning. (Fear is a particularly powerful motivator.)
- Element K has a substantial advantage in this area per the research.
- Element K delivers on this promise at multiple levels:
    - in the way we have designed the student experience;
    - in the way we have designed the training administrator experience;
    - our comprehensive support services;
    - our participation management services;
    - the way our salespeople interact with customers (friendly, low pressure, consultative selling);
    - our corporate culture itself: we are naturally service oriented (this is sustainable as it is built into our corporate DNA).
- Our most formidable competitor was generally known to be pushy and arrogant and only interested in 'making the sale'. (This was a part of their corporate culture.) This positioning would indirectly and subtly bring this weakness to mind.
- Our customers find us to be very easy to work with. (We had extensive anecdotal evidence that we had won many contracts based upon this alone.)
- It felt 'right' and was quickly embraced by every employee with whom I talked about it.

Here is what we now say about Element K:

> Element K brings a unique understanding of how people learn to the business of training. Our understanding comes from a 20-year heritage of innovation in adult career learning for leading corporations. Today, you'll find it in our best-in-class e-learning solution – over 800 courses integrated with a state-of-the-art learning management system, all delivered with a human touch.

This statement is believable because Element K has a rich heritage as a company of training professionals founded by two university professors who wanted to make adult training more interesting and interactive. As training professionals committed to multiple training modalities (including classroom instruction), we would share and want to address these concerns.

Here are some of our proof points:

- Pioneer in adult training for nearly 20 years.
- Sophisticated instructional design model.
- Multiple modalities to accommodate different learning styles, including e-ILT (Electronic Instructor Led Training).
- Extensive online reference materials.
- Personalized learning paths and plans.
- Pre- and post-skills assessment.
- Job role and competency tracking.
- 24/7 student and administrative support (via e-mail, chat and telephone).
- Tools and techniques to help you maximize participation.
- Rated as superior in its ease of use by students and administrators.
- Rated as highly interactive and engaging.
- Element K has won business because its people were easy to work with.
- Element K's culture is service-oriented. We have a passion for delivering quality training. Our knowledgeable, friendly, professional and competent sales people listen to your company's needs and help you develop a training solution that best meets your needs.

Based upon all of this, I held a workshop with our executive team to gain consensus on the following elements of the brand design: target customer, brand essence, brand promise and brand personality. We are now committed to building 'the human touch' into everything we do, from the way our sales force interacts with potential customers and the services we offer to our current customers to the enhancements we make to our learning management system and the personality characteristics we look for when we hire new employees.

Figure 6.4 shows one of our first 'e-Learning with the Human Touch' ads.

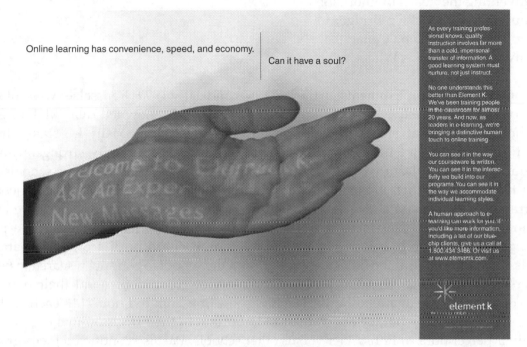

Figure 6.4   *Ad copy for Element K*

So far, the new brand positioning seems to be setting Element K apart from the competition. In less than 18 months since the launch of the Element K brand, it has become one of the top preferred e-learning brands.

Rensselaer Polytechnic Institute

Rensselaer Polytechnic Institute, founded in 1824, was the first degree-granting technological university in the English-speaking world. Rensselaer was established 'for the purpose of instructing persons, who may choose to apply themselves, in the application of science to the common purposes of life'. Since Rensselaer's founding, its alumni have impacted the world in many significant ways:

● inventing television;
● creating the microprocessor;
● managing the Apollo project that put the first man on the moon;
● founding Texas Instruments and creating the first pocket calculator;
● creating e-mail (including using the @ symbol);

- inventing baking powder;
- inventing the Reach toothbrush;
- building the Brooklyn Bridge;
- building the Panama Canal;
- inventing the Ferris Wheel.

Yet, for all of its accomplishments, in the late 1980s and early 1990s Rensselaer was not well positioned (to prospective students) compared to its world-renowned rival, MIT, or even to schools such as Cal Tech, UC Berkeley and Carnegie-Mellon. Many US state schools (Purdue, University of Illinois at Urbana, etc) offered exceptionally strong technical programmes at significantly lower costs than private universities. Ivy League schools and other first-tier liberal arts universities were building their maths, science and engineering programmes. And most states had public universities that provided respectable engineering programmes. This increasingly competitive landscape left Rensselaer in a positioning 'no man's land'. I was on Rensselaer's alumni board of directors and national admissions committee at the time. We worked with the school to conduct research to better understand the college selection process. We interviewed students (and their parents), some of whom chose to attend Rensselaer and some of whom did not. With each of these groups, we explored what factors were most important in their decision-making process, and their perceptions of Rensselaer versus other schools. We also conducted focus groups with alumni and business people to better understand their impressions of Rensselaer.

Here is what we found: Almost everyone who knew of Rensselaer perceived it to be a first rate technical school. Many people put it in the same class as MIT. People 'in the know' were genuinely impressed with the school and the calibre of its students, academics and its research. But there were drawbacks:

- Rensselaer is in Troy, NY (not a garden spot by any stretch of the imagination), while MIT is in Boston.
- Rensselaer is not as well known or prestigious as MIT. It does not have the same name cachet.
- Rensselaer is much more expensive than state engineering schools – before financial aid. After financial aid, it can be comparable or even less expensive.
- Rensselaer was known to be a 'boot camp'. It's been said, 'you don't go there to have fun'.
- The curriculum was perceived to be too narrow compared with liberal arts schools.
- The school had a lopsided male to female ratio (13 to 1 when I attended in the mid-to-late 1970s, 3 to 1 today).
- A significant portion of Rensselaer's students (mostly those who had used Rensselaer as a backup school to MIT and similar schools), felt inferior to students at their first choice schools.

Further, those with no connection to the school had no impression of the school. Awareness was nil among the general US population.

These were significant hurdles. And yet, looking at the school itself, there were also a number of very strong advantages:

- a rich history of alumni who have made major contributions to society;
- a vital, engaged campus community;
- a strong student leadership development programme;
- innovations in entrepreneurship (one of the first and perhaps best known business incubators and a strong student entrepreneurship programme);
- award-winning innovations in educational techniques;
- thriving interdisciplinary research centres;
- certain programmes were ranked among the best available in the world;
- an increasingly strong reputation throughout the world (interestingly, the university's reputation was stronger in many other countries than it was in US Midwestern states!).

The university had also embarked on a significant long-term commitment to enhance the student experience, addressing everything from administrative procedures, counselling, and breadth of course offerings to quality of instruction, the male-to-female ratio, and campus aesthetics. Gauging from student surveys over time, the efforts were producing significant results.

Here are the key insights that led to Rensselaer's very powerful current positioning:

- Rensselaer's students have always been serious about their chosen fields of endeavour and their studies.
- Rensselaer's faculty, students and alumni want to make a difference in the world.
- Rensselaer is and has been a leader in technological innovation.
- Rensselaer's alumni, throughout the school's history, have made major lasting contributions to society.
- Rensselaer was emerging as a leader in entrepreneurship, especially technological entrepreneurship.
- 'Technological creativity' seemed to capture the essence of the school and the spirit of those associated with the school throughout its 175-year history.
- Rensselaer wanted its new positioning not only to capture the school's unique competitive advantages but also to inspire its students and give them confidence. (In the mid-to-late 1970s, under George Low's leadership, the school informally adopted the slogan, 'Rensselaer: Where imagination can achieve the impossible'.)

So Rensselaer's tag line, 'why not change the world?^{SM}', was born.

Confident? Yes.

Aspirational? Yes.

Inspirational? Yes.

Accurately reflecting the school's strengths and those of its alumni? Yes.

An invitation to like-minded individuals and organizations to 'come join Rensselaer in its quest'? Yes.

Effective in recruiting an increasing number of highly qualified students? Yes. Rensselaer's most recent entering freshman classes are the most qualified and talented in the last couple of decades. And each class seems to be more qualified than the prior class. As one measure, the Class of 2005 arrived on campus with average SAT scores of 1307, a leap of 25 points over that of the previous class.

And the most important question: Are students satisfied with Rensselaer and its recently articulated positioning? Yes. Today, Rensselaer is thriving. In early 2001, it received a gift of $360 million – the largest single gift (at that time) ever made to a university. It is building a $60 million biotechnology and interdisciplinary studies centre to expand its research portfolio and a $50 million Electronic Media and Performing Arts Centre to showcase its world-leading electronic arts programme.

GEICO Direct Insurance

When BrandForward conducted its insurance industry brand equity study, it uncovered a few things about the insurance industry:

- The insurance industry is highly fragmented. While there are dozens of companies whose names consumers recognize, less than a handful receive significant unaided first mention.
- While there is high behavioural loyalty, there is low attitudinal loyalty.
- Consumers have a low emotional connection to insurance brands.
- Less than one in five people indicated that their insurance company 'has never disappointed them' (one sign of emotional connection).
- While consumers perceive there to be differences between insurance companies, they do not perceive those differences to be significant.
- Price and rates are among the most important points of difference between companies, suggesting the category is commodity-like among many consumers.
- The following are the seven most important consumer benefits in the insurance industry. Of these seven benefits, consumers perceive only two of them to be addressed to any large degree:
  - paying claims fairly and promptly;
  - good rates/prices;
  - honest, trustworthy representatives;

- – accessible, available representatives;
- – knowledgeable, competent representatives;
- – easy to understand policies;
- – cmpany financial stability.
- The following benefits have the widest variation in delivery and therefore provide the greatest opportunities for differentiation:
  - – representatives can provide unbiased recommendations (all insurance categories);
  - – good rates/prices (all categories);
  - – have knowledgeable, competent reps (life insurance);
  - – can establish a personal relationship (home and auto insurance);
  - – strong overall reputation (financial services).
- The sales representative and claims adjusters' points of contact with consumers are critical to the success of insurance company brands.
- There is the most brand preference in the auto insurance category (roughly a third with 'no preference') and the least in the financial services category (two-thirds with 'no preference').
- State Farm is the preferred brand by a wide margin (especially in home and auto insurance). It also has a wide lead in the emotional connection it has created with consumers.
- GEICO is an 'up and coming' brand in auto insurance.
- Prudential is the preferred life insurance brand.

While State Farm seems to be doing many things right, almost all of the other insurance companies seem to lack any significant brand equity. But my story is not about State Farm. It is about GEICO Direct, the up-and-coming auto insurance brand. And, this is a very simple, short story: GEICO began to advertise its brand at a level that was the talk of the industry. And its message was very simple: 'You could save 15% or more on car insurance!'

Figure 6.5   *GEICO's logo*

Figure 6.6   *GEICO's advertising*

In brand building, focus is everything, and GEICO focused on one product segment – auto insurance – and one benefit – low price. And it did so again and again and again with a disciplined consistency. And its brand equity and market share are increasing at rates unknown to other insurance brands. In an industry with little brand equity or differentiation, GEICO decided to build its brand by aggressively focusing on an important brand benefit: low price. Its success was that simple. (In general, I would not recommend trying to own 'low price' as a point of difference. Typically, it is not a sustainable point of difference. Nor does it usually contribute to building brand equity. For a number of reasons that are too involved for the purpose of this case study, it is working for GEICO in the insurance industry now.)

Did you know…?

Research has shown that the media environment affects advertising claims (see Aaker and Brown's study of vehicle source effects of 1972). For instance, quality claims are more effective in elite or prestigious magazines because people associate the claim with the media environment.

Aspirational, upscale, and high status brands have the potential to alienate customers who lack confidence. While these customers might admire these brands, they do not feel comfortable using them. Building warmth, humour, and less formality into the brands to make them more approachable helps overcome this problem.[2]

Table 6.4 *Brand management checklist: brand design*

	Yes	No
Have you carefully defined your target customer on the following dimensions: demographics, lifestyle, values, attitudes, product usage and buying behaviour?		
Is this customer a good target for your brand in the following ways: • market size, profitability and growth rate? • importance of your brand's promise to them? • their alignment with your brand's values (ie your brand stands for something that is important to them)? • the opportunity for add-on sales through brand extension? • their potential loyalty to the brand?		
Do you have profound insight into your consumers' values and motivations?		
Have you considered the intangible ways in which your brand adds value to the consumer?		

Table 6.4   (_continued_)

	Yes	No
Are you constantly monitoring the market for changes in the following: • customer segments? • customer values, attitudes and needs? • customer shopping behaviours? • competitive offerings?		
Can you articulate your brand's competitive frame of reference? Can you describe the universe within which it operates?		
Have you mapped your brand's delivery of key category benefits against competitive brands' delivery of those same benefits? Did you overlay that with a consumer importance scale?		
Do you fully understand the following for all the categories in which your brand operates: 1) the different market segments, 2) the competitive set, and 3) which consumer benefits are 'cost-of-entry' versus 'differentiating'? (These alternatively may be referred to as 'points-of-parity' and 'points-of-difference'.)		
Do you fully understand the decision-making process (rational or not) the consumer uses to purchase your brand?		
Do you know what benefits your competitors' brands own in consumers' minds?		
Do you have a clear understanding of the things competitive brands do that your brand should and would never do?		
Do you know how different consumer segments perceive your brand differently?		
Is your brand relevant to early adopters?		
Have you defined the role, target consumer, essence, promise and personality for your brand?		
If your brand is not the leader in its category, can you identify a way to redefine, reframe or narrow the category so that your brand can be the leader in the redefined category?		
Do you know what the most important problem is that your brand solves for its customers?		
Do you fully understand what factors in your brand's history built it to what it is today?		
Do you have a vision or dream for your brand? Do you know what you'd like it to become well into the future?		

Table 6.4 (*continued*)

	Yes	No
Do you know what story your brand tells? Can you articulate its myth?		
Is your brand vital and vivid? Does it have the ability to build legends?		
Is your brand dynamic? Does it learn, grow, mature, adapt and improve over time?		
Do you know what your brand's timeless qualities are?		
Is your brand's essence aspirational and inspirational, yet concrete enough so that it can own a position in the consumer's mind?		
Does your brand embody certain beliefs, values, attitudes and behaviours that evoke widespread admiration and devotion?		
Do you have absolute clarity regarding what your brand stands for and how it is unique and compelling to consumers?		
Can you identify the one word your brand owns in consumers' minds?		
Do you know what consumers would miss most if your brand ceased to exist?		
Do you know what deeply felt human needs your brand addresses?		
Does your brand dominate the category by owning the 'core' category benefit or does it lead the category by owning the benefit that best defines where the category is headed? (Source: DMB&B Communication presentation at a Sprint Brand Forum.)		
Does your brand stand for something very important to its customers? Does it capture their imaginations?		
Is your brand's promise believable?		
Can you readily verbalize the proof points to your brand's promise?		
Have you identified brand benefits that are invisible to your competitors (and therefore extremely difficult to imitate)?		
Have you defined your brand broadly enough for it to outlive specific product categories and provide flexibility for ongoing extension?		
Are you aware of any elements of your brand's heritage that may limit its opportunities for future growth? If so, have you devised plans to overcome those limitations without alienating current consumers?		
Has your brand struck the optimal balance between maintaining a strong heritage and reinventing itself for the future?		
Have you considered narrowing your brand's focus to clarify meaning and gain market share?		

Table 6.4 (*continued*)

	Yes	No
Can you identify the opportunities you have sacrificed to maintain clarity regarding your brand's promise and positioning?		
Have you considered 'pruning' businesses that are not congruent with your brand's essence and promise?		
Have you identified product or service features that are not valued by the consumer or that do not reinforce your brand's promise? Do you have plans to eliminate these?		
Have you established brand strategies that are consistent with the brand's promise – product, pricing, distribution, communications, etc?		
Have you designed the brand portfolio, including a sub-brand structure?		
Is your brand hierarchy simple enough for consumers to easily understand (preferably no more than two levels)?		
When your brand hierarchy has two or more levels, do you know which name (corporate, parent, endorsed, or sub-brand) the consumer uses to refer to each product or service offered by your organization?		
Do you have criteria to help you decide when you can use an existing brand, when a completely new brand is needed, and when a sub-brand is the right choice?		
Do you find that all of your sub-brands are distinctive? Are you certain that no two sub-brands in your portfolio meet the same consumer needs and deliver the same benefits?		
Are your sub-brand names distinct from one another so that they are not confused for one another?		
Do you use existing brands whenever possible to meet new consumer needs or to enter new product categories, offering instant assurance and maximizing communication efficiency (providing doing so does not dilute the meaning of the original brand)?		
Are you increasingly leveraging your corporate brand as a parent brand?		
Do you find you are spending most of your time creating sustainable competitive advantages (versus matching competitive moves) with your brands?		
Is your brand so well positioned that there are no acceptable substitutes for your products and services?		
Did you know that competitors can and often will reposition your brand in the process of repositioning their brands? Do you know the ways in which they are trying to reposition your brand? Are you actively doing something about this?		

Table 6.4   (*continued*)

	Yes	No
If you are repositioning your brand, are you implementing it in such a way and at such a pace that consumers can 'digest' the changes?		
Have you designed your brand so that it is, as Kevin Keller says, 'memorable, meaningful, transferable, and protectable'?		

NOTES

1   Source: Morgan, Adam (1999) *Eating the Big Fish: How Challenger Brands Can Compete Against Brand Leaders*, John Wiley and Sons, New York.
2   Source: Max Blackston, Observations: building brand equity by managing the brand's relationship, *Journal of Advertising Research*, **32** (3), May / June 1992, pp 79–83.

7

Brand identity standards and systems

When most people think about a brand's identity, they usually think about the name, the logo, and maybe the tag line. But the identity consists of so much more than that: it includes typestyles, colours, symbols, attitude and personality, brand voice and visual style, sounds and other mnemonic devices, characters and other spokespeople, product design, package design, and the list could go on and on. The most powerful brands have a consistent brand voice and visual style from product design and packaging to retail environment and external communication.

Companies such as Procter & Gamble and Unilever practised the traditional model of brand management. These companies managed a large portfolio of stand-alone brands (Bold, Bounty, Ivory, NyQuil, Pepto-Bismol, Scope, Folgers, Pringles, etc) and marketed them separately. While this was highly effective for those companies, it requires substantial marketing resources. Today, more and more manufacturing companies are discovering the power of using their corporate brand names (General Electric, IBM, 3M, Ford, etc) to market their products. These companies have discovered that it is highly efficient to leverage the corporate brand name. The name offers quality assurance and familiarity at a minimum and a coherent umbrella promise (example: 3M – innovative solutions) as well, if executed properly.

BRAND ARCHITECTURE

(Brand structure is also called brand architecture. I have covered brand architecture in greater detail in Chapter 2 on 'Understanding the language of branding'.)

While situations vary greatly and company brand structures are much more complicated than the ideal, I believe in general that a highly efficient and effective brand structure leverages the corporate brand as the parent brand and includes individual sub-brands targeted to different consumer need segments. This two-level structure, if executed correctly, maximizes consumer communication efficiency while clarifying the definition of the corporate brand and making it more vital to an increasingly wider group of consumer segments. Having said that, brand architecture is a highly complex issue, especially for organizations that either span multiple product/service categories and/or are the result of mergers and acquisitions. Some important considerations in developing and revising brand architecture:

- Make sure that the architecture is based upon a careful analysis of key internal and external audiences and not internal organization structures, egos, and the felt need for control.
- It will be extremely important to outline the role of the various levels in the brand hierarchy from the outset.
- It will also be important to think through the extent to which the various brands will link to the parent brand – by name only (endorsed, sub-brand), through common design elements, by sharing the same essence, by sharing the same positioning and differentiating benefits, etc. (I tend to believe that the various brands should almost always relate to the parent brand in the first three ways but not always in the fourth, especially if the brands span a wide variety of product categories or are targeted at completely different customer segments.)

BRAND NAMING

Brand naming is extremely important. Many readers are probably working with brands that have already been named, but in case you are not, here are a few pointers on naming brands:

- People only refer to a person or product using one, or at the most, two names. For instance, I am either Brad or Brad VanAuken. No one calls me Alan Bradley VanAuken (with the exception of my mother, who called me this when she was upset with me when I was a boy). It is just too hard to remember, too cumbersome to say, and unnecessary. Likewise, a car is either a Taurus or a Ford Taurus. People say, 'I drive a Honda' or 'I drive a Honda Accord'. Few say, 'I drive a Honda Accord EX'. People can occasionally remember three levels of names – but rarely more. Saturn is simple. Chrysler New Yorker Fifth Avenue and Oldsmobile Cutlas Sierra are less easy to remember (and can anyone remember what company makes these cars?) How is a Chrysler New Yorker Fifth Avenue different from a Chrysler New Yorker Salon? How is an Oldsmobile Cutlas Sierra different from an Oldsmobile Cutlas Supreme, and how are both of them different from an Oldsmobile Toronado or an Oldsmobile 88 Royal? It gets very confusing very quickly.

- Products that run into trouble are those that have multiple levels of names. For instance, Hallmark co-produced social expression software with Microsoft. Greetings Workshop was from Microsoft and Hallmark Connections (in some cases, this was a sub-set of another suite of products from Microsoft with additional names). What did consumers remember? What did they ask for? Did each consumer use the same name? It might have been easier to call it 'Hallmark Greetings Workshop (brought to you by Microsoft)' or 'Microsoft Greetings Workshop (featuring Hallmark cards)'.

- *Coined names* (such as Xerox and Kodak) are preferred if you have sufficient resources to build their meaning. Coined names are distinct and can be designed to be easy to read, write and pronounce. It is unlikely that any other brand will be confused with yours if yours has a coined name. Because coined names require significant communication over time to build their meaning, they are best reserved for parent brands or other brands that are extremely important to the organization and that will be around for a very long time.

- Many organizations opt for *associative descriptive names*, which may be partly descriptive and usually allude to a key brand benefit. Examples include Amazon, Sir Speedy, Road Runner, Sprint, BrandForward, and Aris Vision Institute. These names tend to work quite well and deliver the added benefit of immediately alluding to the brand's benefit. If you want to get into a product or business quickly with a name that helps reinforce the product's or business's primary benefit, while still maintaining some level of uniqueness, this is the preferred naming option.

- *Generic or descriptive names* are least desirable. They are not distinctive in consumers' minds and they cannot be protected legally. Interestingly, many online companies with generic names have gone out of business, like Auctions.com, Business.com, Buy.com, Computer.com, eToys.com, Food.com, Furniture.com, Garden.com, Mall.com, Mortgage.com, Pets.com, and Stamps.com.[1] (So much for all those once exorbitantly expensive URLs!)

- Generic descriptors are frequently used for sub-brands, when you want most of the credit to go to the parent brand. For instance, at Element K our branding structure features generic descriptor sub-brands because: 1) Element K is a new brand that we need to build quickly; 2) our resources are too limited to build multiple brands; and most importantly, 3) we are touting a blended solution across all of our products and businesses.

Element K's brands

Entity	Name (brand/sub-brand)
Company	Element K
e-Learning division	Element K Online
Courseware division	Element K Courseware
Journals division	Element K Journals
Rochester, NY, learning centre	Element K Learning Center

In summary, coined names are used for products and services that are distinctive, that provide sustainable competitive advantages and that will receive substantial marketing support over time. Associative descriptive names are used for important products or services, but primarily those that need to have their meaning built quickly or that will not receive the sustained level of marketing support required of coined names. Generic or descriptive names are reserved for non-mission-critical sub-brands.

Strong names allude to the benefit, such as Amazon.com, Passion perfume, Ford Explorer or Roadrunner Internet access service. Ideally, any name you choose should be short, easy to spell and easy to pronounce. Say the name out loud and see how easily it rolls off of the tongue and how pleasing it is to the ear. Pay attention to cadence, rhythm and balance. Alliteration and repetition of sounds can add to the strength of the name. Consider Roadrunner, Kodak and Coca-Cola. I prefer a two-syllable word starting with a strong consonant and possessing rich vowel sounds.

Here are some things to consider when naming your brand. Names formed from acronyms or initials are up to 40 per cent less memorable than any type of pronounceable word, real or coined[2].

Perhaps the worst names of all are those built from generic word parts such as 'com' and 'sys' and 'compu' (WorldCom, UniSys). These names seem to be confused with every other brand name created from similar word parts and they are very difficult to recall.

NAMING DECISION TREES

Organizations with more than one brand should develop decision trees to aid people in naming new products and services. The decision tree should outline when an existing brand should be used and when a new brand is necessary. (One of the more exhaustive branding/naming decision trees that I have seen is in Nicholas Ind's book, *Living the*

Brand.) It should also identify the type of brand to be created (sub-brand, endorsed brand, etc) and the naming convention for that brand (coined, associative/descriptive, etc). This should be based upon the following factors:

- importance of the new product or service to the market and to the organization;
- projected life-span of the new product or service;
- unique differentiating benefits delivered by the new product or service;
- intent and capacity to communicate the new brand in a significant way over time.

In general, new brands should be created only when a new product or service delivers on a different brand promise from one of the organization's existing brands. To do otherwise would be costly and confusing to consumers.

BRAND LOGOS

Some logos were created during the era of big department stores and were designed as signatures to fit on the side of buildings, so these logos are more square in orientation than they are horizontal. Many of these now seem outdated (if they have not been updated). Hallmark's logo belongs to this class. Others were designed as corporate logos to reinforce leadership and stability (AT&T, IBM). Many of these now seem cold and sterile. Some logos are more fun – communicating more of a personality (Apple, MTV, Ebay).

Today, logos must be designed with the foresight that they will be used in multimedia environments (from television to the Internet). That means colours, animation and sound sequences (like NBC, Intel, AOL, Harley-Davidson (engine sound), and Maxwell House) should be considered.

THE IMPORTANCE OF COLOUR

Colour is an important consideration in your brand identity system. Colours have a significant impact on people's emotional state. They have also been shown to impact people's ability to concentrate and learn. They have a wide variety of specific mental associations. In fact, the effects are physiological, psychological and sociological. For instance[3]:

- Non-primary colours are more calming than primary colours.
- Blue is the most calming of the primary colours, followed closely by a lighter red.
- Test takers score higher and weight lifters lift more in blue rooms.
- Blue text increases reading retention.
- Yellow evokes cheerfulness. Houses with yellow trim or flower gardens sell faster.

71

- Reds and oranges encourage diners to eat quickly and leave. Red also makes food more appealing and influences people to eat more. (It is no coincidence that fast food restaurants almost always use these colours.)
- Pink enhances appetites and has been shown to calm prison inmates.
- Blue and black suppress appetites.
- Children prefer primary colours. (Notice that children's toys and books often use these colours.)
- Forest green and burgundy appeal to the wealthiest 3 per cent of Americans and often raise the perceived price of an item.
- Orange is often used to make an expensive item seem less expensive.
- Red clothing can convey power.
- Red trim is used in bars and casinos because it can cause people to lose track of time.
- White is typically associated with cool, clean and fresh.
- Red is often associated with Christmas and orange with Halloween and Thanksgiving.
- Red and black are often associated with sexy and seductive, and are favoured by porn sites.
- Black clothes make people look thinner.
- Black is also associated with elegance and sophistication. It also seems mysterious.
- Black is the favourite colour of Goths.

Colours also have a functional impact on readability, eye-strain, ability to attract attention, ability to be seen at night and so on. This is important in choosing colours for signing, Web site pages, prints ads, and other marketing media.

- The most visible colour is yellow.
- The most legible of all colour combinations are black on yellow and green on white followed by red on white. It is no surprise that most traffic signs use these colour combinations.
- Black on white is the easiest to read, on paper, and on computer screens.
- Hard colours (red, orange and yellow) are more visible and tend to make objects look larger and closer. They are easier to focus upon. They create excitement and cause people to overestimate time.
- Soft colours (violet, blue and green) are less visible and tend to make objects look smaller and further away. They are not as easy to focus upon. They have a calming effect, increase concentration, and cause people to underestimate time.

Obviously, colours are an important part of any brand identity system. Testing the effect of a new brand identity system's colours is well advised. It is important to consider that colour associations will vary by individual, and especially culture, due to the cultural context and previous experiences with the colours. All of the impacts of colours are equally true of music, scents and sounds. For instance, studies have identified that music has an impact on supermarket sales, mental concentration, achievement on standardized tests, factory productivity, clerical performance and staff turnover, among other things.

Favourite colours of US consumers

1. Blue.
2. Red.
3. Green.
4. White.
5. Pink.
6. Purple.
7. Orange.
8. Yellow.

Source: Carlton Wagner, founder of the Wagner Institute for Color Research in Santa Barbara, California.

Colour resources online

Alley Katt's Links to Colors: www.alleykatt.com/colors/colorlnk.htm
Color Psychology: http://psychology.about.com/science/psychology/blsub_soimg_color.htm
Color Psychology: www.shibuya.com/garden/colorpsycho.html
Color Matters: www.colormatters.com/
Color Perceptions: www.ibiblio.org/hmake/color/color_perceptions.html
Color Secrets Revealed (book): www.kombu.com/Colbook/, www.aaaimg.com/Colbook/
The Reds, Whites, and Blues of Emotion: Examining Color Hue Effects on Mood Tones: www.clearinghouse.mwsc.edu/manuscripts/184.asp
The Psychology of Color in Marketing: www.nightcats.com/samples/colour.html

TOOLS TO MAINTAIN BRAND IDENTITY CONSISTENCY

To ensure that external audiences are hearing consistent messages about the brand, companies often 'script' their sales and their service organizations. At Element K, the marketing department worked with company management and the ad agency that developed our 'e-Learning with the Human Touch' campaign to craft a detailed script (together with a PowerPoint slide presentation and other presentation aids). This script was designed to reinforce our brand positioning, 'e-Learning with the Human Touch', and we required our sales and service organizations to memorize those scripts.

In addition to scripts, organizations use the following tools to ensure brand identity consistency across the enterprise (and by business partners):

- Published brand identity standards and systems. (Historically, these were printed hard copy manuals and CDs, but more recently they are featured on intranet sites, which offer the substantial advantages of providing instant, low cost universal updates and digital access.) These published standards usually include brand architecture, brand style guides, naming conventions, and a naming decision tree.
- Brand photo libraries.
- Brand message guidelines. These are often divided into *dos* and *don'ts* columns, such as 'Do say "Make a Xerox branded photocopy," but don't say "Make a Xerox".'
- Brand management intranet sites usually include the following items as well:
    - brand essence, promise and personality statements;
    - brand pricing guidelines;
    - brand research summaries;
    - examples of recent brand ads.
- More and more organizations are using digital brand asset management systems to maintain consistency and control throughout their enterprise. These systems are typically fully hosted on the Internet by third parties (ASP model). They provide the ultimate control over decentralized sales and marketing organizations (or retail networks) which develop localized advertising, promotions and other marketing programmes. Two firms that specialize in digital brand asset management are Imation (www.imation.com) and Saepio (www.saepio.com).
- Naming a brand identity manager or specialist is also extremely helpful. This person reviews and approves all new executions of the brand and its sub-brands and all new interpretations of its identity. This person should be well respected throughout the organization, possess strong interpersonal skills, and should be assertive and persuasive.
- Creating a cross-divisional brand identity council composed of key design (and editorial) managers from departments and divisions throughout the organization is also very helpful. The council raises awareness of brand identity issues, builds a consensus around their resolution, becomes a 'brain trust' for the brand's identity and provides peer pressure for interpreting the brand accurately and consistently.

Need help with brand naming and brand identity?

Here are some companies who specialize in these areas:

- Brand naming:
    - Addison Whitney;
    - Ashton Adams;
    - Brand Institute Inc.;
    - Lexicon Branding Incorporated.
- Brand identity:
    - Desgrippes Gobè & Associates;
    - Interbrand Gerstman & Meyers;
    - Landor, Lippincott & Margulies;
    - Lister Butler Consulting;
    - St Aubyn;
    - Strategies International.

Table 7.1 *The brand identity worksheet*

Target customer:	• May include demographics, need segment, usage segment.
Target consumer insights:	• Beliefs and values. • Needs and desires. • Concerns, fears and anxieties.
Brand essence:	• The heart and soul of the brand. • 'Who' not 'what'. • Can be used as an internal mantra. • Form: adjective, adjective, noun.
Frame of reference:	• The category within which the brand is positioned. • Think about one broader and one narrower category than the one which initially comes to mind.
Relevant differentiated benefit:	• Primary brand benefit. • The most compelling benefit is very important to the target customer, a core competency of the organization and not currently addressed or easily replicated by the competition. • Benefit can be functional, emotional, experiential or self-expressive.

Table 7.1 *continued*

Brand promise:	• Form: only (brand) delivers (relevant differentiated benefit) to (target customer).
Proof points:	• Reinforce the brand promise. • Can be advantages highlighted by any of the following: unique product/service functions or features, third part endorsements, side-by-side comparisons, independent research studies, customer testimonials, etc.
Brand personality:	• 6 to 12 adjectives. • Desired by your target customer. • Can be aspirational.
The brand would never do this:	• Something other brands in the category would do but that your brand would never do.
Unique brand behaviours:	• Something your brand would do that few, if any, other brands in the category would do.
Brand myths:	• Positive stories people tell about the brand (whether true or not).
Brand enhancements:	• Three perceptions you are trying to change about the brand.
Brand logo:	Attach if possible.
Brand colours:	• Be very specific including the exact colours for computer and printing based colour systems.
Brand voice:	• What kind of language does the brand use? Is it succinct? Is it practical? Is it idealistic? Is it poetic? Is it authoritative? Is it friendly? Is it familiar? Give examples.
Brand visual style:	• What visual qualities does the brand possess? • Is there a brand photo or art library/archive? • Are certain symbols, shapes, or artistic styles used for the brand?
Tag line or slogan:	

Brand mnemonic device:	• Usually a sound sequence. • Could be a scent. • Could be background music.	Attach if possible.
Other important brand messages:	• Important messages other than the brand promise.	

Table 7.2 *Brand management checklist:brand identity standards and systems*

	Yes	No
As St James Associates says, some brands are "all symbols but no soul." First and foremost, does your brand have a soul?		
Is your brand's name proprietary? Does it differentiate the brand instead of just describing its products and services?		
Is your brand's name suggestive of a key differentiating benefit, but not so narrow as to decrease the brand's ability to claim new benefits in the future?		
Do consumers like your brand's name? Is it memorable?		
Do you avoid generic sub-brand names?		
Do you have comprehensive brand identity standards and systems that address all uses of your brand's identity elements?		
Are those standards and systems actively in use?		
Are they available in manuals, on CDs, and through your intranet?		
Are all business units and sub-brands subject to those standards, with none outside the jurisdiction of the standards?		
At a minimum, does the system include standards for the visual identifier, color, typography, backgrounds, contrast, staging area, relative size, positioning, key applications, and unacceptable uses?		
Is your logotype horizontally shaped? That orientation delivers the greatest visual impact and is a functional necessity when the logotype is used in retail environments.		
Will your system work globally? The meanings of specific words, colors, and symbols in different countries are especially important to understand.		
Does your system include distinctive shapes, colors, typestyles, and voices?		
Does your brand own a color that is different from that of your major competitor?		
Does your system include a slogan or jingle?		
Does it include sounds and other mnemonic devices?		
Is your system effective in multi-media environments?		
Does it address co-branding, co-marketing, brand licensing, strategic alliance and sponsorship situations?		

Table 7.2 *continued*

	Yes	No
Are there simple and consistent ways in which sub-brands relate to corporate or parent brands?		
Are there simple rules for when a brand is endorsed by a corporate or parent brand and when it is not?		
Does everyone agree upon what names, symbols, colors, visual styles, voices, etc. are used across all applications, sub-brands and product lines on behalf of the parent brand and its identity?		
In each point of contact with the consumer (advertising, retail environment, product packaging, etc), have you decided how much emphasis will be placed on the parent brand versus the sub-brand? Have you decided which elements will be associated with the parent brand and which will be associated with the sub-brand?		
Does the system deliver strong brand recall and recognition in all contexts?		
Is the system functional for all intended uses?		
Is the system flexible enough to address even the most complicated situations?		
Does your system address internal applications (memos, employee newsletters and other internal publications, computer screen savers, etc)?		
Does the system reinforce intended brand associations?		
Have you built at least nine random, non-functional design elements into your brand's trade dress to make it easier for you to legally protect your brand?		
Do you confer with intellectual property lawyers when designing new products and brands to ensure what you have created has maximum protection under the law?		
Do you have an ongoing process set up to proactively protect your brand's identity against dilution or confusion, including regular reviews of possible competitive infringements?		
Do you have a corporate brand identity council (or another process) to manage the brand identity on an ongoing basis?		
Do you conduct periodic communications audits to monitor adherence to corporate brand identity standards?		
Is your brand identity system as simple as possible?		
Ultimately, is it immediately clear which brand is the source for all points of contact you have with the consumer?		

NOTES

1　Source: *Wall Street Journal* as quoted in *emarketing magazine*'s April 2001 issue, p 52.
2　Source: Naming Strategies: 33 Tips and Tactics for Generating Names, *The Naming Newsletter*, Rivkin and Associates, http://www.namingnewsletter.com33tips.htm.
3　Primary Source: Color Psychology: Meanings and Effects of Colors, wysiwyg//3/http:// pyschology.about.com

Section 3

Building the brand

8

Driving the consumer from brand awareness to brand insistence

BrandForward believes that the ultimate goal of brand equity building is to move the consumer from brand awareness to brand insistence. Our brand insistence model incorporates five elements that drive a consumer to insist upon a particular brand to meet his or her needs: brand awareness, accessibility, value, relevant differentiation and emotional connection. We believe that these five areas of emphasis and activity are the primary drivers of consumer brand insistence.

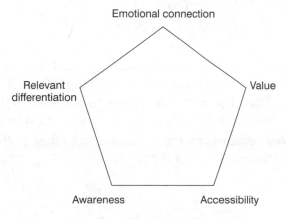

Figure 8.1 *BrandForward's brand insistence model*

BRAND AWARENESS

Brand building begins with awareness. Consumers first must be aware that there are different brands in the product categories in which your brand operates. Next, they must be aware of your brand. Ideally, your brand should be the first one that comes to their minds within specific product categories, and also the first one they associate with key consumer benefits. Consumers should:

- be able to identify which products and services your brand offers;
- be able to identify which benefits are associated with the brand;
- have some idea of where your brand is sold.

McDonald's: the power of the arches

During the 1996 Summer Olympics, a study was done of the most recognized symbols across several nations. What was right up there in the top five behind the Olympic rings but ahead of the Christian cross? The McDonald's golden arches, of course. How did this icon get to be so well recognized? To answer this, you only have to go to a McDonald's restaurant. From the time you turn into the restaurant parking lot and enter the restaurant until the time you are finished eating and leave, count the number of times you are exposed to the arches. Also make note of the most unusual places in which you discover the arches. You will have witnessed the power of an effective brand identity system and icon repetition.

ACCESSIBILITY

Your brand must be available where consumers shop. It is much easier for consumers to insist upon your brand if it is widely available, and slight brand preference goes a long way towards insistence when the brand is widely available. The importance of convenience cannot be underestimated in today's world. (Brands whose marketplace positionings have 'exclusivity' as a key component are an exception to this. In those cases, scarcity and limited distribution can stimulate demand.)

The Coca-Cola Company: the power of brand accessibility

Brand asset value

In 1997, *Financial World* valued the Coca-Cola brand at $48 billion. (More recently, it was valued at $72.5 billion. For the sake of comparison – Microsoft's brand was valued at $70.2 billion, IBM at $53.2 billion, and Intel at $39.0 billion.)

What does that really mean? If all of Coke's plants were burned to the ground, if every one of its employees were to quit, if all of its retail distribution was lost to competitors, if every single remaining tangible asset was sold, the person who owned rights to the Coke name and trademark could go to any bank in the world and, based on the value of that trademark, borrow money to completely rebuild the company. In other words, the Coke name alone is worth some $72.5 billion dollars – more than the value of all the company's other assets combined. After all, it's Coke that consumers insist upon, not any of the other stuff.

From the three A's to the three P's

Coca-Cola used to focus its strategy on the three A's: availability, acceptability and affordability. While these provided for tremendous growth, they also led to lowered entry barriers. Today, Coca-Cola's mantra is the three P's: preference, pervasive penetration, and price-related value.

The power of brand accessibility

If you were another soft drink company, you might define your competitive frame of reference as the cola market or the soft drink market or even the beverage market. But Coke thinks of its business and its market share in terms of 'share of human liquid consumption'. This makes water a competitor. In fact, a Coke executive has said that he will not be satisfied until 'there is a Coca-Cola faucet in every home'. Coca-Cola's mantra is 'within an arm's reach of desire'.

Another indication of Coke's drive for accessibility, beyond the vending machines which seem to be everywhere, is illustrated in a recent trip I took to Peru. We had spent several days travelling down Rio Madre de Dios on a riverboat, moving deeper and deeper into the Amazon river basin, jungle, and Manu World Biosphere Reserve. When we finally encountered a riverside village of indigenous people and thatched huts, what was waiting for us? A Coke sign and fresh Coke.

Coca-Cola is serious about brand building

Each month, Coca-Cola tests 20 brand attributes with 4,000 consumers to measure movement. The company also compensates (bonus and other compensation components) a large portion of its senior managers based on brand preference.

One final Coca-Cola fact

Coca-Cola's 1995 annual report reported that the second most recognized expression in the world after 'OK?' is 'Coca-Cola'.

VALUE

Does your brand deliver a good value for the price? Do consumers believe it is worth the price? Regardless of whether it is expensive or inexpensive, high end or low end, it must deliver at least a good value.

IMPORTANT THINGS TO KNOW ABOUT PRICING[1]

Reference prices

People often compare a product's price to a 'reference price' that they maintain in their minds for the product or product category in question. A 'reference price' is the price that people expect or deem to be reasonable for a certain type of product. Several factors affect reference prices:

- Memory of past prices.
- Frame of reference (compared with competitive prices, pre-sale prices, manufacturer's suggested prices, channel-specific prices, marked prices before discounts, substitute product prices, etc). Creating the most advantageous (and believable) competitive frame of reference is essential to achieving a price premium.
- Prices of other products on the same shelf, in the same catalogue, or in the same product line. The addition of a more premium priced product typically increases sales of other lower-priced products in the same product line.
- The way the price is presented – for instance, absolute number versus per quart, per pound, per hour of use, per application, for the result achieved, etc; also, four simple payments of $69.95 versus $279.80; for automobiles: total purchase price versus monthly loan payment versus monthly lease payment.
- The order in which people see a range of prices, as when a realtor uses the trick of showing the poorest value house first.

Price sensitivity

It is extremely important to be able to estimate the impact of price changes on sales and profits. That is, it is important to know how a price change will impact consumer response, competitive response and unit volume. Many business people erroneously believe that a price increase is the most cost-effective revenue generating marketing tactic. I have heard generally intelligent business people share their excitement about how a price increase will drop to the 'bottom line' dollar-for-dollar. Most of the time, this is simply not true.

People display different price sensitivities to different products in different situations. Often people are relatively price insensitive, but only within a relevant price range. Once a price exceeds that range, people become very sensitive. Raising the price across that threshold is akin to walking off of a cliff.

The following factors decrease price sensitivity:

- relevant brand / product differentiation;
- marketing and selling on factors other than price;
- convincing consumers that quality differs significantly among products and brands in the category;
- self-expressive or 'image' products or brands;
- brand advertising;
- situations in which price is a signal to quality – usually for relatively new or unknown products or brands;
- when it is difficult to ascertain a 'reference price' within the category;
- when there are significant switching costs – in dollars, time, effort, risk or emotional impact;
- product categories for which the risk of failure is an important issue;
- when the price is insignificant relative to the total budget or discretionary income;
- for businesses, when the item's price does not significantly contribute to the price of the products and services that they sell;
- when the price falls within the expected price range for products in the category;
- new markets;
- offering 'value added services' versus 'price discounts' to motivate purchases.

The following factors increase price sensitivity:

- price promotions, especially when people are able to stock up on the price-discounted items;
- mature and declining markets.

Price segmentation

Price segmentation (offering different prices to different market segments) increases overall revenues and profits, and is particularly beneficial to industries that have high fixed cost structures. Obviously, price segmentation works better to the extent to which there are real customer need segments and to which you can effectively isolate those segments.

Prices can be segmented in the following ways:

- By time (higher hotel room rates for holidays and other peak tourist seasons).
- By location (higher prices in locations with less competition or in which less price-sensitive shoppers shop, orchestra versus balcony seats in a theatre).

- By volume (volume discounts for large orders).
- By product attribute (first class versus coach section on aeroplanes; solid brass versus plastic faucets).
- By product bundling; for example:
  - selling software in product suites versus by the program;
  - selling e-learning by library versus the individual course;
  - fixed price versus a la carte menus;
  - 'fully-loaded' models versus 'basic' models with additional options available;
  - single admission ticket at theme parks versus charging per ride.
- By customer segment (brand-loyal versus price-sensitive versus convenience-oriented, or image-conscious versus economy-oriented).

Other price/value considerations

- Pricing strategy should consider these factors:
  - perceived customer value;
  - competitive response;
  - channels of distribution;
  - cost parameters;
  - congruence with the brand position.
- Constantly explore new ways to uniquely add customer value to your products and services.
- In creating greater customer value, always ask, 'How can we make it quicker, easier, less risky, or more pleasant to do business with us?' Ask, 'What could we do that would favourably surprise and delight our customers?'
- Communicate the value of services that you provide for free.
- Providing value-added products and services at 'no charge' is superior to price discounting as a short-term purchase incentive because it preserves the value of the brand.
- Be careful to price your products and services to reward brand-loyal (versus brand-switching) behaviour.

Pricing is becoming an increasingly sophisticated discipline. These three topics (reference prices, price sensitivity, and price segmentation) are just a few of the important considerations when developing pricing strategies and tactics. (Introductory pricing (skimming versus penetration, trial pricing), product mix pricing, fixed and variable price components, price adjustments (reason, amount and frequency), pricing to meet buying system requirements, loss-leader pricing, prestige pricing and even-odd pricing are other pricing approaches/considerations of note.) I would highly recommend reading *The Strategy and Tactics of Pricing* by Thomas T Nagle and Reed K

Holden (1995) (see References and further reading section) to better understand how to develop effective pricing strategies and tactics. Online pricing resources include www.pricing-advisor.com and www.profitablepricing.com.

RELEVANT DIFFERENTIATION

Relevant differentiation is the most important thing a brand can deliver. Relevant differentiation today is a leading-edge indicator of profitability and market share tomorrow. Does your brand own consumer-relevant, consumer-compelling benefits that are unique and believable? Today, services and the 'total brand experience' often become the differentiators.

The power of breaking consumer compromise

I believe 'breaking consumer compromises' is one of the most powerful concepts in business today. Introduced by George Stalk Jr, David K Pecaut, and Benjamin Burnett in a *Harvard Business Review* article in late 1996 (see References), it states that the best way to create breakaway business growth is to identify all the ways in which a business has made compromises with the consumer and then break them all so that that consumer gets exactly what he or she needs and wants.

CarMax and the used car industry

A powerful example they use is CarMax and the used car industry. An industry outsider (Circuit City) carefully analyzed the very large and profitable used car industry to identify all the consumer compromises: limited variety at any one place, no maintenance records, limited knowledge about the car's history, high pressure sales tactics, perceived lack of honesty and so on. By breaking all of these compromises, Circuit City gained a substantial market share very quickly with its CarMax business.

The greeting card industry

Another example is the greeting card industry. Most of the major greeting card companies raised their card prices much faster than the rate of inflation over several years until the average price of an individual card exceeded $2. This invited deep discount card shops into the industry. Factory Card Outlet (selling all cards for under $1) and others have gone from a zero share of market to over 20 per cent of the market in less than 10 years. (These stores have introduced other compromises, however, which will limit their long-term share to about 25 per cent of the market – unless they can keep on reinventing their successful business formula.)

Another greeting card industry example is share shift from card shops to the mass channels. As more and more women entered the workplace (the vast majority of working age women today), the convenient hours of grocery stores, chain drug stores, and Wal-Mart broke the compromise consumers faced in card shops (with their traditional 10 am to 5 pm hours, which they have extended more recently).

Reinventing your business

The trick is to constantly reinvent your business even if you think you have something to lose by doing so. That is why it is often the most difficult for an industry insider to transform the industry by breaking compromises. Consider Kodak. It must have been difficult for Kodak to enter the digital imaging world with a passion when most of its current business is based on chemical photography. And, it was very difficult for Hallmark, in the late 1990s, to introduce a very large selection of 99 cent cards (Out of the Blue, children's seasonal, and Hallmark Warm Wishes greeting cards) with the very real concern of possible trade down. But, to their credit, Hallmark did it, and broke the consumer compromise.

EMOTIONAL CONNECTION

As we have discussed, the consumer first must know your brand and then he or she must like your brand. Finally, the consumer must trust your brand and feel an emotional connection to it.

People become emotionally connected to a brand for a number of reasons:

● The brand stands for something important to them.
● The brand is intense and vibrant. It connects with people on multiple levels across several senses.
● The brand is unique.
● The brand is admirable.
● The brand consistently interacts with them. It never disappoints them.
● The brand makes them feel good.

There are many innovative ways to achieve this emotional connection, from advertising and the quality of front line consumer contact to consumer membership organizations and company-sponsored consumer events. Ultimately, emotional connection will come from positive shared experiences with the brand over time. While this trust is built over time, offering an unconditional guarantee is a quick way to reduce the risk of a new unknown brand and to generate some minimum level of trust immediately.

Other loyalty inducing approaches

The brand encourages frequent, habit-forming interaction (as long as the interaction is pleasant or beneficial and not against people's wills).

The brand finds ways to build cumulative value for customers over time, especially if the value is not transferable to the use of competitive products and services.

In his book, *The Dream Society,* Rolf Jensen makes the case for a shift from an information society to a dream society in which imagination and storytelling become the primary drivers of value. In this book, he identifies six emerging emotion-based markets:

- adventure;
- community (togetherness, friendship and love);
- providing and receiving care;
- self-expression ('Who am I?');
- peace of mind;
- standing for something (convictions).

Any brand that seeks to create emotional connection should find ways to tap into these and other underlying human motives.

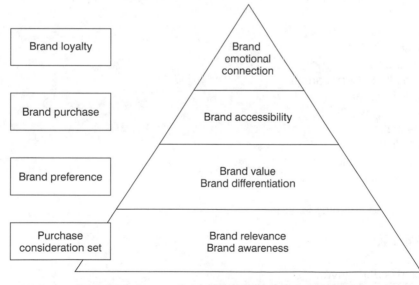

Figure 8.2 *Creating an emotional connection*

Brand emotional connection

You know you have a vital, relevant, compelling brand when customers think or say the following things about your brand. (These are taken from real customer feedback on brands with strong emotional connection.)

- It affects people at a visceral level.
- It 'gets in your blood'.
- It evokes strong emotions.
- It speaks from the heart.
- It speaks to the heart.
- It opens up people's sense of what is possible.
- It creates a sense of possibility.
- It opens up a whole new world.
- It is inspiring.
- It is empowering.
- It is invigorating.
- It helps people see that they can make a difference.
- It makes people believe that they can change the world.
- It helps people articulate what they have been trying to say.
- It is the first time that people feel as if they really have been heard.
- It is unique.
- It is fresh.
- It is original.
- It is one of a kind.
- It breaks all of the rules.
- It breaks down all the boundaries.
- It is 'a breath of fresh air'.
- It defines the category.
- It is quintessential.
- It sets the standard.
- It stands apart from all the rest.
- It can't be categorized.
- It is in a class all of its own.
- No one else is doing anything like that.
- It has new ideas.
- It is very influential.
- It is seminal.
- Everything else is derivative.
- It reinvents the category.
- It is genuine.
- It is sincere.
- It is real.
- It is pure.
- It is trustworthy.

- It is approachable.
- It is endearing.
- It stands for something.
- It believes in something.
- It is passionate.
- It has a distinctive attitude.
- People in that organization love what they do.
- It is powerful.
- It possesses great energy.
- It is entertaining.
- It is elegant, beautiful and/or haunting.
- It is admirable.
- It is visionary.
- It possesses a timeless quality.
- It possesses a universal quality.
- It has successfully stood the test of time.
- It is still relevant years later.
- It is as it is meant to be.
- It is 'bigger than life'.
- It has a presence that you can't ignore.
- It demands to be heard.
- It is legendary.
- It is enshrouded in mystery.
- There is a certain mystique about it.
- It is profound.
- It is captivating.
- It is otherworldly.
- It is mesmerizing.
- It is indescribable.
- The only way that people can fully understand the brand is by experiencing it for themselves.
- It is unstoppable.
- It is extraordinary.
- It is flawless.
- It is genius.
- It is a 'crowning jewel'.
- It is riveting.
- It is 'mind blowing'.
- It doesn't get any better than that.

WHAT BRAND?

What brand has built enormous equity without huge advertising budgets?

What brand has defined its business not narrowly as a product, but broadly as an experience and a state of mind, despite the fact that the vast majority of its revenues result from one single product category?

What brand has created tremendous brand loyalty by creating a social organization for owners of its products?

What brand sponsors frequent events for owners of its products, which the company's management attends in order to understand the consumer, his/her experience, and his/her needs first hand?

What brand proactively leverages publicity as a key component of its marketing plan?

What brand tried to legally protect the sound its product makes as a key element of its brand identity system?

What brand, having been on the brink of bankruptcy twice since the 1960s, has achieved a stunning transformation into a world-class brand?

What brand evokes so much loyalty in its consumers that many of them tattoo its logo on their bodies?

Harley-Davidson, of course.

MANAGING BRAND EQUITY: A CASE STUDY

While serving as director of brand management and marketing at Hallmark, I spent the better part of three years developing and refining a brand equity framework and scorecard for Hallmark. As awareness of the Hallmark brand was very high and its image was very positive, we were less interested in measuring and managing these aspects of the brand's equity than we were in identifying the attributes that drove customers to insist upon the brand. This ultimately led to what is now BrandForward's brand insistence brand equity model (as addressed earlier in this chapter) with key drivers: awareness, accessibility, value, relevant differentiation and emotional connection. Hallmark scored extraordinarily high on awareness, accessibility and emotional connection. While relevant differentiation was constantly a focus (as it should be for all established brands), we primarily focused on improving value. While Hallmark's greeting cards were actually less expensive than competitors' cards, they were universally thought to be more expensive. People perceived Hallmark cards to be priced between $2.75 and $2.95 ($1 higher than the actual average price paid), while they perceived mass channel brands' cards to be priced at $2 (very near the actual average price paid after in-store discounts). So people connected the following in their minds:

'Hallmark = the best = expensive' (or 'When you care enough to send the very best'). This perception was reinforced in several ways.

People were especially price conscious in card shops (Hallmark's primary channel at the time) as they assumed products would be more expensive there. Card shops seldom, if ever, offered price discounts. People shopping in Wal-Mart, with its promise of 'Always the low price – always', its prominent 'X% off' displays, and, in the case of greeting cards, its generic brands, are less likely to be on the lookout for high prices.

Also, in a card shop's typical market basket of three greeting cards, card prices were obvious (a total bill of $12 easily translates to $3 a card). This is versus a typical mass channel market basket, which may total nearly $100 comprised of a wide variety of items.

Our brand equity measurement system identified this as an issue in two ways: Hallmark received a mediocre score on 'value' and the system identified 'expensive' as Hallmark's only negative brand association.

Altering price perceptions for a leading premium brand is a tricky exercise. It is kind of like diffusing a bomb. The trick is to snip the right wire – the 'the best = expensive' wire, not the 'Hallmark = the best' wire. Changing Hallmark price perceptions was also critical to the success of our strategy of launching Expressions From Hallmark to the mass channel (see the Hallmark case study in the section on 'Leveraging the brand').

After our brand scorecard identified 'value' as an issue, we got management's buy-in to develop and test aggressive measures to alter the 'expensive' price perception. Here is what we did:

- We developed two lines of 99 cent cards as proof points: children's (occasion and non-occasion) cards and 'Out of the Blue', a new line of 'anyday' friendship cards. We devoted 248 skus and 8 liner feet of product to this new line, which provided a proof point of (and statement about) our commitment to the new line.
- Because we knew our competitors could not match this, we created pocket identifiers (signing above each card on the display) highlighting the cards that were under $2 (65 per cent of Hallmark's cards, only 11 per cent of our competitors' cards).
- We prominently featured '99 cent' signs at appropriate places throughout the card department.
- We advertised the fact that Hallmark now had 99 cent cards.
- Introducing 'Expressions From Hallmark' cards to Wal-Mart and other mass channel stores reinforced the point that Hallmark must not be that expensive (borrowing upon Wal-Mart's 'low price' brand perceptions).
- We did all of this as part of a test market in Las Vegas.
- We tested the impact of this action on many brand equity components in that test market, not just 'value'. For instance, we tested brand preference, quality perceptions, and brand insistence itself, to validate that increased 'value' led to increased brand equity and insistence.

Here is what we found from the Las Vegas test market:

- Greeting card category price perceptions improved significantly.
- All Hallmark brand equity measures increased significantly.
- People gave Hallmark credit for listening to their concerns about price.
- Hallmark sales and market share increased significantly.

Based upon the success of this test market, we launched this programme throughout the United States, and we achieved the same results throughout the United States. This is a simple example of how a brand equity measurement system led to actions that significantly improved brand perceptions, sales and market share.

Did you know...?

- Everything else being equal, people are less sensitive to price changes for brands with large market shares than for competing brands with smaller market shares.

- The average person can only bring three to four brands to mind for a given product category. In low involvement categories, these brands receive a major advantage. (Low involvement categories are those categories in which not much time or effort is invested in the purchase choice. These tend to be low price, low risk categories.)

- If your brand has high top-of-mind awareness, it is a good indication that it is firmly in most consumers' consideration sets (the set of brands a consumer considers when making a purchase choice).

Table 8.1 *Brand management checklist: driving the consumer from brand awareness to brand insistence*

	Yes	No
Was your brand first to market?		
Was it the first to communicate with consumers in significant ways?		
Is your brand the top-of-mind brand in its product/service category?		
Is it the only brand that comes to mind for its primary differentiating benefit?		
Do consumers perceive your brand to be easily accessible and convenient?		
Have you carefully crafted brand pricing strategies and tactics based upon a solid understanding of contribution margins, consumer price sensitivities, reference prices, likely competitive responses, and basic pricing principles?		

Table 8.1 (*continued*)

	Yes	No
Does your brand deliver a good value for the price? Do consumers think your brand is worth the price?		
Is your brand differentiated in at least one highly relevant and compelling way?		
Does your brand touch people at some deep emotional level? Does it stand for something important to them?		
Does your brand achieve any of the following: • Make people feel more in control? • Is it nostalgic of something from their childhood? • Does it make them feel warm and safe? • Does it offer a sensual experience? • Does it make them feel smart or frugal or important when they use it? • Does it make them feel like 'masters of the universe'? • Does it help them play out unfulfilled fantasies? • Does it make them feel as though they have become the people that they had always wanted to be? • Does it make them feel more connected to the group they most admire? • Does it make them feel superior to others?		
Is your brand the most preferred brand in its category?		
Do your customers perceive your brand to be vital, popular or leading-edge?		
Do people like your brand?		
Do people trust your brand?		
Is your brand on most potential customers' shortlists? Is it typically the only brand that they consider?		
Are your customers attitudinally loyal to your brand?		
Do people enthusiastically recommend your brand to others?		

NOTES

1   Much of this section (especially the list of factors that decrease and increase price sensitivity) is informed by Thomas T Nagle and Reed K Holden's book, *The Strategy and Tactics of Pricing* (1995). It also largely draws upon my experience crafting pricing strategy for Hallmark.

9

Brand advertising

Advertising is one of the most frequently used and powerful communications mediums for brand building. How then does one maximize the effectiveness and efficiency of this medium?

SELECTING AN AD AGENCY[1]

First, if you do not have an advertising agency, select one. Begin by thoughtfully defining what is most important to you in an agency, and clarify where you need the most help. This will be an important touchstone throughout the remainder of the process.

Cut out your favourite magazine ads and tape your favourite television commercials. www.adcritic.com is a good place to find great ads, as are One Show and *Communication Arts* awards books. Also, most cities have ad clubs that judge and recognize the best ads from local agencies. Check with these clubs as well. Once you have selected several ads that you like, find out which agencies created them. Of those agencies, find out which are already working for your competitors. Rule them out. Talk with marketing peers at other companies about their perceptions of the agencies that are left. Ask about the agencies' capabilities in each of the following areas: product, company and market place knowledge, creative, strategic insight, media planning and production. (I have found that the two most important aspects of an effective agency are strategic insight and translating that insight to creative communication.) Contact the top three to four of those that are left.

When you meet, ask to see their best ads. Have the agencies demonstrate how they would address your most pressing strategic issues. You might also ask each agency to create three campaigns to move your brand forward. (Be sure to pay each of the agencies for their work. This protects you if you use an agency's ideas but do not end up hiring that agency.) You should also look for the agency that you can best work with based upon personal chemistry.

Some other notes

Do not assume that going with the biggest well-known agency is best. Unless you have an enormous advertising budget, you are likely to be assigned to their 'C team' and may not be happy with the 'C team's' work.

There are significant advantages to choosing an agency that has strengths in multiple areas: strategy, creative, media planning and buying, direct marketing, online marketing, Web site design, trade shows and so on. It will make it easier to manage your overall marketing budget and, more importantly, all of your communication will be likely to be consistent and 'on brand'. Unfortunately, very few agencies are tops in more than a few aspects of marketing. I prefer to work with a small number of 'best in class' agencies. This requires a strong coordination effort including frequent (quarterly) 'brand champion summits' (in which all agency partners are invited to remain informed and aligned with the strategy and key messages), well-thought out and accessible brand identity standards, and an accessible brand image library. It is particularly important to coordinate the efforts of advertising strategy and creative with that of media planning and buying, if these functions are performed by separate agencies. The two agencies should meet often and learn to work well together.

I have found that some agencies are best at (and enjoy most) the development of new breakthrough campaigns. They are critical to your brand's success but also tend to be more expensive. Other agencies do not have a 'strategic bone in their bodies' but provide on-spec collateral pieces at a fraction of the cost. I use both types of agency. Some agencies try to address both needs at different hourly rates using different individuals and processes. Sometimes that works. Sometimes it doesn't.

THE IMPORTANCE OF A WELL DESIGNED BRAND TO BRAND ADVERTISING

As you begin to work with an agency (even during an agency review), you will make greater strides if you have already designed and positioned the brand. Remember, your brand's promise should leverage all three of the following: 1) a compelling point of difference in the consumer's mind; 2) your organization's unique strengths; and 3) your competitors' vulnerabilities. This implies that you have identified the brand's target consumer, essence, promise and personality. The brand promise, in turn, implies that you understand your brand's competitive frame of reference and the consumer's benefit structure within that frame of reference. The brand design and positioning will drive brand advertising and every other brand marketing activity. Make sure your ad agency thoroughly understands and embraces your brand's design. (While you should take the lead in crafting your brand's design, ideally your ad agency should be actively involved in the process, including immersing themselves in the underlying consumer research.)

SPECIFYING THE MARKETING OBJECTIVE FOR ADVERTISING

The next step in advertising development is specifying the marketing objective for the advertising. That is, what do you want the advertising to achieve? Do you want it to increase brand awareness, attract new customers, increase brand loyalty, encourage add-on purchases, motivate people to switch from competitive brands to your brand, increase frequency of use, reinforce ongoing use?

As an example, the marketing objective for Hallmark's brand insistence advertising campaign in the mid 1990s was very simple and tactical: to get consumers to flip the card over and look for the brand name on the back cover.

Next you augment the brand promise with proof points (reasons to believe).

Convince:	Target customer
That your brand uniquely delivers:	Relevant differentiating benefit
Because:	Proof points[2].

During your brand positioning work, you should have developed the brand promise including identification of the brand's relevant differentiating benefit. Proof points may include product features and attributes (including the design itself or its formula or ingredients).

WRITING THE AGENCY BRIEF

The marketing objective and the brand promise with its proof points are key elements of the agency brief, a document that communicates the strategic direction of a new advertising campaign. Once you have completed the agency brief, your ad agency will use the brief to develop campaign ideas/concepts (storyboards, print ads, and so on). They will probably show you several different campaign ideas.

Here are the elements of the agency brief:

Agency brief

Background/overview: (provide history, context, and a general overview of the competitive environment and the problem).

Target customer: (be as specific as possible).

Marketing objective: (desired tangible result, usually in target customer's attitude or behaviour – intended effect with quantifiable success criteria).

- **Current state:** (what the customer thinks today).
- **Desired state:** (what we want them to think *and* what we want them to do).
- **Customer insight:** (key insight that could lead to changed brand attitudes or behaviours).

Assignment: (deliverable, timing and budget).

Product or service: (if product/service-specific).

Brand essence: (the 'heart and soul' of the brand expressed as 'adjective, adjective, noun').

Brand promise: (Only [brand] delivers [relevant differentiated benefit]).

- **Proof points** (reasons to believe).

Brand personality, voice and visual style: (from the positioning statement – list of adjectives that describe the brand, for instance, *voice:* down-to-earth, assertive, confident, warm, sarcastic, witty, reassuring, eloquent, simple, etc; *visual style*: bold, bright, energetic, soft, textured, ornate, understated, nostalgic, futuristic, etc).

Mandatories: those items that are givens. It is best to provide as few constraints as possible. I usually specify the brand identity standards and system as the only mandatory. There may be legal or regulatory mandatories as well.

EVALUATING ADVERTISING EFFECTIVENESS

When evaluating the potential effectiveness of different campaign ideas, I use the following questions:

All advertising

- Does the ad clearly identify your brand? Does it do so immediately and throughout the ad?
- Does the ad clearly and forcefully communicate your brand's unique promise?
- Does the ad feature a tag line that reinforces the brand's promise?
- Are the ad's tone, voice and style true to your brand's essence and personality?
- Does the ad reinforce your brand's identity?

- Does the ad connect with the reader on an emotional level? Does it win the reader's heart or capture his or her imagination?
- Is there something about the ad that makes the reader admire the brand?
- Is your ad significantly different from that of your competitors? Does it look and feel different from anything else featured in the same media?
- Does the ad reinforce the positive value and values of your brand?
- Does the ad seem truly inspired?
- Is your ad so powerful that it has the potential to keep your competitors awake at night worrying about your brand?
- Is the ad persuasive?
- Could no competitor make the same claim? If you inserted a competitor's logo in the ad, would it make no sense or be unbelievable?
- Does the ad lead the reader / viewer to believe that he or she will be better off in some way for having interacted with your brand? Does it create a more favourably perceived end-state for him or her? Does it leave a vivid picture in his or her mind?

Did you know...?

Psychologist Erich Dichter found that consumers are more apt to relax and accept advertiser recommendations when the tone is that of a friend or an unbiased authority.[3]

Print advertising

Benefits of print advertising are its good reach and frequency, that it can handle complicated propositions, reaches consumers in a receptive context, and can be very targeted:

- Does the headline immediately 'grab' the reader? (In advertising guru David Ogilvy's book *Ogilvy on Advertising* (1985), Ogilvy states that five times as many people read headlines as read body copy.) Ideally, the headline is nine words or less.
- Does the headline promise an important benefit? (Ogilvy also states in *Ogilvy on Advertising* (1985) that ads with headlines that promise benefits are read by four times more people than those that don't.)
- Is the body copy long enough to provide the reader with useful information and ample proof points for your brand's promise? Long copy is more effective than short copy. This is particularly true for business-to-business advertising. (Alternatively, Roper

Starch Worldwide, which maintains a database of more than 2,000,000 print ads, has found that excessive copy reduces the effectiveness of ads and recommends keeping ad copy to 50 words or less. With whole generations having now grown up on 'sound bytes' of information, some cohort groups will respond better to shorter copy.)

● Increasing white space around the ad or the headline increases the ad's effectiveness.

Ranking order of magazine advertising size impact

1. Three single-page ads following each other on the right side.
2. Two single-page ads in different sections of the same magazine on the right side.
3. Double-page spread.
4. Single-page ads on right.
5. Single-page ads on left with strip on right.
6. Single-page ads on left.
7. Checkerboard ads on right.
8. Checkerboard ads on left.
9. Half-page ad, upper right.
10. Half-page ad, lower right.
11. Strip on both right and left sides.
12. Half-page ad, upper left.
13. Half-page ad, lower left.
14. Third-page block, lower right.
15. Strip (one column) extreme right.
16. Strip, extreme left.

Source: A study performed by the PreTesting Company.[4]!

Television advertising

The benefits are: broad reach, greatest ability to dramatize the brand):

● Do you try to grab people's attention immediately so that they do not become preoccupied with other activities?
● Do you have enough time to tell a story with your commercial? (Two-minute commercials are more powerful than 30-second commercials.)
● Have you carefully selected the music for your commercial? (Music can make or break a commercial.)
● Have you consistently used a sound or visual mnemonic to reinforce the brand in your commercials?

Radio advertising

The benefits are: very efficient, a good frequency medium, coverage flexibility):

- Does the first five seconds 'grab' the listener?
- Have you chosen the right voice?
- Does the dialogue sound natural?

Outdoor advertising

The benefits are: very low CPM, a true local medium, ability to communicate a single 'idea' effectively:

- Does the billboard have no more than seven words? Does it have less than five? ('Got Milk?') Remember, motorists often have to 'get it' (your message) in a second or less!
- Is the ad 'big' in every way? Is it outrageous? Does it turn heads? Does it pique the reader's curiosity? Does it shock the reader? Does it make the reader laugh?

SUCCESSFUL ADVERTISING APPROACHES

Effective general ad techniques:

- A good ad will always dramatize your brand's most important benefit.
- Simpler ads are usually more powerful.
- Create copy in smaller chunks – sentences, paragraphs, etc.
- Natural and 'real life' writing or dialogue.
- Subtly tapping into people's fears and anxieties.

Here are some print advertising techniques that have proved to be effective:

- Try to evoke the reader's curiosity. Begin by asking a provocative question and/or feature an image that piques the reader's curiosity.
- Put quotes around your headlines.
- Romance/dramatize your product or service.
- Try to trigger multiple senses – use words that help people feel, hear, smell and taste your product.
- Tell a story.

- Communicate 'news.'
- Provide information that is useful to the reader.
- Always write in the present tense.
- Be as specific as possible.
- Include customer testimonials (they should seem natural, not scripted or polished).
- Know how readers read (from right to left top to bottom in the United States) and place your headlines, illustrations, captions and copy accordingly.
- Use white space to focus the reader's attention on something important.
- In his book *Secret Formulas of the Wizard of Ads*, Roy H Williams indicates that savvy photographers and graphic artists have known for some time that there is a spot on a piece of artwork to which the eye is irresistibly drawn, roughly between the middle and upper right corner of the artwork.
- Use words that sell: at last, now, new, introducing, announcing, finally, limited, save, free, win, easy, guarantee, breakthrough, wanted, etc. (Keep in mind that as consumers become more sophisticated and savvy, there may be instances where these words might be clichéd or overused, and thus might not be as effective.)
- Avoid metaphors, analogies, puns, double entendres, "insider" references, and other non-straightforward language. Alliteration is sometimes effective.
- Avoid jargon, dialect, acronyms and model numbers, especially in the headline.

Here are some successful approaches to television advertisements[5]:

- Company leader as brand spokesperson (examples: Richard Branson of Virgin Atlantic, Dave Thomas of Wendy's, Lee Iacocca of Chrysler, Ben Cohen and Jerry Greenfield of Ben & Jerry's).
- Interesting character as brand spokesperson (Mr Whipple of Charmin).
- Customer testimonial.
- Visualization of the brand benefit and/or the 'reason why'.
- Product demonstration (demonstrate product usage and show brand benefit).
- Torture test.
- Problem–solution.
- Before–after. To some large degree, advertising sells the hope of an improved future with the use of a particular brand of product or service. Before–after advertising reinforces this hope.
- Competitive comparison, although it is usually not wise to identify the competitive brand by name.
- Slice-of-life vignette (tells a story about the benefits of the brand).
- Presenter/'talking head' (in which a person attempts to persuade the viewer about the benefits of the brand).

The following will probably result in bad brand advertising:

- Design by committee.
- Opinionated reviewers and approvers who do not understand marketing.
- Writing ads that appeal to you rather than the target consumer.
- Using flowery language that sounds good but that means nothing. (This is a common ailment of neophyte copywriters. Substance is good. Using an economy of words is good. Simple, persuasive copy is good. Fluff and filler are bad.)
- Focusing on reach versus frequency. (See discussion on reach versus frequency later in this chapter.)
- Assuming that business-to-business advertising is significantly different from consumer advertising ('It needs to be factual and informative, not emotional.'). Don't forget, business decision makers are people too. And people are ruled as much by their hearts as by their heads. Harding's 1996 study of buyers in 10 corporations demonstrated that corporate buyers overwhelmingly rely on personal and emotional reasons over rational ones in their purchase choice.
- Jingles. Unless they are very, very good (and most are not very, very good), they will distract from the brand message.
- Celebrity endorsements: they tend not to be believable.
- Making claims that your brand cannot support.

When building the brand, the best advertising vehicles to use tend to be radio, television, and with the widespread emergence of broadband, the Internet, due to the auditory elements. These vehicles create a slower build but are more effective in the long run. Trade magazines and shows and direct marketing (mail, e-mail, etc) are effective for business-to-business marketing because the target audiences typically are geographically dispersed but highly targeted. Newspapers and the radio are often used to promote brand-building events, as they can efficiently and effectively deliver a more immediate message. Radio advertising should be scheduled for immediate effect, and radio ads should be scheduled to run just before or during a sale or other event.

ADVERTISING RESEARCH

While advertising is part art and part science, there is more science to it than one might realize. There are many 'rules of thumb' that ad agencies and advertisers have developed over time, based on experience or research or both. I have found the following types of research to be important to creating strong brand advertising:

- Qualitative research (focus group, mini-group, one-on-one, anthropological, etc) to better understand the target customer's hopes, needs, desires, aspirations, fears and concerns.

- Brand preference testing (before and after exposure to the ad). Asking people what they would tell others about your products and services before and after exposure to the ad is also insightful. (David Ogilvy's book, *Ogilvy on Advertising* (1985), states that people whose brand preference increases after having seen an ad are three times more likely to purchase the brand then those whose preference does not change.)
- The split run technique. This technique allows you to test two forms of the ad in the marketplace to determine which one is the most effective.
- Occasionally, you may want to understand how existing loyal customers are responding to your ads, especially if your ad's intent is to attract new customers. For instance, are the ads offering new customers something that you are not offering existing customers? Are the ads promising something that current customers have found not to be true? Are your ads helping existing customers to feel better about your brand? Are they reinforcing the wisdom of having purchased your brand?

When measuring the effectiveness of your ads, increased top-of-mind awareness and purchase intent are the two most important measures. Other measures tend to be: more specific changes in customer attitude or behaviour based upon the specific marketing objective for the ad.

Keep in mind, too, that because advertising's effect is gradual and cumulative (much like the growth of a child), it is difficult to measure the effect of an individual ad on sales or market share. That (and for diagnostic reasons) is why it is important to measure the effect of ads on attitudes. Ad recognition and recall and message takeaways also help diagnose an ad (which is particularly important when an ad is not working).

A word of caution regarding advertising research: it is unwise to delegate this task to your advertising agency. It is best to conduct it yourself or to employ a third party to conduct it. Checks and balances are a good thing. And, to mix metaphors, there is no sense in 'hiring the fox to guard the chicken coop'.

If you are interested in learning more about advertising research, I would suggest that you go to the Advertising Research Foundation's Web site (http://www.arfsite.org/) and consider subscribing to their *Journal of Advertising Research*. Another source is the American Marketing Association's *Journal of Marketing Research* (www.marketingpower.com).

ADVERTISING RULES OF THUMB

- Try to budget between 8 and 12 per cent of revenues on advertising and other marketing activities. (This obviously varies significantly by company and industry. An average company spends approximately 6 per cent of sales on advertising alone. Advertising expenditures for computer and office equipment are as low as

0.09 per cent versus 16.8 per cent for toys, dolls and games.[6] Industrial companies tend to spend less on advertising (1 per cent to 5 per cent typically) than consumer products companies.)

- You should spend more on advertising and marketing if the following conditions exist[7]:
    - You are building a new brand.
    - You are launching a new product or service.
    - Your product offering is large and complex.
    - You charge premium prices.
    - You sell products and services in a 'low involvement' category (typically low priced items for which there is little risk of failure).
    - You are selling commodity products (advertising will be the primary differentiator).
- Spend approximately $1 on proactive publicity for every $10 you spend on advertising.[8] (PR budgets are 1 per cent of a company's revenues on average.) It will multiply the effectiveness of your advertising. (Advertising in trade magazines also gives you a relationship with the publications, alerts you to editorial opportunities, and sometimes will impact your brand's presence in articles.)
- Production costs are usually 10 per cent of the media buy.
- Know what your brand's 'share of voice' is – or the amount of advertising (or consumer communication) dollars your company spends compared to competitors for a given product category. It is a good rough measure, despite its flaws, which include:
    - its focus on traditional advertising spending only;
    - competitors are usually in different portfolios of businesses and it is difficult to break the spending out for the same categories across all competitors;
    - advertising effectiveness for the same level of spending varies widely.
- It is nearly always more productive to focus on frequency versus reach. Many will say that it is more efficient to focus on reach because there are diminishing returns with each new ad exposure. That is, the advertising response curve is usually concave. This is particularly true if your goal is to create an immediate sale of a ubiquitously purchased consumer product. In that situation, reach almost always delivers 'more bang for your buck'. However, if your funds are limited and your audience is highly targeted, you would do better to focus on a reach schedule of 3+, seeking out media with significant audience overlap.[9] For brand building purposes, I usually focus on advertising frequency targeted at those who are most likely to influence the remainder of the market: primary target opinion leaders and 'hard core' users.
- Ads produce better results if they highlight or dramatize the brand's unique compelling benefit.
- The most effective ads combine a subtle emotional appeal with a practical benefit.[10]
- The more an ad can get people to identify with one of its characters, the more powerful its effect will be.

- If the ad is designed so that people overhear something rather than being told about it, they will be less rigorous and defensive in their analysis of the message[11].
- If a significant portion of your product's sales results from repeat purchases, it may be more important for your advertising to reinforce the purchase than to persuade people to purchase your product for the first time.
- Carrying a particular brand voice and visual style (and mnemonic device) from one ad campaign to another increases the effectiveness of the new ad campaign.
- Scents have the greatest ability to evoke memories. Music has the second greatest ability to do so. Both are mnemonic devices.

What comes to mind when you hear the following?

1. You deserve a break today.
2. Be all that you can be.
3. Just do it.
4. It's the real thing.
5. Where's the beef?
6. It takes a tough man to make a tender chicken.
7. We try harder.
8. Oh, what a feeling...
9. You've come a long way, baby.
10. Mmm mmm good.
11. It's where you want to be.
12. It takes a licking and keeps on ticking.
13. Don't leave home without it.
14. A different kind of company. A different kind of car.
15. The Uncola.
16. Melts in your mouth, not in your hand.
17. When you care enough to send the very best.
18. We do it your way at...
19. All the news that's fit to print.
20. Put a tiger in your tank.
21. Snap! Crackle! Pop!
22. We bring good things to life.
23. It's not just a job – it's an adventure.
24. The thrill of victory. The agony of defeat.

Answers
1. McDonald's.
2. US Army.
3. Nike.
4. Coca-Cola.
5. Wendy's.

6. Perdue.
7. Avis.
8. Toyota.
9. Virginia Slims.
10. Campbell's.
11. VISA.
12. Timex.
13. American Express.
14. Saturn.
15. 7-Up.
16. M&Ms.
17. Hallmark.
18. Burger King.
19. The *New York Times*.
20. Esso.
21. Rice Crispies.
22. GE.
23. US Marine Corps.
24. ABC's Wide World of Sports.

- Repeatedly featuring a product's packaging in advertising makes it more noticeable at point of purchase (and therefore, more likely to be purchased).
- 15-second commercials are seldom effective as it is difficult for them to break through the clutter and they are far too short to tell a story. They are best used as reminder commercials (reinforcing messages from previous longer commercials).
- The following factors have been shown to increase advertising effectiveness:[12]
  - differentiating brand message;
  - product demonstration (use, result and benefit);
  - total time viewed.
- The following factors have been shown to decrease advertising effectiveness:[13]
  - detailed component or ingredient information;
  - multiple propositions.
- For manufacturers, advertising can affect sales in two ways: it persuades the end consumer to purchase your brand, and it persuades the intermediary (retailer) to carry your brand, increasing the brand's accessibility.

- Persuasive ads diminish in their effectiveness over time. This argues for front-loading GRPs (gross ratings points) to maximize the effect.[14]
- There is a strong correlation between how much a company spends on advertising and its share of market.
- Brand familiarity and popularity increase with increased advertising.
- Advertising affects purchase decisions by affecting the order in which alternatives are evoked (top-of-mind awareness) and the desirability of a particular alternative (positioning). The former is the most important effect. It puts an alternative in people's consideration sets.
- Over 70 per cent of the impact of advertising on market share results from increasing brand awareness (versus creating or building brand image).[15]
- As the number of messages in an advertisement increase, two things happen: demand increases and recall decreases. The ratio of these effects varies by media and for high and low involvement categories.
- It is extraordinarily difficult to try to change the consumer's mind about your brand. You would do best not to try. If you must, link the change in perception to something that consumers currently believe about your brand.
- Themes and slogans that reinforce the current brand image generate awareness faster than those that support a new positioning.
- In general, the more unique the message, the more successful its communication.
- Highly recalled messages tend to be the result of well funded long-standing advertising campaigns.[16]
- The more often a brand repeats a claim, the more likely people are to believe that the claim is true, especially if there is no evidence to the contrary.
- For low involvement categories (in which the alternatives are often virtually identical), advertising can tip the balance in favour of the advertised brand. For these categories, it is particularly important that the ads break through the clutter and focus on one simple message.
- For high involvement categories, advertising plays less of a role overall. Typically, its role is to put the brand in the consideration set, not to influence the final buying decision.
- People actively seek out information in high involvement categories. Print media, more information, and longer copy work well with this audience.
- It is acceptable, and even preferable, to include a 'call to action' in brand advertising. (An impact on short-term sales results will help you justify the expenditure.)

Advertising quick assessment tool

- Does the headline/opening grab people?
- Does the ad clearly and forcefully communicate the intended brand benefit?
- Is the ad distinctive and 'ownable'?
- Does the ad feature a strong reason why (proof points)?
- Does the ad communicate something admirable about the company?
- Will this ad resonate with the target audience?
- Does the ad connect with people on an emotional level?
- Does the ad reinforce the brand essence, promise and personality?
- Does the ad reinforce the brand identity standards?

MEDIA PLANNING

It is best to leave media planning to media planning professionals. The following are some of the things that they will consider when they develop a media plan for you:

- Reach (percentage of people – or target audience – exposed).
- Frequency (number of times, on average, a person is exposed).
- Impressions (the number of times the target market comes in contact with a media vehicle).
- CPM (cost per thousand exposures) – measures efficiency.
- CPMTM (cost per thousand target market exposures) – measures effective efficiency.
- Identifying the most appropriate media vehicles (audience fit with target market, environmental fit with advertising message).
  - For instance, Web sites and trade shows provide a high capacity to process information when customer information needs are high, while short television spots are best used when information processing needs are lower.[17]
  - Some media are more appropriate when the purchase decision is based primarily on facts, while others are more appropriate when feelings and emotions are the key influencers.
- Evaluating vehicle effectiveness (clutter, distractions).
- Adjusting potential exposures to actual exposures (for television, it has been found to vary from 50 per cent to 70 per cent).
- Developing a media strategy and schedule that maximizes advertising response (against the advertising objective).

When we conducted laddering research[18] at Hallmark, we discovered that most product and brand benefits ultimately supported the underlying need to preserve self-esteem.

Different benefits may have followed different paths to that end, but ultimately, the need that they fulfilled was the same fundamental one – to preserve self-esteem. While the following data is from a study conducted decades ago, I believe it points out that some of the most powerful motives are fundamental ones. Some of the most effective advertising over time has tapped into these motives. (Also consider communication that taps into any of the higher order needs from Maslow's hierarchy of needs: affiliation, esteem or self-actualization.)

Table 9.1 *The relative strength of motives*

Motive	Value	Motive	Value
Appetite – hunger	9.2	Gregariousness	7.9
Love of offspring	9.1	Taste	7.8
Health	9.0	Personal appearance	7.8
Sex attraction	8.9	Safety	7.8
Parental affection	8.9	Cleanliness	7.7
Ambition	8.6	Rest – sleep	7.7
Pleasure	8.6	Home comfort	7.5
Bodily comfort	8.4	Economy	7.5
Possession	8.4	Curiosity	7.5
Approval by others	8.0	Efficiency	7.3

Source: *Psychology in Advertising* by Albert T. Poffenberger, PhD, Chicago: A W Shaw, 1925, p 85 (in which he sites a study by Daniel Starch).

THE ART OF PERSUASION

There are certain techniques that advertisers, politicians, salespeople, speechwriters, preachers, and others have long known to be effective in persuading people. Social psychologists have studied many of these in great detail. Anthony Pratkanis and Elliot Aronson, in their book, *Age of Propaganda: The everyday use and abuse of persuasion* (2000), outline four basic strategies to effectively influence others:

- defining/structuring how an issue is discussed (setting the agenda, creating the frame of reference);
- establishing credibility (authority, likeability and trustworthiness);

- vividly focusing the audience's attention on the key point the communicator intends to make;
- arousing emotions in a way that can only be satisfactorily addressed by taking the communicator's desired course of action.

In his book *Influence: The psychology of persuasion* (1993), Robert B Cialdini, PhD, focuses on six principles of persuasion:

- reciprocation (people try to repay favours out of a sense of obligation);
- commitment and consistency (people behave in ways that support an earlier action or decision);
- social proof (seeing other people doing something makes it more acceptable and appealing);
- liking (people are more likely to say yes to people and brands that they know, like and trust);
- authority (people are inclined to yield to authority);
- scarcity (people are more motivated by the thought of losing something than by the thought of gaining something).

Cialdini indicates that many approaches lead to 'liking': physical attractiveness (which studies have shown to be a function of body/facial symmetry), similarity (people feel comfortable with and can relate to you), compliments, familiarity (through contact and cooperation), and direct or indirect association with other likeable entities.

Both books are quite interesting and well worth reading, if only to help you better understand how third parties attempt to persuade you on a daily basis.

Other considerations in creating highly persuasive communication

- Always design the message to play off of the audience's preexisting beliefs and values. To be effective, your point of departure must be from a place of agreement.
- Try to define the issue in a way that your brand can't help but 'win'. This is why it is so important to choose the optimal 'frame of reference' in brand positioning.
- Sometimes, just asking the right questions can reorient people's thinking about a topic in your favour.
- Comparisons/contrasts alter perceptions of the items being compared/contrasted. When I moved to Rochester, my realtor first showed me a number of overpriced houses that required much work. When we got to the houses that she wanted me to buy, they seemed even more appealing than they might have otherwise if she hadn't first shown me the other inferior houses. This concept is also used in establishing reference pricing. Create reference prices that make your price seem more reasonable or even a 'bargain'.

- Label, categorize or describe competing brands or approaches in ways that cast them in a negative light. Be careful with this approach. While it is an effective technique (that is, it usually works), in the long run, it may cast a less favourable light on your brand.
- Making people feel as though they are a part of a group (assigning brand labels, brand-as-a-badge) helps sell products and brands.
- Fear and guilt sell. (Example: 'When you care enough to send the very best.')
- Paint vivid pictures of desired or dreaded end states with words or images or both.
- Let people touch, try, use and otherwise interact with your product or brand before they buy it. Once they have done so, they are much more likely to want to purchase it. This works for a wide variety of situations: from automobile test drives and in-home free trial use to staying overnight on the campus of a college that you are considering attending (assuming the experience is positive).
- Neurolinguistic programming (NLP) is a well-studied technique that increases persuasion. Through NLP, you can establish a strong rapport with the audience by mirroring the mannerisms and expressions of the audience. After you have done this, you can more easily lead them in a direction of your choice.
- 'Largest', 'fastest growing', 'most popular', 'highest rated', and other similar claims provide strong third party endorsements for a product or brand. (Alternatively, they may be perceived to be puffery by a jaded audience unless you back them up with credible proof points.)
- Repetition increases the effectiveness of communication.

Did you know...?

The memory of images decays less rapidly than the memory of words. The implication is that pictures are often more effective than words. The more effective option is 'dual coding', or the use of visual and verbal cues together. The most effective option is when the visual and verbal cues are designed to say the same thing, or when they are completely redundant.

Other aids to memory include:

- communicating the most important points first and last in the overall communication;
- repeating a key point again and again in a communication;
- presenting the key point in a catchy song, phrase or slogan that the customer will repeat over and over again in his or her memory;
- presenting the communication in the atmosphere, environment, or mood in which you intend the customer to recall the communication.[19]

Note: Sound remains in our short-term memory over five times longer than images do. That is why sound is an even better aid to memory.[20]

ONLINE ADVERTISING RESOURCES

Here is a list of online advertising resource, including brief descriptions (including some taken straight from the Web sites themselves).

www.adforum.com/ – AdForum is the Internet's leading portal to the advertising, marketing and communications industry, with direct links to more than 16,796 agencies in 134 countries.

www.warc.com/ – the World Advertising Research Center (WARC) provides knowledge and data to the global advertising, marketing and media industries, through its websites, hard copy publications and conferences.

www.oneclub.com/OneShow – The One Show is an annual advertising competition judged by a group of the advertising industry's most reputable creative directors. Every year, a different team of top creatives is put together to judge ads sent in from all over the world.

www.commarts.com/CA/ – Founded in 1959, *Communication Arts* is the leading trade journal for visual communications. It is the largest design magazine in the world and showcases the top work in graphic design, advertising, illustration, photography and interactive design. The magazine has an audited paid circulation of 74,834.

www.shots.net/ – shots.net is a dedicated site for professionals involved in the advertising and production industry. Collected over the past 10 years, shots.net presents the finest archive of creative talent: over 4,000 of the most original spots – with credits, to search and view on your computer.

www.adcritic.com – AdCritic.com is a business-to-business and business-to-consumer knowledge resource for the advertising industry and related industries. Peter Beckman, Founder, CEO and Chief Technology Officer of AdCritic.com, developed the concept of AdCritic.com to be a premiere screening service for television commercials using broadband video in 1999. AdCritic.com is well-positioned to serve a need for agencies seeking creative talent, for creative talent to be found, and for consumers to give valuable feedback, survey data and rating of advertising collateral.

www.ecreativesearch.com – A comprehensive database of directors, production, and post-production services from around the world, plus thousands of spots and credits. eCreativeSearch is a subscription-based Internet service for the commercial broadcast production industry. It provides access to a searchable and comprehensive database of directors, production companies, music and other talent, and support services, as well as commercials. You get the most efficient tool to search for the right director or a specific commercial – saving you valuable time and money.

www.clioawards.com/ – The Clio Awards Web site wants to make this site your first stop for news about Clio and its 41-year history, and eventually for all relevant news about the world of creative advertising.

www.effie.org/ – Introduced by the New York American Marketing Association in 1968, EFFIE has since become recognized by agencies and advertisers as the pre-eminent award in the advertising industry. It is the only national award that honours creative achievement in meeting and exceeding advertising objectives. In short, it focuses on effective advertising, advertising that works in the marketplace.

www.aaaa.org/ – Founded in 1917, the American Association of Advertising Agencies (AAAA) is the national trade association representing the advertising agency business in the United States. Its membership produces approximately 75 per cent of the total advertising volume placed by agencies nationwide. Although virtually all of the large, multinational agencies are members of the AAAA, more than 60 per cent of the membership bills less than $10 million per year.

www.aaf.org/ – The American Advertising Federation protects and promotes the well-being of advertising. It accomplishes this through a unique, nationally coordinated grass-roots network of advertisers, agencies, media companies, local advertising clubs and college chapters. To accomplish these objectives, AAF initiatives include the following:

- Advertising Hall of Fame.
- Advertising Hall of Achievement.
- ADDY(r) Awards.
- American Advertising Conference.
- American Advertising Federation's Executive Summit.
- Government Affairs Conference.
- Great Brands Campaign.
- Most Promising Minority Students Program.
- NSAC: College World Series of Advertising
- Principles and Recommended Practices for Effective Advertising in the American Multicultural Marketplace.

www.ana.net/ – The Association of National Advertisers, Inc. (ANA) is the industry's premier trade association dedicated exclusively to marketing and brand building. Representing more than 300 companies with 8,000 brands that collectively spend over $100 billion in marketing communications and advertising, the Association's members market products and services to consumers and businesses.

www.arfsite.org/ – Founded in 1936 by the Association of National Advertisers and the American Association of Advertising Agencies, the Advertising Research Foundation (ARF) is a nonprofit corporate-membership association which is today the pre-eminent professional organization in the field of advertising, marketing and media research. Its combined membership represents more than 400 advertisers, advertising agencies, research firms, media companies, educational institutions and international organizations. The principal mission of the ARF is to improve the practice of advertising, marketing and media research in pursuit of more effective marketing and advertising communications.

www.iaaglobal.org/ – The IAA is the only global partnership of advertisers, agencies, the media, and related services. Its mission is to:

- promote the critical role and benefits of advertising as the vital force behind all healthy economies and the foundation of diverse, independent media in an open society;
- protect and advance freedom of commercial speech and consumer choice;
- encourage greater practice and acceptance of advertising self-regulation;
- provide a forum to debate emerging professional marketing communications issues and their consequences in a fast-changing world environment;
- take the lead in state-of-the-art professional development, education and training for the marketing communications industry of tomorrow.

www.cahners.com – Cahners is a leading provider of critical information and marketing solutions to business professionals in targeted industry sectors. Their market-leading properties include more than 135 business-to-business publications, over 125 Web sites, and a range of services, including Web development, custom publishing, research, business lists and industry events. Cahners is a member of the Reed Elsevier plc group – a world-leading provider of information-driven services and solutions. CARR (Cahners Advertising Research) Reports – found under the Research/CARR Reports tab, provides a wide variety of free downloadable reports on specialized business publications, advertising effectiveness and other advertising-related business results.

www.adage.com – For more than 65 years, *Advertising Age* has been the pre-eminent source of marketing, advertising and media news, information and analysis.

www.ciadvertising.org/ – The Center for Interactive Advertising at the University of Texas at Austin. This site contains research and resources in the areas of Internet advertising, electronic commerce and advertising education.

www.magazinescanada.com/ – Magazines Canada: the source for the Canadian magazine industry, including research summaries and archives.

www.ahaa.org/ – The Association of Hispanic Advertising Agencies. The mission of AHAA is to promote the growth, strength and professionalism of the Hispanic marketing and advertising industry to a diverse audience of business, government and educational institutions.

www.aadslogans.co.uk/index.html – ADSlogans Unlimited. Home of the Advertising Slogan Hall of Fame, runs the world's most comprehensive advertising slogans database. A unique global resource for advertisers and ad agencies comprising many thousands of English-language advertising slogans, taglines, claims, straplines, theme lines, endlines, payoffs, base lines, slogos (the slogan by the logo) and catchphrases.

Advertising glossaries

http://advertising.utexas.edu/research/terms/
www.ad-up.com/new/adup_ad_defs.html
www.atlantamusicgroup.com/adterm.html
www.doadvn.com/news_terminology.html
www.comcept.ab.ca/meccaglen/advertising_terms.html

Table 9.2 _Brand management checklist: brand advertising_

	Yes	No
Have you conducted extensive customer research prior to developing your ads?		
Do you have a carefully crafted brand promise? Have you identified the most powerful (believable) proof points for that promise?		
Does your ad agency fully understand and embrace your brand design and plans?		
Do your other external marketing agencies embrace them as well?		
Is there centralized management of the client/agency relationship?		
Do your ads immediately capture people's attention?		
Does your advertising clearly communicate your brand's promise? Do your ads clearly and forcefully communicate the intended brand benefit?		
Are your ads distinctive and 'ownable'?		
Do your ads feature a strong 'reason why' (proof points)?		
Do your ads reinforce your brand's essence, promise and personality?		
Have you kept your ads simple and devoid of meaningless detail?		
Do your ads connect with people on an emotional level?		
Are your ads focused on building brand awareness and differentiation?		
Are your brand's ads unique?		
Are your ads clever enough in and of themselves to create brand buzz?		
Do you have a way to measure the effectiveness of your ads? Is your advertising effectiveness measured by a party other than your ad agency?		
Have you maximized the frequency of your ads?		
Have you been consistent in advertising your brand over time? Have you communicated a consistent brand message over time?		

Table 9.2 (*continued*)

	Yes	No
Do your brand's successive advertising campaigns share the same brand identity and mnemonic device (to provide a bridge)?		
Do you know how your advertising-to-sales ratio compares to that of your direct competitors? Is it higher?		
Do you know what your brand's share of voice is? Is it higher than or equal to its share of market?		
Do you know how effective your advertising is, not only in growing your brand's share of market but also in maintaining or growing the health of its product category? (This is especially important if you are the share leader in the industry.)		
Does everyone in your organization understand that brand advertising is an investment leading to increased revenues and market share over time?		
Does your organization only reduce your advertising budget as a last resort in down markets? Do you realize that maintaining or increasing advertising in a down market increases brand equity and share of market?		

NOTES

1 Much of this is adapted from an approach David Ogilvy outlines in his book, *Ogilvy on Advertising* (1985), pp 66–69, combined with my personal experience.
2 Adapted from the Advertising Strategy Statement as presented by Richard D Czerniawski and Michael W Maloney in *Creating Brand Loyalty: The management of power positioning and really great advertising*, p 162 (1999).
3 Source: Emanuel Rosen, *The Anatomy of Buzz*, p 210 (2000).
4 As reported by the *MPA Research Newsletter* no 60 (Magazine Publishers of America) as featured on the Magazines Canada Web site (http://www.magazinescanada.com/research_archives/7_Ad_Postioning_60/1.shtml)
5 Source: Czerniawski and Maloney (1999) *Creating Brand Loyalty: The Management of Power Positioning and Really Great Advertising*, AMACOM, New York. Ogilvy, David (1985) *Ogilvy on Advertising*, Vintage Book, New York.
6 Source: Paul A Scipione, Too much or too little? Public perceptions of advertising expenditures, *Journal of Advertising Research* 24 (6), December 1984/January 1985, pp 22–26.
7 Source: Lutner, William (2001) *The Marketing Plan: How to Prepare and Implement It*, AMACOM, New York.
8 Source: Christian Harper, Managing Director, BSMG Worldwide.
9 Source: Hugh M Cannon, Addressing new media with conventional media planning, *Journal of Interactive Advertising*, **1** (2) (Spring 2001), p 12.

10   Source: David N Martin, *Be The Brand*, p 22 (2000).

11   Source: Sutherland, Max and Alice Sylvester (2000), *Advertising and the Mind of the Consumer: What Works, What Doesn't and Why*, Allen & Unwin, St. Leonards.

12   Source: David Stewart and David H Furse, Analysis of the impact of executional factors in advertising performance; *Journal of Advertising Research*, **21** (6 December 1987 / January 1988), pp 45–50.

13   Source: David Stewart and David H Furse, Analysis of the impact of executional factors in advertising performance; *Journal of Advertising Research*, **40** (6 November / December 1988), pp 85–88.

14   Source: Margaret Henderson Blair, An empirical investigation of advertising wearin and wearout, *Journal of Advertising Research* (2000).

15   Source: Paul Georgiou and Stephen Miller, 10 years of advertising tracking, *Rent-A-Car Business Advertising Research Foundation Advertising and Brand Tracking Workshop* p 7 (1996).

16   Source: Paul Georgiou and Stephen Miller, 10 years of advertising tracking, *Rent-A-Car Business Advertising Research Foundation Advertising and Brand Tracking Workshop* p 10 (1996).

17   Source: Hugh M Cannon, Addressing New Media with Conventional Media Planning *Journal of Interactive Advertising* (2001).

18   Laddering is a research technique that probes consumers to better understand underlying basic human values the brand addresses. It investigates benefits that underlie product attributes, consequences that result from the benefits, and values that underlie the consequences. The results are often mapped to outline the brand's benefit structure.

19   Source: Debbie MacInnis, *How to Make a Web Site Memorable* [Online] www.marketingprofs.com/print.asp?source=/Tutorials/memorableweb.asp

20   Source: Roy H Williams, *Secret Formulas of the Wizards of Ads* (1999).

10

Non-traditional marketing approaches that work

Advertising is usually the most important element in any brand marketing plan, but many companies are finding that other approaches are also effective. Some have pursued these approaches out of necessity, being unable to support national advertising campaigns, while others are just more innovative than most in developing their marketing repertoires.

The following are some examples of non-traditional marketing techniques:

- Membership organizations (Harley Owners Group (HOG), Hallmark Keepsake Ornament Collectors Club, Pond's Institute).
- Special events (HOG Rallies, Saturn Owners Homecoming, Jeep Jamboree).
- Museums and factory tours. Examples include the World of Coca-Cola Museum in Atlanta and Las Vegas; Kellogg's Cereal City USA in Battle Creek, Michigan; the Crayola Factory tour and store in Easton, Pennsylvania; the Hallmark Visitors' Center in Kansas City, Missouri; the Ben & Jerry's factory tour in Waterbury Center, Vermont; Hershey's Chocolate World in Hershey, Pennsylvania; The Vermont Teddy Bear factory tour and store in Shelburne, Vermont; MacWorld Expo (85,000 make this pilgrimage!) and the annual Saturn owners homecoming in Spring Hill, Tennessee.
- Theme parks (Disney World, Cadbury's Theme Park, Legoland, Busch Garden, Knottsberry Farm).

Did you know...?

Lego opened its third Legoland in March 1999 in Carlsbad, California. When Legoland Windsor opened in 1996, Lego's toy business in England grew by double digits. Find out more about Legoland at www.legoland.com.

- Flagship stores (Niketown, Warner Brothers Store). A more recent phenomenon: new ultra-deluxe flagship megastores from fashion designers DKNY, Donna Karan, Gucci, Hermes, Hugo Boss, Hickey Freeman, Louis Vuitton, Prada and Tommy Hilfiger.[1]
- Limited distribution for product launches. Create a sense of scarcity. Focus on those outlets known to be frequented by enthusiasts.
- Sponsorships (Rolex and high-end sports events such as horse eventing, yacht races, polo; Continental Arena, Allstate Arena).
- Sponsorship ambush. Converse was an official sponsor of the summer Olympics in Los Angeles in 1984. Nike upstaged Converse, however, by creating a huge tribute to the Olympics on walls near the Olympic stadium. In 2000, Reebok was an official sponsor of the Olympics. Nike upstaged Reebok by contracting with many athletes to wear Nike branded athletic wear. In both instances, Nike received a much greater 'share of mind' than the official sponsors in its category. (Of course, using this technique says something about the brand that uses it. The technique is not compatible with many brands' intended personalities.)
- Larger than life brand owners. At the December 1999 Brand Master Conference, Sixtus Oechsle, the Manager of Corporate Communications and Advertising for Shell Oil Company, said that 40 per cent of a company's reputation is based on the reputation of its CEO. Examples include Martha Stewart (of Martha Stewart and K-Mart), Richard Branson (of Virgin), Anita Roddick (of the Body Shop), Dave Thomas (of Wendy's), Bill Gates (of Microsoft), Ted Turner (of TNT), Jeff Bezos (of Amazon.com), Steve Jobs (of Apple), Michael Eisner (of Disney), Lee Iacocca (of Ford).
- Frequency programmes (Hallmark Gold Crown Card, Continental Airlines OnePass).
- Businesses with a social conscience (Ben & Jerry's, the Body Shop, Toms of Maine, Paul Newman products).
- Cleverness that creates buzz. Consider Wendy's 'Where's the Beef?'; the Dairy Council's 'Got Milk?' and Absolut Vodka's advertising of its bottle shape.
- Cause-related marketing (McDonald's Ronald McDonald House, American Express alleviates world hunger).

- Special events, especially community-based and grass-roots events (Adidas holds streetball festivals and track and field clinics).
- Proactive publicity. This can be one of the most powerful and cost-effective marketing tools. Publicity is free, approximately six times as many people read articles as read ads, and articles are more credible as they are perceived to be third party endorsements versus self-promotion. And the average salary of an in-house copywriter is very low compared with the average ad agency fee to create an ad. Here are some examples of proactive publicity:
  - When Hallmark launched the industry's first personalized, computer-generated cards, we sent some to talk show hosts.
  - Easyjet invested a large portion of its marketing dollars in a lawsuit against KLM claiming unfair competitive practices, positioning itself as the underdog on the side of the public.
  - Trivial Pursuit marketers sent games samples to celebrities featured in the game and radio personalities who had an affinity for trivia.

How to get the news media to cover your story

- add to discussions on current 'hot' issues or topics;
- reference prominent people, places or things;
- have visual impact;
- be dramatic;
- be unexpected, controversial or outrageous;
- directly impact a publication's readership;
- have a 'local' angle;
- tie into a holiday or special occasion;
- represent a significant milestone or a major honour.

16 sure-fire ways to impress the media

1. Demand that reporters run your entire news release 'as is' with no editing, including your pithy headline.
2. Tell reporters that you have an 'exclusive' story for them only. Then send it to all the other media outlets also to give them 'exclusives'.
3. Let reporters know your story would make a good cover story. Unlike you, sometimes they just don't realize the importance of it.

4. In an interview, use the words 'No comment' as often as possible because reporters appreciate not having to write down as much stuff.

5. Always demand to review the story ahead of time. That way you can make sure it comes out correctly.

6. If you say something you wish you hadn't, quickly follow up by saying, 'That was off the record'. Don't bother to let them know when you are 'on-the-record' again. Keep them guessing.

7. Let the reporter know that you consider all media people a bunch of liberal, pot-smoking, bleeding hearts, but that you are graciously willing to give him/her a chance to handle your story. He or she will appreciate your honesty.

8. Let reporters know you are well connected to the editor/publisher/station manager/ owner and tell them you hope you won't have to go over their heads.

9. Pretend you genuinely care about reporters' deadlines. Then ignore them.

10. Constantly tell reporters that all information is 'proprietary'. This will eliminate a lot of needless facts in your story.

11. Make sure to tell reporters that you never read their newspaper or watch/listen to their station because they always get things wrong.

12. After the interview, contact them hourly to determine the status of the story.

13. When the story runs, call the reporter and tell him/her to send you a copy. Reporters consider it part of their job to respond to your needs.

14. Always let a reporter know that your company is a BIG advertiser and helps pay their salary. This is a sure-fire way to impress them and guarantee a favourable story.

15. If you say something stupid, or if the story is negative, always claim you were misquoted, or that they edited out your real remarks. Demand a retraction!

16. If a reporter does a good job and writes a great story, don't bother to thank him/her. That's why they make big bucks. It is enough of a reward for them to have worked with a REAL media professional.

Courtesy John Landsberg of Bottom Line Communications: www.BottomLineCom.com.

● Outrageous marketing breakthroughs. I recommended the following to a non-profit organization whose mission was to encourage women over 40 to get mammograms annually. They wanted a message that would 'break through'. I suggested they feature a bare-chested woman with a double mastectomy on outdoor signs along major highways, and use shocking copy such as, 'Over 40? Don't wait until it is too late. Get a mammogram today', or, 'Which pain is worse? Over 40? Get a mammogram today'. (Imagine the buzz this would create.) To create buzz about the movie *Frenzy*, Alfred Hitchcock floated a dummy of himself down the River Thames.

- Brand as a badge (Nike swoosh, BMW). For this to work, the brand must stand for something the consumer wants to say about himself or herself.
- Co-branding (K-Mart and Martha Stewart, Hallmark Confections and Fannie Mae Celebrated Collection).

Figure 10.1   *An example of co-branding*

- Ingredient branding (Dolby, Nutrasweet, Intel, Kevlar, Lycra, Nylon, Gore-Tex and Culligan).
- Contests (Crayola: Kids Colouring Contest and new crayon colour contest).
- Brand magazines and newsletters (*Crayola Kids*).
- Network marketing (Primerica, MCI's Friends & Family, Amway, Mary Kay, Avon, Tupperware).
- Colossal ads (500 foot high working Swatch watch draped from tallest skyscraper in Frankfurt, Germany).
- Word of mouth, folklore, testimonials and referrals. (Saturn's television commercial spreading the news about one of its dealers flying to Alaska on a rented plane to replace a part on a recalled car in the customer's own garage.)
  - Focus on hard core users, opinion leaders and what Emanuel Rosen in *The Anatomy of Buzz* (2000) calls 'network hubs' – they read, they travel, they attend trade shows and conferences, they serve on committees, they participate in best practices benchmarking studies, they speak, they write books, articles, newsletters and letters to editors, they teach courses, they consult, they advise others.
  - Expose people to things that make great 'cocktail party talk'.
  - Give them sneak previews, 'inside information', 'behind the scene stories', and factory tours. Let them meet the product designers.
  - Ask your employees to spread the word to everyone they know. Give them free products as a perk. This will attract people who like the product category and brand. It will also familiarize them with your brand's products so that they can make better sales people.

The power of word of mouth

In his book, *Eating the Big Fish: How challenger brands can compete against brand leaders* (1999), Adam Morgan indicates that people enthusiastically share information for one of four reasons: 1) bragging rights; 2) product enthusiasm; 3) aspirational identification; or 4) news value.

Stories and anecdotes make a point real to people and embed it in their memories. Brand stories and anecdotes can become legends. As they are told and retold, they can raise the brand to a mythological level. Stories are often told about consumer experiences that far exceed expectations. This could be the result of extraordinary customer service or some other incredible experience with the brand. Going out of your way as an organization to create these experiences will pay huge dividends: word-of-mouth marketing can not be underestimated. Ideally, you create experiences that reinforce your brand's point of difference.

For instance, a Hallmark card shop owner cared so much for one of her customers that when the customer could not find what she was looking for in the store, the owner drove several miles away to a few other Hallmark stores until she found what the customer was looking for. She hand delivered it to the customer's house that evening, at no charge, reinforcing Hallmark's essence of 'caring shared'. Now that is the stuff of legends. Delivering this type of service, even occasionally, generates significant word-of-mouth brand advocacy.

- Many companies have discovered that the channel QVC is a great way to promote new products.
- Neiman Marcus catalogue. BMW offered a limited edition of its Z3 Roadster with a 'Specially equipped 007' dash plaque in the catalogue. They sold all 100 cars, and there were still approximately 6,000 people on the waiting list!
- Airline radio and television shows.
- Unusual advertising media. Companies have used everything from sidewalks (written in chalk), walls above men's room urinals, and posters on bulletin boards, to the sides of trucks and buses, athletes' clothes, and crop art (images created by ploughing fields in certain patterns). In France, PlayStation inserted sick air bags in magazines to communicate the realism of its latest Formula One racing game. A German company is now printing advertising messages on toilet paper.
- The Internet, particularly Amazon.com, which I cover in greater detail later in this book.

TRADITIONAL MARKETING TECHNIQUES 'ON STEROIDS'

Here are some traditional techniques taken to an extraordinary level of success:

- Packaging (Gateway's cowhide pattern on its boxes, Absolut vodka's consistently advertised distinctive bottle shape, Ty Nant's use of cobalt blue bottles to break into the mineral water category, Voss' use of aesthetically pleasing cylindrical glass bottles to do the same, *New York Times* use of blue bags for home delivered papers).
- The product itself (Apple's iMac, Chrysler's PT Cruiser). Never underestimate the power of design to differentiate!
- Vehicles, uniforms and signing. Coca-Cola, FedEx, and UPS use trucks as billboards. UPS uses their delivery people's distinctive brown uniforms. Lucent displays large branded signs in front of each of its offices.
- Point-of-sale signing and merchandising. Mass displays of Coca-Cola cases at the end of aisles (in grocery and other mass channel stores) are designed to bring the brand to the top of the customer's mind. Signs, posters and coasters featuring a particular brand of alcohol are intended to accomplish the same in bars and taverns.
- Free product trial. AOL did this very successfully by distributing hundreds of millions of free software disks featuring one month's service free. Element K is doing this with e-learning IDs featuring run of site (over 800 courses) for free for three months. This works especially well with low variable cost items for which there is some perceived risk of purchase.

SMALL BUSINESS MARKETING TECHNIQUES

- Conduct demonstrations, classes and workshops. A restaurant's chef can teach a cooking class for a continuing education programme or for a department or cooking supply store.
- Speak at conferences and for professional associations. Join your local chapter of the National Speakers Association and register with speakers' bureaux. Publicize your speaking engagements.
- Hold contests.
- Write articles for newspapers, periodicals and professional journals.
- List yourself as an expert (*Radio-TV Interview Report, Yearbook of Experts, Authorities and Spokespersons*, Broadcast Interview Source, Inc., ProfNet, etc).
- Be a guest on or host a local radio or television show on your area of expertise.
- Network online and offline (in professional associations, conferences, trade shows, benchmarking groups, chambers of commerce, usenet groups, chats, online forums, etc).

- Publish newsletters (online or offline).
- Write a book.
- Hire a publicist.
- Maintain relationships with the press.
- Get involved in civic organizations.
- Donate money to local charities, especially complementary causes.
- Volunteer to judge competitions
- Wear branded shirts and other clothing
- Cross-promote with complementary or nearby businesses.
- Give away insignia merchandise (featuring your business's name, logo, tag line and contact information).
- Write letters to new residents introducing them to your business (perhaps offering them a free or reduced-price trial).
- Script your customer service and tech support people to cross-sell and up-sell products and services as appropriate. (Be careful not to over-encourage people to do this. They should only do this in the most helpful way as appropriate.)

BUSINESS-TO-BUSINESS TECHNIQUES

- Create and actively interact with customer advisory boards. Invite the most influential opinion leaders to participate.
- Create and actively interact with strategic partner boards.
- Create external 'expert councils' for all major new products. Invite the most knowledgeable and influential outside experts to participate; involve them in the product design itself.
- Hold conferences and seminars, inviting current satisfied customers, prospective customers and internal and external industry experts. Present case studies, the latest innovations, let the experts speak, and allow time for networking.
- For software companies, 'beta test' your software with major influential customers and those that would provide compelling case studies and testimonials.
- Hold product launch parties for important customers.
- Record testimonials from your most supportive customers and subtly interweave these with the background music that plays when people are on hold at your company. (This could become annoying to some people who are waiting to speak to a customer service or technical support rep regarding a major problem. Hopefully, they are not on hold for long!)
- Develop and disseminate a portfolio of customer case studies to reinforce specific brand benefits to specific target customers.

- Publish and widely disseminate white papers to position your organization and brand as experts in your field.
- Develop a speakers' bureau and actively orchestrate speaking engagements at key industry events: conferences, trade shows, industry association meetings and so on. At Element K, we started a local chapter of Toastmasters and assigned the speakers' bureau responsibility to a specific individual.
- Actively seek industry association committee assignments and board positions.
- Constantly keep the following people and organizations aware of your brand and its latest accomplishments:
  - industry analysts;
  - financial analysts;
  - resellers and other strategic partners;
  - your organization's professional partners: lawyers, accountants, management consultants, advertising agencies, etc;
  - people who write about your industry for the general business press;
  - people who write books about your industry;
  - other opinion leaders.

Table 10.1 *Distribution of business marketing budget*

	%
Trade magazines	23
Trade shows	18
Direct mail	10
Promotion/market support	9
Dealer/distributor materials	5
General magazine advertising	6
Internet/electronic media	9
Directories	5
Telemarketing/telecommunications	3
Publicity/public relations	7
Market research	4
Other	1
Total	100

Source: *Cahners Advertising Research Reports*

DIRECT MARKETING

Direct marketing is a very specific sub-discipline with its own rules within marketing. It offers several advantages to the marketer:[2]

- It allows you to target specific people.
- It enables you to tailor your message for each person.
- It is action-oriented.
- It is confidential.
- It is economical.
- You can track and measure the response rate and the return on investment.
- You will be able to significantly and continuously improve its effectiveness over time.

The three most important elements of direct mail response are the list, the offer and the creative. Of the three, the list is by far the most important.

The list

- You will have the most success with your current customer list (typically, it provides 2 to 10 times the response rate of a rented list). Beyond that, always seek out frequently updated lists.
- Use a list broker that you trust.
- Profile your current (or prospective) customer base (behavioural and demographic characteristics) and compare that with the profiles of the various lists that you are considering.
- Test each of the lists that you are considering (ask for free names or rent the minimum number of names possible).

The offer

- Provide an incentive for the recipient to act immediately ('free'…, free product trial, per cent off, premiums, sweepstakes; for B2B: kits, white papers, research reports).
- Maximize the perceived value of the offer.
- Provide an easy way to respond (free phone number, postage-paid response card, coupon or Web site address).
- Code the response devices to be able to track the effectiveness of the offer.
- Make the offer time-sensitive in some way.
- Specify a response deadline (not too short, not too long).
- Provide a guarantee if appropriate.
- Avoid offers that are vague, generic, offered by most of your competitors, or seem too good to be true.
- Test responses to various offers.

The creative

- Use the Johnson Box area (top right corner of the letter) to plainly state your offer.
- Start the letter with a powerful, attention grabbing, benefit-driven statement.
- Talk to the recipient in his or her own language – be conversational.
- Use the word 'you' as much as possible.
- Always use the active voice.
- Write long copy, but use short words, sentences and paragraphs.
- Maximize subheads to call-out important offers, benefits and points of differentiation.
- Sell benefits, not features.
- Appeal to the head and to the heart.
- Personalize the letter to the extent possible.
- Your copy should be sympathetic to the recipient's problems.
- Use words to paint a picture: help the recipient to envisage a desired or undesired end state.
- The fear of loss is more powerful that the hope of gain.
- Including testimonials and case studies often helps.
- Include a strong, clear call to action.
- The problem–solution construct almost always works: think about the five P's: picture, problem, promise, proof and push.
- Always use a PS (restate your proposition here). After the Johnson Box, this is the most read portion of the letter.
- Test various versions of the copy.

Other considerations

- Personalize the envelope.
- Design the envelope / packaging to maximize its possibility of being opened.
- Dimensional packaging has a much higher chance of being opened.
- Test envelope solutions.
- Time the mailing for maximum response.
- Carefully time follow-up contacts to substantially increase response rates.
- Always take the opportunity to thank your current customers – again and again.

Online Direct Marketing Resources

www.directmailquotes.com/expertadvice/index.cfm
www.directmailtips.com
www.mailinglistbuyingguide.com
www.wordsthatsell.com.au/wordsthatsell2.htm

www.the-dma.org (Direct Marketing Association, United States)
www.dma.org.uk (Direct Marketing Association, UK)
www.adma.com.au (Australian Direct Marketing Association)
www.cdma.org (Canadian Marketing Association)
www.nmoa.org/index.htm (National Mail Order Association)

Direct marketing information for a fee
http://directmail-bootcamp.com/
www.301directmailtips.com/index.html

CUSTOMER RELATIONSHIP MANAGEMENT (CRM)

Customer Relationship Management (CRM) is huge. Most companies use it to increase customer loyalty and retention, and it will continue to grow with the emerging accessibility of the Internet and e-mail worldwide.

Relationship Marketing International characterizes the shift from mass marketing to relationship marketing as follows:

Mass marketing	*Relationship marketing*
transactions	relationships
volume	value
mass production	mass customization
assumed needs	actual needs
acquisition	retention
independent contracts	integrated contracts
impersonal communications	personal communications
remote	intimate

While CRM potentially results in significant benefits to an organization, a recent Conference Board report on the subject (www.conference-board.org) indicates that only a quarter of all firms report that their CRM projects have been 'very successful'.

Since CRM would be best covered by a book, not a chapter or section of a book, here are some popular books on this topic:

- *Relationship Marketing for Competitive Advantage: Winning and keeping customers* by Adrian Payne, Martin Christopher, Helen Peck and Moira Clark.
- *Relationship Marketing : New strategies, techniques and technologies to win the customers you want and keep them forever* by Ian H Gordon.
- *Customer Equity: Building and managing relationships as valuable assets* by Robert C Blattberg, Gary Getz and Jacquelyn S Thomas.
- *Romancing the Customer: Maximizing brand value through powerful relationship management* by Paul Temporal and Martin Trott.
- *Customer Once, Client Forever* by Richard A Buckingham.
- *Developing Knowledge-Based Client Relationships, The Future of Professional Services* by Ross Dawson.

IDEATION AND CREATIVE PROBLEM SOLVING

The mostly highly admired brands are usually unique, original, fresh and leading edge. In fact, many have invented or reinvented entire categories. To be that kind of a brand, an organization must be highly innovative. Innovative brands with innovative products, services and marketing approaches typically make extensive use of creative problem solving and ideation (idea generation) techniques.

Creative problem solving usually requires two distinct phases: divergent thinking (ideation) and convergent thinking (idea analysis and evaluation). The purpose of ideation is to generate as many ideas as possible in as condensed a timeframe as possible.

Brainstorming is the most popular ideation technique. Brainstorming requires the following components to be successful:

- A well defined problem.
- Two or more people together in a room. Ideally, you have a mix of people from different disciplines, including someone who knows nothing about the subject (to offer perspective) and a subject matter expert. Also, participants should be screened for divergent thinkers with diverse experiences who are willing to actively share their thoughts and ideas.
- Relaxation training, autogenics, psychodrama, sociodrama and other techniques can help prepare people to ideate effectively. The intent is to break down mental blocks and preconceived notions and to get people to relax and to feel confident and safe from criticism. A warm-up exercise also helps to get people to think about things in new ways, to encourage 'boundary-less' thinking.
- Providing participants with crayons and paper, play-dough, clay, Tinker Toys and other activities often helps people open up in their thinking.

- The exchange of ideas to generate more ideas.
- Session ground rules: no criticism or judgments allowed.
- The facilitator ensures that each person's ideas are drawn out.
- No ideas are filtered out by the session facilitator: all are captured as presented, typically on a flip chart.
- The facilitator keeps the session moving so that people do not have time to make premature judgments.
- The facilitator interjects questions to stimulate additional ideas when ideas are waning. Facilitators should have prepared a set of conceptual blockbusting questions before the session. 'What if it was bigger? What if it was the opposite of what it is? What if we morphed it? What if it was only one-dimensional? What could we do to solve the problem if we had no money to do so? What could we do if we had unlimited financial resources? What if it was round? What if it was red? What is the high-tech solution? What is the low-tech solution? How would environmentalists solve the problem? How would farmers solve the problem? How would Albert Einstein solve the problem? How would a five-year-old girl solve the problem? How would the Chinese government solve the problem? How would your cat solve the problem? How does nature address this? What if you were the problem? What would you do? What if you were the solution? How would you feel?' And so on.

Other ideation techniques include the following:[3]

- visualization, guided imagery, fantasizing and envisioning the future;
- attribute listing, discovering connections between those attributes;
- mind mapping, diagramming relationships;
- questioning the problem and its assumptions, broadening the problem, looking at the problem at a meta-level;
- applying ideas from one context to another (metaphorical thinking);
- creating connections for two previously unconnected items (bisociation);
- forced relationships (or forcing an association between the problem or solution and random words);
- conceiving of two unrelated entities occupying the same space (homospatial thinking);
- stopping to further consider associations that initially make us laugh (laughter results from the unexpected connection between two things);
- sketching and doodling;
- stream of consciousness writing;
- experiencing the problem emotionally, intellectually, spiritually and physically;
- incubation (walking away from the problem after intensely thinking about it);
- living a life of diverse experience.

Online ideation and creative thinking resources

www.bsu.edu/classes/flowers2/brainstorming.htm – Five brainstorming structures by Jim Flowers

www.bsu.edu/classes/flowers2/beyond.htm – Ideation: It's more than just brainstorming by Jim Flowers

www.stemnet.nf.ca/DeptEd/g7/ideation.htm – Idea generating activities (Ideation) paraphrased from Hutchinson and Karsnitz

www.zideas.com/cps_methods.htm – How Might We? An Introduction to creative problem solving methods

www.directedcreativity.com/ – Paul . Plsek's Directed Creativity™". Creative thinking for serious people™". (Includes a creativity bookstore.)

www.b822.org.uk/exercises.htm – B822 creativity, innovation & change: creativity enhancing exercises and sites

www.brainstorming.co.uk/ – Change your life and career with advanced brainstorming

http://members.home.net/garbl/writing/creative.htm – Garbl's creativity resources online

http://members.ozemail.com.au/ caveman/Creative/index2.html – Creativity Web: resources for creativity and innovation

www.mindbloom.net/ – MindBloom: the creativity site

www.tmius.com/3crecorn.html – TMI USA: Creativity corner: unbind your mind

www.bemorecreative.com/ – Bemorecreative.com: thinking, working and living more creatively.

Did you know...?

- In general, it is much more important for a brand to focus on gaining the zealous support of its primary customers than it is to try to gain the business of a much broader audience. If the primary customers are 'brand fans', others will follow.

- Risk taking, innovation, breaking industry rules, products that overperform and services that exceed customer expectations strongly contribute to brand vitality. 'Adequate', 'suffice', and 'good enough' are not a part of a vital brand's vocabulary.

- The products and services that achieve the most 'buzz' and that benefit the most from 'buzz' are innovative, leading-edge, and of superior quality – often creating a new standard for customer experience.

Table 10.2 *Brand management checklist: non-traditional marketing approaches that work*

	Yes	No
Is marketing perceived to be an investment (versus a cost) at your company?		
Are there clear objectives and performance targets for each marketing programme you initiate?		
Do you know the payback or return on investment (or better yet, the marginal return on investment) for each of the following marketing strategies: increasing household penetration, increasing capture, increasing conversion, incenting trial, encouraging repeat purchase, increasing share of requirements,* increasing price premium, reinforcing purchase (post purchase), increasing brand loyalty, and increasing brand advocacy? (Note: Don Schultz, Angora, Inc, and Targetbase can help you measure marketing ROI.)		
Have you made a conscious decision regarding how much you should spend on marketing activities in total?		
Is your marketing focused on consumer 'pull' (versus trade 'push')?		
Is there agreement that the majority of your marketing resources will be spent on brand building versus product sales promotion?		
Are you spending more on brand building than you are on trade deals? Do you know the answer to this question without having to research it first? If you are not happy with the spending balance, do you have specific, realistic plans to change the balance?		
Do you know your consumers as well as you know your products?		
Do you know what consumers value most about your brand?		
Do you know who your best customers are? Do you know why they are your best customers? Have you designed programmes to retain those customers? Are you actively trying to increase share in your high profit, heavy user market segment?		
Do you have a database of your best customers?		
Have you established a robust customer relationship management (CRM) system?		
Do you use an innovative mix of marketing elements tailored to achieve your brand's key objectives, instead of relying primarily on advertising?		
Do you stick with marketing programmes that are working well (versus changing them whenever someone new arrives on the job)?		
Are your consumer and trade marketing efforts integrated across all marketing elements?		

Table 10.2   (*continued*)

	Yes	No
Are your marketing programmes and consumer communications seldom if ever diluted, compromised, or killed by multiple layers of review and approval?		
Do your marketing plans and programmes include the following elements: products, packaging, pricing, sales, advertising, promotion, publicity, distribution, signing, merchandising, point-of-purchase materials, product placement, marketing events and sponsorships?		
Have you carefully designed your promotions to reinforce the brand promise (versus primarily delivering price incentives)?		
Does your packaging reinforce the brand promise and other key brand messages?		
Are customer service departments and customer contacts always included in your marketing programmes?		
Do you know all of the points of contact your brand has with consumers? Are you measuring the quality of contact at all of those points? Are you actively managing what you are communicating at each of those points of contact?		
Do you provide brand training for all people who come in contact with your consumers on behalf of your brands (whether they are your employees or not)?		
Do you create brand and product scripts for your salespeople, customer and technical service representatives and other front-line employees?		
Do you leverage point-of-purchase as a major consumer communication platform?		
Is your brand available wherever and whenever your consumers want it (versus being channel-constrained due to internal or trade issues)?		
Do you use your Web site to transact business and to communicate key brand values and to create an emotional connection with the consumer?		
Does your Web site provide an engaging interactive experience for your consumers?		
Do you use database marketing?		
Do you use proactive publicity to build the brand?		
Do you use event marketing?		
Do you use cause-related marketing?		
Do you use word-of-mouth marketing?		

Table 10.2   (*continued*)

	Yes	No
Have you identified the industry opinion leaders and 'network hubs'? Do you communicate with them on a regular basis?		
Have you created flagship stores to showcase your brand and its promise?		
Have you created factory tours, a visitor's centre, or a company museum to communicate your brand's promises to the public?		
Have you considered creating consumer membership organizations to increase emotional connection and loyalty to the brand?		
Have you created other ways (online and offline) for your customers and potential customers to interact with one another on a regular basis?		
Have you considered establishing your brand as a consumer badge? Do you offer insignia merchandise to increase the brand's badge value?		
Are there media to which your brand has privileged access, such as magazines, television programming, radio stations, television networks, billboards, theme parks, retail stores, Web sites? Are you fully exploiting them?		
Do you leverage secondary brand associations to build brand equity (co-branding, endorsements, sponsorships, licensing, etc)?		
Do your marketing programmes build brand awareness?		
Do your marketing programmes communicate brand essence, promise, personality, and other intended associations?		
Do they create an emotional connection with the consumer?		
Do they communicate good value?		
Are they memorable and engaging?		
Do they clearly communicate differentiating benefits that are relevant and compelling to the consumer?		
If you are marketing your brand globally, have you considered how the brand's geographic origin affects consumers' perceptions of the brand? (Often, countries and regions have their own 'brand images' which may influence the perceptions of brands from those places.)		
Do you know which of your marketing programmes provide the highest return on investment? Do you know which ones provide the lowest? Based on this, are you constantly adjusting your programme mix? (Note: Media Market Assessment at www.mma.com can help you measure your programme efficiency.)		

Table 10.2 (*continued*)

	Yes	No
Does you organization frequently use creative problem solving and ideation techniques to promote innovation? Does the organization encourage 'out of the box' thinking?		
Do you measure business innovation? Do you have a constant stream of consumer relevant innovations?		
Do at least 20 per cent of your annual revenues result from new products and services?		

* Or share of wallet or share of dollar. The concept is to identify the percentage of every unit or dollar sale within a category that goes to the brand in question.

NOTES

1   Source: Designer stores, in extra large, *Wall Street Journal*, June 6 2001, p B1, B12
2   Source: Ray Jutkins, *13 Platinum Advantages Direct Response Marketing Offers the 21st Century Marketer*, [Online] http://www.directmailquotes.com/expertadvice/
3   Source: Diane Mongomery, Kay Sather Bull and Sara Leigh Kimball, *Stimulating Creativity in Computer Mediated Learning: Individual and collaborative approaches*, [Online] http://home.okstste,edu/homepages.nsf/toc/EPSY5720cm119 (accessed 4 August 01)

11

Brand building on the Internet

The advent of the Internet has expanded the possibilities – and the requirements – for brand building.[1] The organization that ignores the Internet as a brand-building medium does so at its own risk. Web sites are effective at building brand relevance, differentiation, and loyalty, but they should not be relied on to build awareness and recognition. Why? Because consumers must seek out your site – your site is not broadcast (like television).

Kristin Zhivago likened consumer behaviour on the World Wide Web to providing a pond of water and inviting consumers to 'come for a swim'. She continues by saying, 'Prospects can visit your pond anytime they like, stay as long as they want, and dive in as deeply as they want'.

COMPARING BRAND BUILDING IN CYBERSPACE TO BRAND BUILDING IN THE 'BRICKS AND MORTAR' WORLD

The following are other ways in which brand building in cyberspace is different than brand building in the 'dirt world':

- Web sites offer two-way (versus one-way) communication.
- Ability to customize content depending on the situation.
- A wide variety of brand building elements come together to create a total brand experience in one medium.
- The consumer is in control – he or she selects what he/she wants to see and for how long.

- It is easier to gather far more information on the consumer – although something must be provided to the consumer in return – information, incentives, etc.
- Instant feedback is possible – and is sometimes desired by the customer.
- Results are easier to measure.

THE INTERNET 'LEVELS THE PLAYING FIELD' FOR SMALL COMPANIES

In some ways, the Internet favours smaller companies:

- In the 'dirt world', product accessibility is primarily driven by number of retail locations – and large companies have many such locations. In cyberspace, only one Website is needed – which doesn't necessarily require the resources of a large company.
- Smaller companies are usually too small to have functional silos and therefore can deliver a more coherent brand message, environment and experience on the Internet.
- Smaller companies are often much quicker and more agile (a very important attribute on the Internet).
- Web sites of smaller companies are usually much more critical and important components of their businesses.

Conversely, aspects of the Internet definitely favour larger enterprises, including the rising cost of keeping site content fresh, maintaining a high site search engine ranking, and placing online ads.

THE INTERNET INCREASES CONSUMER POWER

The Internet also increases consumer power in the following ways:

- Consumers choose where they go and what they see.
- The Internet makes price comparisons easy – especially with the emergence of intelligent agents (intelligent agents search the Web for specified items and notify the user where the items can be found and at which prices).
- The Internet provides people with mechanisms to communicate with one another and to band together, thereby increasing their influence and buying power. (New technologies even make it easier for people to communicate with each other on your site without your knowledge or permission.)
- The Internet makes it much easier for people to make their complaints public.

Open mike: the Internet increases the power of consumers

www.baddealings.com

www.ecomplaints.com

www.thecomplaintstation.com

www.untied.com www.planemad.com

www.sucks.com (Corporate America Sucks)

www.wal-martsucks.com

INTERNET USER SEGMENTS

Ketchum Interactive, the global public relations agency, has identified four different Internet user segments (see Table 11.1) based on their approach to finding information on the Web. These segments should clearly impact an organization's site design and Internet strategy.[2]

Table 11.1 *Internet user segments*

	Adventurer	Expert	Investigator	Wanderer
Is the user brand knowledgeable?	Yes	Yes	No	No
Does the user know what he/she is looking for?	No	Yes	Yes	No
Segment summary	'There was nothing there to draw me in because I wasn't looking for a product, I was just looking for stimulation.'	'If I'm looking for information, I just want to get it without unnecessary detours. What's frustrating about the Web is that you go places you weren't expecting and it wastes your time.'	'Don't insult me when I come to your site by advertising to me. You've already got me in the store, so give me some help. Ask smart questions that could help diagnose what I really need.'	'The Web is a place to go to make sure I'm not missing out on something.'

Table 11.1 (*continued*)

	Adventurer	Expert	Investigator	Wanderer
Ways to appeal to segment	Entertainment, special promotional offers and participation in virtual community activities	Fast downloads, easy navigation, intuitive site maps and search capabilities	Consultative navigation, search tools that link needs with the appropriate information, products or services	Create a 'buzz' about the site, provide opportunities for community members to interact over time

WEB SITE OBJECTIVES

Organizational Web site objectives vary, but typically the objectives include one or more of the following:

- Make it easier for consumers to do business with us (accessibility).
- Reduce our costs of doing business (customer value and business profitability).
- Enhance our relationship with our customer (creating emotional connection).
- Build our brand.

Regardless of the objective, effective Web sites should accomplish the following:

- Drive site traffic.
- Reinforce the brand essence and promise.
- Create an engaging, interactive, interesting, informative and helpful consumer experience.
- Create a sense of community.
- Give the consumer reasons to return to the site on a regular basis.
- Get the consumer to bookmark the site.
- Unobtrusively capture consumer information to build a database.
- Integrate content and commerce.
- Generate incremental sales (online and in the 'dirt world').

BUILDING A STRONG WEB SITE

Successful Web development begins with the database and then backs into design. Questions such as 'what information will be collected?' and 'where will it be stored for easy retrieval and utilization?' must be raised early on. The site should be thought of as a two-way communication mechanism rather than a static receptacle for information.

A well designed Web site attracts and informs, compels transactions (inquiries, subscriptions, and orders), and delivers a high-quality experience. It is imperative that you think about all communication and information paths, mapped to your database, before writing a single line of code. Keep in mind, too, that a successful Web site must work for a wide variety of technical platforms: operating systems, browsers, plug-ins, monitor sizes and resolutions, e-mail programs and so on. Your Web site should be developed by professional Web site developers to ensure that it is platform-independent.

Before beginning to design your organization's Web site, it is very important to identify the different people who will use it: customers, potential customers, industry analysts, financial analysts, reporters and editors, resellers, prospective employees and so on. Ideally, you will perform anthropological research on each user group to determine how it uses the site (or at least make the site designers put themselves in each user group's shoes) and design the content and navigation accordingly. You should also have human factors engineers review the site for user functionality.

The following are also important considerations when building a strong Web site:

- The site must download quickly. The average person will only wait 10 seconds or less for a page to download.
- The home or splash page must capture the user's attention and invite him or her deeper into the site.
- Use your home page to communicate your purpose, personality and point of difference. Use plenty of white space and minimal copy. Provide clear navigation to copy-dense pages.
- The site must be rich in useful or interesting content, which must be frequently updated and refreshed to keep people coming back to the site.
- Keep the user active (he or she wants to click and scroll, not read).
- In general, the user should be able to reach any page in three clicks or less.
- Use concise, factual and bulletized copy.
- Provide a clear, easily accessible site map.
- Provide a site search engine.
- Architect intuitive site navigation.
- Ideally, every page should have home, search and site map buttons.
- Provide an FAQ (frequently asked questions) section.
- Provide activities to unobtrusively build a database (games, contests, sweepstakes, surveys, newsletters).
- Consider personalizing the site to the user's preferences: wallpaper, first page viewed, customized content.
- Create 'New', 'Hot', or 'Sale' sections to alert frequent visitors to new or timely content.

- Create a feedback loop through e-mail (be sure to staff the e-mail for timely response). An immediate autoresponder message followed up by a personalized response is ideal.
- Offer customer services (such as a store locator service, checklists and consultative or diagnostic tools).
- Consider adding a database that is searchable against multiple criteria. This is a very powerful feature.
- Provide entertainment.

CREATING A BRAND-BUILDING SITE

To create a brand-building site, the following considerations are also necessary:

- The domain name (URL) should be the brand name (to provide intuitive site access). People are increasingly trying to the type the name as the URL. If that does not work, they then use a search engine.
- Own the URLs for all variations of the brand name, including acronyms, abbreviations, misspellings, etc. Also consider owning the .com, .org, and .net URLs. Redirect people who use those URLs to your site.
- Protect your domain name through ongoing surveillance and enforcement. (www.Cyveillance.com and www.Cobion.com provide this online service.)
- Weave a story about the brand's history, heritage and character.
- The site must be true to your brand's identity and attitude. Your brand should not take on a new persona in cyberspace just to be 'hip'.
- Brand-building sites should avail themselves to the full spectrum of brand identity elements; not just name and logo, but also typography, colours, design and graphic elements, brand voice and visual style, theme lines, animation, sound, etc.
- Consider using a brand sound icon as a mnemonic device. Use good judgment to ensure the sound is pleasing and not distracting or annoying.
- A well branded site will have a consistent look and feel across all of its pages. Ideally, the brand name and logo appear in the upper left corner on each page.
- Brand-building sites should establish a sense of community and create an emotional connection with the brand.
- Consider featuring pictures and video clips of the 'people behind the brand' to create an emotional connection with people using your site:
    - corporate officers;
    - product designers;
    - customer service reps;
    - newsletter authors;
    - advice columnists;
    - other satisfied customers.

CREATING COMMUNITY ONLINE

The following are effective community building techniques:

- Directories (with hypertext links to specific pages on other sites).
- Bulletin Boards. They are less expensive and more controllable than chat rooms.
- Chat rooms.
- Surveys/reviews.
- Daily tips, tricks or rules of thumb.
- Daily quotes (especially related to the Web site's main topic).
- Personal user lists kept on your site.
- Guest books.
- Matching people with like interests (search and browse techniques).
- Custom published Web magazines.
- Extranet sections (password protected areas for clients/members with value added services).
- Site opinion postings.
- Online events.
- Featuring regularly updated news headlines on topics related to the site's purpose.
- Searchable library of articles by subject matter experts.
- Become a portal site – that is, an entry site for people looking for information and links on a particular topic.
- Track where consumers are going. Ask them what they like. Change the experience based on their responses. (www.siteintelligence.co.uk provides a detailed analysis of how people use your Web site.)
- Provide ample opportunities for community members to interact with each other over time.
- Several companies specialize in helping Web sites create online communities, including RealCommunities and PeopleLink.

ONLINE NEWSLETTERS: PERHAPS THE MOST POWERFUL ONLINE MARKETING TECHNIQUE

Online newsletters are one of the most effective tools for keeping your brand in people's minds and creating an emotional connection with your brand. They provide global reach 24 hours a day for free. Because of that, you can afford to use them to advertise to non-respondents indefinitely. The more people receive e-mail ads, the more they revisit Web sites. According to CyberAtlas, as many as 70 per cent of Internet users say visiting a Web site regularly would influence their decision to place orders.

Here are some more tips for creating successful newsletters:

- They should be free.
- Let people opt in (don't spam). That is, give them a simple way to subscribe, and let their subscription be their decision.
- Communicate your privacy policy when people subscribe to your newsletters.
- Provide useful, fresh content each issue.
- Provide hypertext links to useful sites and to deeper areas in your site.
- Include a small ad in each newsletter. Specific offers with hypertext links are the most effective.
- Explicitly inform people how to unsubscribe to the mailing list. Better yet, provide a simple way to do so in each newsletter.
- Do not send more than one newsletter a week.
- Add your newsletter to other sites' online periodical listings (with a hypertext link to your subscription form).
- Encourage readers to pass the newsletter on to anyone else who might be interested in the topic. (Testing this approach with BrandForward's newsletter indicates that the power of suggestion is real.)
- Always include brand access information (URL, address, e-mail address, telephone number, etc) in the newsletter.
- Copyright all newsletter content.
- Feature the 'enrol' button in the upper right hand corner of each Web page – this will substantially increase subscription rates.

One caution: Since the late 1990s, newsletters have burgeoned in their popularity as a marketing tool. Increasingly, people will weed out newsletters to which they had previously subscribed based upon the immediate value added to them. This will make it more and more important for publishers to focus on delivering useful content in a quick and interesting way if they wish to stay on people's 'reading short lists'.

E-MAIL BLASTS[3]

E-mails are like direct mail without the cost of stamps and printing. Cross/up/retention e-mail blasts can be extremely lucrative. However, successful e-mail letters are not identical to their snail mail counterparts. Responses generally occur within 48 hours, and copywriting is different.

To create copy that generates results, start with a clear offer and convey it in the subject line. The subject line, not the copy, is the most critical component of a successful response rate because it determines whether the e-mail will be opened or immediately discarded. Test many subject lines in all campaigns and keep a list of top performers.

Next, make the first line of copy succinct and interesting. Like the subject line, it also determines whether the rest of the e-mail will be read or discarded. Tell people what you are offering, what it will do for them and why they should read further. Keep the copy short and use bullet points to convey information rather than long sentences. Keep all information on bullet points on a single line.

Finally, deliver a powerful, time sensitive call to action with a link to an order page or Web response form. Track gross and net response rates (e-mails opened versus target response) so you know where improvements can be made in the sales cycle.

WEB SITE PROMOTION

Once you have a strong brand-building site, you will want to promote it online and offline. The first thing you will want to do is submit your site to search engines and online directories. (In January 2001 the NPD Group, a leading marketing information provider, conducted a study to compare the effectiveness of search listings versus banner ads and titles. Search listings outperformed banner ads and titles by two to one or more on awareness, likelihood to read and click, and favourable opinions.)[4] There are three approaches to this: you can do this yourself with the help of online site promotion resources, you can hire a company that specializes in search engine and directory placement, or you can do both. I recommend doing both.

To get you started, the following are some of the better search engine and directory placement resources:

- www.searchenginewatch.com
- www.searchengineforums.com
- www.selfpromotion.com
- www.jimtools.com
- www.associate-it.com
- www.directhit.com
- www.announceitamerica.com
- www.dmoz.org
- www.Webposition.com.

Web site ranking on search engines is a function of many variables, and each search engine uses a different set of criteria. A few years ago, it was fairly easy to get a high search engine ranking by adding the appropriate keywords to your site's tags. With more and more sites added to the Internet each day, search engines have become much more sophisticated in how they rank sites, so achieving a high ranking has become much more difficult.

Specialists use a variety of techniques including 'gateway' or 'jump' pages. These pages, which provide hypertext links to your site, are optimized to appeal to specific search engines. Considering this increased sophistication, I recommend hiring specialists to improve your Web site's ranking. Having said that, there are a few things you should know about how to improve your Web site's chances for a high ranking. Remember to do all of these before you submit to search engines.

- The location and frequency of keywords are important. Including them in your site's title and tags will typically improve your Web site's ranking.
- Link popularity, or the number of links to your site, is also very important in increasing your site's ranking. That is why it is important to negotiate reciprocal links with other sites.
- Well thought through and persuasive Web page titles and descriptions will also help.
- Finally, consider using text to describe all graphic elements on your site. Many search engines index these. Also, using texts makes your Web site more accessible to blind people (as the text can be read and converted to the spoken word).
- Most search engines have grown wise to 'spamming' and will penalize sites that use invisible or tiny text among other approaches.

Here are some companies that specialize in maximizing Web site search engine rankings:

- www.OneUpWeb.com
- www.eiCommunications.com
- www.top-10.com
- www.1stplaceranking.com.

Whether you outsource site placement or not, it will benefit you to do the following on a regular basis:

- Monitor your listings frequently. Check your ranking placement.
- Using Virtual WebTrends or other similar software, study your log files to see which search engines send you the most traffic.
- Check your competitors' sites to see how they rank using your keywords.
- Analyze the pages with the highest rankings using your keywords. (Work with your Webmaster to view the pages' code, or right click 'view source' on the Web page to view its underlying code.)

Once you are listed with search engines and directories, you will want to promote your Web site in other ways as well. The following are effective online site promotion techniques:

- Banner ads.
- Keyword advertising, or ads that appear only when people enter specific keywords into a search engine.
- Directory advertising, or advertising on pages with specific directory topics.
- Signature line (brand name/logo, tag line, address, telephone number, URL, etc) included in all e-mail.
- Virtual storefronts in Web malls and virtual shelf spaces within stores on other sites.[5]
- Set up an affiliate programme (perfected by Amazon.com).
- Be a part of portal sites.
- Apply for awards (start here: http://websiteawards.xe.net/).
- Submit your website to 'What's New' websites (such as www.whatsnu.com).
- E-zine ads. Advertise in your own and other people's newsletters/e-zines.
- Lead forum discussions.[6]
- Online media relations (www.prweb.com).
- By-lined articles for E-zines and other Web sites.
- Webcasting.[7]
- Micro-sites – or small sites created to promote a particular product or service. Movie studios do this for each new film they release. Conference companies often do this for each conference they produce.
- Place notices in chat rooms and on bulletin boards.[8]
- Participate in Usenet newsgroup discussions.
- Post ads in targeted discussion groups.
- Join online mailing lists (www.list-universe.com, www.topica.com, etc).
- Invite site users to return to your site with a follow-up e-mail message.
- On your site, suggest that users bookmark your site.
- Make it easy for people to suggest your Web site to a friend (simple pre-written e-mail messages).
- Include 'send to a friend' buttons on every digital product or give-away item.
- Design a page on your site to serve as a useful or interesting home page then make it easy for people to specify it as their home page.
- If your product is created on or distributed by the Web, make it 'sticky'. That is, include an ingredient brand label (such as 'I used Photoshop') and/or a hypertext link back to your Web site on the product itself. (A year and a half after its launch, Hotmail had signed up 18 million subscribers with little to no advertising. A simple line at the bottom of every e-mail message helped them achieve this – 'Get your free e-mail at Hotmail.com').
- To create a powerful viral program, invent a product that meets a need, exceeds expectations of quality, make it unique, offer it for free, and make it easy for people to give

away. (Hotmail, again, is a great example.) Create a conversion strategy once you build a database of users, to migrate as many as possible into paying customers. This could include offering something free for a 30-day trial period, and then sending follow-up conversion e-mails with a first time user discount.

- If possible, build something into your online product or experience that makes it more valuable to the user if they share it as broadly as possible. (For instance, the more friends and family members that I can get to join ICQ, the more valuable the service becomes to me.)
- Highly creative and entertaining multimedia games and greetings designed to spread like wildfire throughout the Internet (examples: dancing baby, elf bowling and dancing hamsters).
- Submit free content to other sites in exchange for a link to your site.
- Reciprocal links:[9]
  - A top strategy for obtaining reciprocal links is to create strategies that bring qualified sites to you, rather than going to them. Advertise a cross-linking program on your site, e-zines, and other media.
  - The second best way is by approaching sites with an effective e-mail. Do not blast the same e-mail to multiple site contacts. The response will be abysmal. Hand pick sites you like and sign up for their e-zines and special offers. Write them a personal letter and congratulate them on the quality of their site and content. Thank them for the commitment to a quality user experience. Tell others about their site and pass along their e-zines and other content to others. Let them know that you are promoting their site already. Then, tell them a little about your site and the experience and value you offer. Let them know how many visitors you have. Translate this to value to them: more traffic and qualified leads, leading to more profitability with no cash outlay, which can be achieved simply by providing cross links to your respective Web properties, and some mutual promotional activities.
  - For added ROI on your efforts, test directing some links to lead forms, offer pages or specific site pages, rather than the home page.
- Newsletters (previously discussed).

BANNER ADS

Banner ads are the most prevalent form of online promotion. Banner ads should be evaluated using the following metrics:

- increased brand awareness;
- brand attributes communicated;
- increased purchase intent.

'Click throughs' have decreased in importance as a measure, because much of the brand-building benefit is derived from people just seeing the ad and absorbing its message. I use banner ads to increase advertising frequency against a highly targeted audience (by placing them only on highly targeted pages on highly targeted sites).

The following are some tips for maximizing the effectiveness of those ads:[10]

- Animated banners with a question or a call to action are the most compelling. Rich media banner advertising will probably be the standard by the time this book is published.
- Keep the message simple with as few words as possible.
- Use bold colours (assuming they are compatible with your brand's identity).
- Always anchor your brand mark at one end of the banner – preferably the left side.
- Include your URL in the banner.
- Always have a 'click here' tag line at the end of the banner.
- Incorporating the word 'free' increases response.
- Ad size should be under 10k and 468 x 60 pixels.
- Mentally engage the viewer.
- Target and test your creative.
- Seek out contexts within which there is minimal clutter surrounding your banner ad.
- As with any advertising, increase the frequency of your banner ad.
- Learn what works best by constantly testing and modifying the ads: measure results, modify the ads and measure the results again.
- Changing your banner ads every few weeks maintains click throughs – otherwise they decay with time.

A final word on online advertising: when online, the consumer is in control. He or she does not have to put up with invasive advertising, the worst of which are interstitial or 'pop up' ads. (Do you wait for those ads to fully load before you close them? I don't. My automatic response is to close them as soon as they come up, especially when they are interrupting an activity such as writing an e-mail message or filling out a form.) For that reason, I strongly believe that online advertising will evolve to less intrusive forms, integrating persuasive messages and appropriate hypertext links with useful content sought by people. (Some studies have found that click-through rates for text-based links are 4 to 10 times higher than for banner ad links.) I also believe that online advertising will increasingly integrate interactive and entertaining elements as well. In fact, the future of advertising online may be the seamless blending of information, entertainment and persuasive commercial messages in the places where people are engrossed and absorbed in the medium and particularly receptive to the messages. (While this is likely to be particularly effective, it will raise potential ethical issues, especially regarding advertising directed towards children.)

Do not forget to promote your Web site offline as well. Offline promotion should focus on all of the things it normally would for a 'dirt world' brand, plus it should drive traffic to the Web site. Given that, your offline marketing plan should include advertising, promotion, publicity, and other standard marketing elements. In addition, and most importantly, include your Web site's URL in *all* external communication (advertising, business cards, letterhead, etc). And don't forget to include e-mail addresses in appropriate external communication as well. List your site with reference publications. Finally, tell everyone about your Web site. Word-of-mouth marketing works.

BRANDFORWARD CYBERBRANDING 2000 STUDY (™)

BrandForward conducted its seminal Cyberbranding 2000 Study(™) in March of 2000. We designed the study to address the questions marketing executives most often ask about brands and the Internet:

● How does brand building on the Internet differ from brand building in the 'bricks and mortar' world?
● What opportunities and vulnerabilities exist for pure Internet brands and for 'bricks and mortar' brands conducting commerce in cyberspace?
● How do people shop online and what is the role of brand in that process?
● How can companies best build and leverage brands online?

In a study that surveyed 1,548 Internet users in the United States, we answered these and many other questions. The study explored three top e-commerce categories: books, toys and games, and clothes/apparel, and identified patterns that are applicable to all product categories. It compared brick and mortar brands in cyberspace to pure Internet brands on 12 different dimensions of brand equity including awareness, accessibility, quality, value, emotional connection, relevant differentiation, personality, vitality and loyalty. It identified how people shop online and the role of brand in that process. It also ranked the importance of 23 factors to the success of e-commerce sites.

The following are some of the findings:

● The brand name is the single most important way people arrive at Web sites at which purchases are made. Roughly half of all consumers arrive at a Web site by directly typing in the site's URL (domain name). (If one considers bookmarks to be a sign of brand loyalty and counting searching on product or store name, approximately three-quarters of all people arrive at Web sites where purchases are made by using the brand's name.)

Table 11.2 *How online consumers arrived at Web sites where purchases were made*

	Books %	Toys and games %	Clothing %
Directly to site via URL	46	45	54
Link from another site or newsletter or e-mail	13	19	14
Search engine on product name	5	9	N/A
Search engine on category name	2	9	6
Search engine on store name	2	4	4
Search engine directory of hypertext links	1	0	1

- Top-of-mind awareness of brick and mortar brands far exceeds that of pure Internet brands. (As discussed earlier, awareness is the cornerstone of brand equity. Without it, a brand is unable to differentiate itself or create an emotional connection with people.)
- Approximately 15 per cent of all consumers arrive at Web sites at which purchases are made through links from other sites and online publications.
- The same factors drive brand equity in cyberspace and the bricks and mortar world: awareness, accessibility, value, relevant differentiation and emotional connection, but again they manifest themselves differently in cyberspace.
- The same factors are important in shopping online and in bricks and mortar retail: product quality and selection, convenience and price / value – and again, they manifest themselves differently in cyberspace. For example, the Internet has more convenient hours (24 hours a day, 365 days a year) and, in some instances, a faster way to find a particular product (witness Amazon.com's sophisticated search and browse techniques). But bricks and mortar stores offer the convenience of instant gratification – the ability to take the product home with you immediately after you purchase it and return it en route to home or work without having to contend with the hassles of shipping it.
- When consumers are made aware of a bricks and mortar brand's cyberspace presence, many dimensions of that brand's equity are significantly enhanced. This is particularly true for bricks and mortar brands in whose product categories there are no dominant Internet brands.
- Bricks and mortar brands with e-commerce capability are perceived to be more accessible than cyberbrands. The ability to return goods purchased on the Internet to a bricks and mortar store provides a substantial advantage.

- Cyberbrands are perceived to be more 'innovative/leading edge' and less 'old fashioned/traditional,' and 'boring'. They are also perceived to be less 'friendly', 'dependable', and 'trustworthy' (largely due to lower brand awareness).
- Some characteristics of an Internet site that are important to consumers when deciding to make a purchase are clearly marked prices, secure payment methods, inexpensive shipping, no hassle return policies, detailed item descriptions and pictures of items.
- E-commerce sites will eventually win on information, interactivity, and price (and on some dimensions of convenience). Bricks and mortar brands must significantly enhance the store experience (especially its tactile and olfactory elements) to remain viable.
- Amazon.com is one of the few pure Internet brands that has achieved a level of brand equity that puts it on a par with bricks and mortar brands.

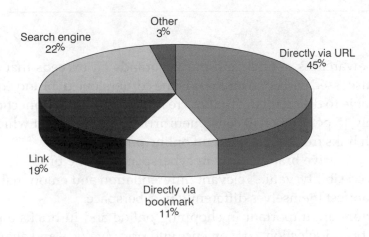

Base = those who purchased Toys & Games over Internet in past 3 months

Figure 11.1 *How customers arrived at a toys and games site*

Implications of the Cyberbranding 2000 Study (tm) findings are as follows:

- It is essential that bricks and mortar brands have a cyberspace presence.
- A bricks and mortar brand that is new to the Internet still has the potential to dominate a product or service category online if it has a strong brand name, it acts quickly, and it can adapt itself to a successful cyberspace business model.
- Pure Internet brands are extremely vulnerable to bricks and mortar brands due to their very low awareness. They must forcefully and relentlessly build brand awareness through every method possible, including offline. Amazon.com's relentless publicity and affiliate programmes and AOL's market saturation approach to software distribution should be considered seriously as models. (In the early-to-mid 1990s, AOL had

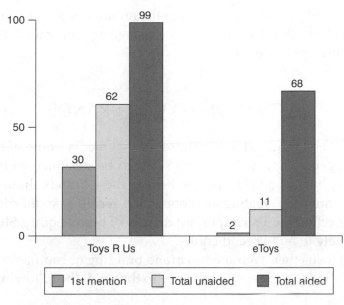

Base = Internet users who purchased category via any means in past year.

Figure 11.2 *Brand awareness for toys and games*

only 300,000 subscribers to CompuServe's 1 million subscribers and Prodigy's 500,000 subscribers. In 1994, AOL began saturating the market with free software disks offering one month's service free. In so doing, AOL surpassed its competitors in far less than a year, reaching 23 million subscribers just a few years later.)

● Your brand's URL must be the brand name. You should own URLs for all variations of your brand's name (abbreviations, misspellings, etc) and direct people from those URLs to your brand's primary URL.

● Create as many links to your site as possible.

● Bricks and mortar brands should work towards integrating their cyberspace and bricks and mortar processes and systems, especially those that affect customers. (This study found that offering 'bricks and mortar' returns for online purchases offers a company substantial advantages. For example, Barnes and Noble has improved at integrating this service across its 'bricks and clicks' components of its business.)

● Shopping on e-commerce sites must offer an advantage over doing the same in the bricks and mortar world. Identify the added value and make sure you build it into your site.

● Pure Internet brands are much more successful if they can claim leadership in a specific product or service category. Two approaches to this are:
   – Becoming dominant in a new category made possible by the Internet (for which there is no good bricks and mortar world counterpart). Example: Backup.com.

- If there is already a dominant brand in the online category in which you intend to operate, narrow the definition of the category you intend to own. Example: VarsityBooks.com (textbooks).

A CAUTION TO WEB BRANDS

As more and more Web brands advertise in traditional media, some of them have created ads featuring outrageous stunts. These ads seem to be designed to break through the clutter and create high recall quickly. People behind these brands should understand that brand building is more than creating awareness and recall. *Relevant* differentiation, trust and emotional connection are also important drivers of brand equity. Shooting gerbils out of cannons is not likely to build brand equity.

Companies often focus their Web sites on brand building or commerce, but not both. My strong recommendation is to integrate the two. To that end, the following is a brief section on online stores.

ONLINE STORES

According to IntelliQuest, a marketing research organization for the technology, Internet, and wireless industries, the following are the top five reasons why people do not buy online:

- Worried about fly-by-night retailers (81 per cent).
- Don't want to deal with the hassle of returning something (72 per cent).
- Worried about using their credit card online (69 per cent).
- Think they are going to get a bunch of junk mail (63 per cent).
- Want to see / touch what they buy (62 per cent).

However, people are getting more comfortable about shopping online. According to Greenfield Online and *Business Week* Online, people's concerns are as shown in Table 11.3.

The following are key success factors for online stores:[11]

- Don't keep shoppers waiting.
- Provide various methods for quick product search: by price point, product category and brand name.
- Build trust:
  - Feature name brand products.
  - Provide for easy telephone contact (free phone number).
  - Feature customer testimonials.
  - Prominently display your privacy policy.

Table 11.3   *Concerns about shopping online*

	July 1999 %	December 1999 %
Can't see and touch items	56	41
Can't return items easily	47	32
Credit card safety	43	35
Shipping charges	39	33
Can't ask questions	33	22
Don't know which Web sites to use	18	7
Takes too long to load screens	10	9
Too difficult to find items	10	3

- – Offer a no hassle return policy.
- – Provide an unconditional guarantee (or at least a performance guarantee).
- – Feature pictures of your merchandise.
- – Communicate product sizes and dimensions.
- – Use a secure server and encryption technology – make the consumer aware of this.
- – Cover the $50 credit card liability in case of credit card fraud.
- – Don't hide the price.
- Create a foolproof shopping cart and checkout process.
- Retain customer information for return visits.
- Follow-up with e-mail (autoresponders and human generated).
- Provide online customer service chat rooms (like www.1800Flowers.com).

LEARN FROM STRONG BRAND-BUILDING WEB SITES

As you surf the Internet, think about your favourite Web sites. What makes them your favourite sites? What keeps you coming back to those sites? Visit those sites. Identify the features that appeal to you. Notice the site navigation. Notice how the brand identity elements are used throughout the site. After that, if you are still looking for examples of brand building sites, the following are a few others to visit:

- **Amazon.com:** this Web site has gained more publicity than any other – and no wonder: *Advertising Age*, in its December 13 1999 issue, named Amazon.com founder Jeff Bezos 'Marketer of the Year'. And while the brand is still in the red, it is doing many, many things right from a marketing perspective. Applying BrandForward's brand equity model, Amazon.com has addressed every key driver of brand insistence.

- *Awareness:* at 60.1 per cent of all US adults, Amazon.com has the highest awareness of any Internet business. It is no coincidence that it is also the number one Internet advertiser – not counting all the publicity it generates.
- *Accessibility:* Amazon.com is available 24 hours a day, 7 days a week, 365 days a year – with quick shipping and delivery. Its myriad browse and search approaches make it much quicker and easier to find what you are looking for on its Web site than in most retail stores. They even keep multiple shipping addresses and credit cards on file to simplify the shopping process. Their extensive Amazon Associates programme has extended their online reach even further, often tapping into sites with highly targeted interests and traffic.
- *Value:* on the price side of the ratio, all hardcover books are 30 per cent off and all paperback books are 20 per cent off. They also have a bargain book section in which you can save up to 80 per cent and a '10 for under $10' section. On the other side of the value ratio, you can listen to music samples and they offer complimentary shipping upgrades, free Post-it notes, magnets and bookmarks (with their logo), free gift wrapping (except for Christmas), book reviews, special orders, many ways to browse or search products, etc.
- *Relevant differentiation:* Amazon.com revolutionized the way we buy books (and other products). It owns that spot in our minds. Plus it has many unique features: personal wish lists, customized recommendations, purchase circles and even your own customized store.
- *Emotional connection:* they have personalized suggested book lists (by subject). They maintain your complete order history, which you can access at any time. They let you write online reviews of their books, CDs and other products. Clearly, they are using every brand insistence driver to their advantage.

- **Patagonia.com:** through visuals and words, this site exudes the essence of the Patagonia brand. The 'About Patagonia' section prominently features a statement of its brand's essence ('Committed to the Core') along with paths to sub-sections on 'our culture', 'sports we do', 'design philosophy', and 'enviro action'. The 'our culture' section features 'our roots' (company heritage and vision), 'field reports' (adventure essays) and 'Patagoniacs' (profiles and pictures of their employees living the brand) sub-sections. Given these features and the site's consistently distinctive brand voice and visual style, it's nearly impossible for you not to comprehend Patagonia's essence after having visited their site.
- **Nextmonet.com:** this site sells fine art for the home and office. It allows you to search their collection by any combination of the following criteria: style, medium, subject, colour, artist, price, size and artwork title or keyword. It allows you to select your

favourite art and organize it by your own customized 'rooms' for later reference. Its complex set of search criteria helps you search the collection based upon a variety of needs or problems to be solved. Its SmartArt section gives an overview of art appreciation including collecting basics (such as collecting strategies, authenticity, value and conservation).

- **Winespectator.com:** this site is full of useful features for the wine enthusiast. It provides wine search, wine ratings, vintage charts, wineries search, wine chat, contests, a weekly poll, personal wine list, restaurant search, food and wine matching, menus, bulletin boards on 20 topics, daily wine news, and other features. It is the easiest way to maintain your personal wine list and it includes reviews, ratings and 'drink before' dates for each bottle of wine.

- **Morningstar.com:** this investment site allows you to track multiple self-defined portfolios in one of several modes, including a completely customized mode (with frequently updated net worth). Its X-ray feature allows you to view your portfolios in various other ways (diagnostics, stock overlap, asset class, stock style, stock sector, stock type, stock stats, fees and expenses, world regions, bond style and overview). The Web site also features news, updates and alerts (based on your portfolio), forums (topic, stock or fund specific) and Morningstar University.

- **Travelocity.com:** this full service travel site offers the following features: find/book a flight, find/book a rental car, find/reserve a hotel, vacations and cruises, special deals, and a destination guide. You can search for a flight in one of three ways: best fare, best itinerary (date/fare combination), or schedule. The site maintains a personal profile for you, including frequent flyer numbers and meal and seat preferences. It provides the following travel tools: review your reservations, check your ticket delivery status, edit your personal profile, fare watcher e-mail, weather and maps.

- **Ebay.com:** this site redefined commerce. Now anyone can auction off anything to anyone else throughout the world 24 hours a day, seven days a week. They even offer a personal shopper service, alerting you to when new items that match your search criteria arrive. The site features an easy search function, seller feedback/rankings, seller's other auctions, message boards, a library (with a section dedicated to collectibles). On November 30 1999, the site offered 3,456,220 items for sale in 2,568 categories. The bold, colourful logo reinforces the brand's vitality.

- **Disney.com:** this site is massive with immense amounts of content – much of it with full animation and sound. The site looks and feels like Disney and features the following: games, music, activities, stories and Club Blast (for kids).

- **Smarterkids.com:** this site allows you to shop by the child's age range, theme, brand, subject, format and character. It highlights teachers' favourites, parents' favourites, best sellers, picks under $20 and great gift ideas. It even has three speciality centres: special needs centre, gifted and talented centre, and grandparents centre. It has a gift registry and you can create a customized 'My Kid's Store'. It even features a family resource centre with advice, news, activities and resources, including a learning styles survey and early development checklists. Their products are reviewed and rated by professional educators. Clearly, this site is not just another online toy store. It was carefully designed with the customer's needs in mind – to help children learn, discover and grow.

- **Crayola.com:** this site looks and feels like Crayola, with a strong and consistent brand identity, including lots of colour (a key part of its essence). It features separate sections for parents, educators and kids. It also provides a wide variety of searchable creative ideas for Crayola product use.

- **Hallmark.com:** Hallmark's first generation site focused on creating an emotional connection between Hallmark and its consumers. It featured a storytelling bulletin board, joke of the day, weekly comic strip, ornament collectors bulletin board, personal Hallmark Gold Crown card point totals, address book, occasion reminder service, artist profiles, store locator service, keepsake ornament screensavers and many other endearing features. The second-generation site is much more focused on commerce, but still offers many of the original features. You can talk keepsake ornament collecting or join the Maxine club online.

- **Women.com:** this site has attempted to become a community network for women. It features message boards, chat, experts, clubs (walking, stork, investment, book and entrepreneurs), community news, team profiles and free stuff. It also features multiple channels including career, cars, entertainment, family, fashion and beauty, food, health, home and garden, horoscopes, money, news and trends, pregnancy and baby, sex and romance, small business, tech and Internet, travel, weddings and basically anything and everything that may be of interest to women. Some of the more interesting features include makeover-o-matic, the relationship game and dates from hell.

- **Garden.com:** Garden.com is now defunct. When it went out of business, its URL was purchased by Burpee, presumably to divert garden.com traffic to Burpee's site. I still use this site as an example because it was very smart about merging content and commerce. Whatever your gardening needs were, garden.com addressed them. The site featured a plant encyclopedia, garden planner software, a plant finder (with exhaustive criteria – like hardiness zone, sun exposure, soil composition, soil pH, soil moisture, flower colours, foliage colours, season of bloom, planting time, type of plant, care required, height, width, fragrance, butterfly attracting, hummingbird attracting, deer resistant, rabbit resistant, etc), a daily tip, to do lists, a garden doctor, chat, a gardeners forum, free postcards and other services. The site was very well designed with easy navigation. As with Amazon.com, it featured sophisticated search and browse functions. Its most notable feature was that almost all of its free services eventually led to products that you could purchase instantly online.

There are many common elements that make these Web sites 'strong brand building Web sites'. These common element include:

- strong and consistent brand identity, voice and visual style;
- robust and intuitive search and browse techniques;
- features specifically designed to appeal to the target customer, including customer problem-solving features;
- creative ways for customers to put a piece of themselves on the site (investment portfolio, personal wine cellar, product wish list, etc).

A FINAL CAUTION

A final caution: poorly thought out and executed Web sites can hurt brand equity. Apply the same thoughtfulness and quality standards to your organization's Web site as you do to its products, services and other marketing programmes. Some companies will permit spelling, typographical, or grammatical errors on their Web sites that they would not tolerate in other media. Some companies also seemingly ignore broken links and leave amateurish 'work in progress' pages up for indefinite periods of time. It is amazing how many companies outsource development and maintenance of their Web sites with little direct input or oversight.

Your organization's Web site is its most visible face to the public. Make sure it is building your brand's equity, not depleting it. (For a fee, www.atwatch.com will watch your Web site and alert you to problems in the following areas: average and peak response times, missing content, site down, broken links, hackers and public postings about your site.)

THE IMPACT OF THE INTERNET ON BRANDS: A SUMMARY

- An Internet presence has become an essential requirement for brand building.
- A Web site can create an integrated brand experience that consistently reinforces the brand positioning.
- The Internet will drive brands without a compelling point of difference (or a strong value proposition) out of business.
- Brands more than ever will help people break through the over-communication clutter.
- The Web site itself is just one element of brand building on the Internet.
- You can and should integrate commerce and brand building online.
- A well-known brand name is the most important factor in directing people to your e-commerce site (top-of-mind awareness is the desired end).

- To be successful, e-commerce sites must deliver superior value to their bricks and mortar competitors. There are four primary ways in which the Internet can add value: information, entertainment, convenience and cost savings. For instance, Amazon.com delivers superior convenience in finding and purchasing books.
- Brands that integrate a bricks and mortar presence with a 'cyberspace' presence will be formidable competitors.

Top sources of Internet-related facts, information, and research

- **www.nielsen-netratings.com/corporate_default.jsp** – Nielsen/Net Ratings.
- **http://wreportus.mediametrix.com/clientCenter.html** – Jupiter Media Metrix: United States – purchased by Nielsen/Net Ratings.
- **www.forrester.com** – Forrester Research.
- **www3.gartner.com** – Gartner (including Gartner Dataquest).
- **www.iconocast.com** – ICONOCAST.
- **www.cyberdialog.com** – Cyber Dialog.
- **www.doubleclick.net** – DoubleClick.

Other online marketing resources
- **www.brandforward.com** – features 21 categories of brand resources and links.
- **http://iabcanada.com and www.iabuk.net** – Interactive/Internet Advertising Bureau.
- **www.mbinteractive.com/site/iab/study.html** – IAB branding study.
- **www.millwardbrown.com** – Measuring brand impact on the WWW.
- **www.dminteractive.tmp.com and www.channelseven.com** – Advertising ideas.
- **www.adbility.com** – Banner advertising.
- **www.infogate.com and www.marimba.com** – 'Push' companies.
- **www.Webtrendslive.com** – Website traffic analysis package.
- **www.broadvision.com** – e-Business platform and tools.

Table 11.4 *Brand management checklist: brand building on the Internet*

	Yes	No
Is your domain name (URL) your brand name?		
Do you own URLs for all variations of your brand name? Do you redirect people who enter those URLs to your site?		
Do you contract with someone to protect your brand name and trademark online? (Namesake.com and Cyveillance.com provide this service.)		
Does your Web site reinforce your brand's essence, promise and personality?		
Is your brand's identity consistently presented throughout the site?		
Does your site weave a story about your brand's history, heritage, character or attitude?		
Does your Web site create an engaging, interactive, interesting, informative and helpful consumer experience?		
Do you use animation (such as Macromedia's Flash and Shockwave) throughout your site to make it interesting?		
Do you use audio on your site?		
Do you feature streaming video on your site (using programs such as Quick Time or Real Audio)?		
Does your site download quickly?		
Do you keep your site visitors active (they want to click and scroll, not read)?		
Can users get to almost any page on your site in three clicks or less?		
Is your site's copy concise, factual and bulletized?		
Do you have a site map that is easy to find and use?		
Do you have a site search engine?		
Is your site's navigation intuitive and consistent?		
Does every page on your site have 'Home', 'Search', and 'Site Map' buttons?		
Does your site work for a wide variety of technical platforms (operating systems, browsers, plug-ins, monitor sizes and resolutions, e-mail programs, etc)?		
Does your site create a sense of community? Does it provide ample opportunities for community members to interact with each other over time?		
Do you personalize your site to your site visitors' preferences (wallpaper, first page viewed, customized content, etc)?		

Table 11.4 (*continued*)

	Yes	No
Do you give consumers reasons to return to your site on a regular basis?		
Do you offer customer services (such as store locator service, checklists and consultative or diagnostic tools)?		
Does your site have directories with hypertext links to specific pages on other sites?		
Does your site have a searchable library of articles by subject matter experts?		
Does your site have bulletin boards?		
Does your site have chat rooms?		
Do you feature simple surveys and reviews on your site?		
Do you keep personal user lists on your site?		
Does your site match people with interests (through search and browse techniques)?		
Does your site feature user opinion postings?		
Do you sponsor online events on your site? Do you lead forum discussions on your site?		
Does your site have an extranet section (password protected area for clients/members with value added services)?		
Do you publish a free online newsletter?		
Do you provide activities to unobtrusively build a database (games, contests, sweepstakes, surveys and newsletters)?		
Do you know which word combinations people most often use in search engines to find Web sites like yours? Do you know how your site places in search engine rankings for those key phrases? Do you monitor your listings and check your search engine rankings frequently?		
Does your site's ranking place it on the first page or two of a search engine's results? If not, are you actively pursuing ways to increase your site's search engine ranking?		
Have you listed your site in search engine directories?		
Do you check your competitors' sites to see how they rank using your keywords?		
Do you analyze the pages with the highest search engine rankings using your keywords?		
Is your site featured in portal sites? Is your site a portal site?		

Table 11.4 (*continued*)

	Yes	No
Do you actively seek reciprocal links with other sites?		
Do you submit your site for awards?		
Do you advertise online?		
Do you use banner ads, keyword advertising, or interstitial advertising?		
Are your banner ads compelling?		
Do you post ads in discussion groups? Do you place notices in chat rooms and on bulletin boards?		
Do you write by-lined articles for other Web sites?		
Do you place e-zine ads?		
Do you maintain good online media relations? Are you (or is someone from your company) listed as a subject matter expert in online expert lists?		
Do you create micro-sites to feature specific products, services or events?		
Do you have virtual storefronts in Web malls and virtual shelf spaces within stores on other sites?		
Do you include a signature line (brand name/logo, tag line, address, telephone number, URL, etc) in all your outgoing e-mail as a standard business practice?		
Do you include your Web site's URL in all external communication (advertising, business cards, letterhead, etc) as a standard business practice?		
Do you promote your brand's Web site offline (through advertising, publicity, published articles, word-of-mouth, etc)?		
Are you a student of the World Wide Web, constantly noting effective techniques that other sites use?		
Do you visit your competitors' sites often to better understand how they are interacting with their customers?		
Do you carefully track who is on your site, where they came from, what they look at and how they found your site (through programs that analyze your log files)?		
Do you ask your consumers what they like and what they don't like? Do you change the site experience based on their responses?		
Do you use cookies to capture additional information on site visitors and to provide them with customized content when they return to your site?		
Do you use a combination of cookies and surveys to compare site/page/ad exposure to brand awareness and perception?		

NOTES

1 Source: Kelly Anthony-Rodriques, *Brand Management: From print to broadcast on the Web*, Seybold San Francisco/Publishing '98 Web Publishing Conference, Tuesday, September 1, 1998.

2 Source: Steven M Cristol and Bob Johnson, *Building Brand Equity on the World Wide Web*, Summary of a presentation to the Business Week Corporate Branding Symposium, Chicago, June 17, 1997.

3 Courtesy of Jeff Kuzmich, Element K Internet marketing manager.

4 Source: 'Search Listings Outperform Banner Ads and Tiles!', www.goto.com/d/about/advertisers/slab/jhtml.

5 Source: Steven M Cristol and Bob Johnson, *Building Brand Equity on the World Wide Web*.

6 Source: Joseph Jobst, *Branding on the Net* [Online] http://linz1.net/freep19.html

7 Source: Steven M Cristol and Bob Johnson, *Building Brand Equity on the World Wide Web*.

8 Source: Steven M Cristol and Bob Johnson, *Building Brand Equity on the World Wide Web*.

9 Courtesy of Jeff Kuzmich, Element K Internet marketing manager.

10 Primary source: www.aibn.com/brandbuild.html and Rex Briggs, digital marketing and measurement pioneer (at the Second Annual Online Marketing International Summit, April 23–26 2001).

11 Source: *Brand Interaction: The oft-neglected element of online branding*, by Rob McEwen, principal of This Quarter, a direct-marketing consultancy, and former founder and CEO of M2K, an integrated marketing agency. (Accessed 23 October 1999.)

12

Developing a brand-building organization

One of the most difficult tasks in brand management is transforming the organization from one that does not understand the scope or importance of brand management to one that embraces and actively builds the brand as a critically important source of sustainable competitive advantage. Key to this transformation is the organization's brand promise.

The following comment is typical of what I hear from marketing executives at more and more companies these days: 'We conducted exhaustive consumer research. We carefully positioned our brand. We developed and instituted comprehensive brand identity standards and systems. We are running our new advertising campaign. Now what do we do? How do we get the rest of the organization to understand and care about the brand and its promise? How do we get the organization to deliver on the promise? How do we make the brand promise real?'

Brand management guru, David Aaker, posed the following very important question when he visited Hallmark a few years ago: 'Until everyone from your CEO to your receptionist can accurately and consistently articulate your brand's promise, how do you expect your customers to?'

Certainly, the brand promise drives your marketing communication and your brand identity standards and systems. But it must do much more than that. Your products and services, every point of contact your brand makes with consumers, and the total consumer experience your brand creates must reinforce your brand's promise. This has tremendous organizational implications. How can an organization deliver against its promise if its front line employees do not know (or care about) what its brand stands for?

At Hallmark, we did a number if things to incorporate the brand at every level of the organization:

- We worked with our public affairs and communications department to include key brand concepts and messages in all internal and external publications and executive speeches.
- We worked with the training department to build brand strategy modules into all internal training programmes, especially new employee orientations.
- We gave Franklin Planner page finders featuring the brand essence and promise to all employees.
- We created a brand management and marketing intranet site so all employees could easily access brand plans, brand research, brand identity standards and other brand information.

NEGATIVE EXAMPLE: UNITED AIRLINES RISING

A way to illustrate the importance of developing a brand-building organization is through an example of when it is not working. A good example is the United Airlines 'United Airlines Rising' advertising campaign in 1997. This campaign was meant to communicate to the public that United was aware of their problems and was making an effort to raise their service to meet consumers' expectations. But the campaign backfired on them when they first launched it. Why? Because just as United was making promises about its new customer satisfaction philosophy, its flight attendants were threatening a labour action (called CHAOS(™), or 'Creating Havoc Around Our System(™)') and the Association of Flight Attendants stated, 'No raises, no rising'. To add insult to injury, United's customer relations department was also so unresponsive to complaints that a disgruntled customer created the Web site www.untied.com, a site featuring complaints from other United Airlines passengers.

In 1998, The Conference Board conducted a study on *Managing the Corporate Brand*. In that study, they discovered four organizational support factors were critical to brand strategy success. They are:

- CEO leadership and support;
- a distinctive corporate culture that serves as a platform for the brand promise;
- the ability to obtain support from a broad spectrum of employees;
- the alignment of brand messages across functions.

At the Institute for International Research's December 1999 Brand Masters Conference in Palm Beach, Florida, Sixtus Oechsle, Manager, Corporate Communications and Advertising, Shell Oil Company, indicated that in a study of sources of brand favourability, Shell Oil found that interaction with company employees had the greatest impact (much greater than brand ads or news) on brand favourability.

COMMON ORGANIZATIONAL BARRIERS TO BRAND BUILDING

Here are some of the most common problems that organizations encounter when trying to implement new brand management programmes:

- Senior management is not focused on the brand.
- Senior management has a short attention span and fails to provide the support and resources necessary for the branding to occur.
- Some senior leaders do not believe in the brand management concept.
- The organization is highly fragmented and resistant to change.
- The organization is internally focused.
- Difficulties in shifting people's focus from their functional 'silos' to cross-functional ownership of the brand.
- The organization's culture does not reinforce the brand.
- The organization's operations and systems do not support the brand.
- The brand message is just one of many among a myriad of corporate messages.

BRAND BUILDING REQUIRES MORE THAN ADVERTISING AND BRAND IDENTITY MANAGEMENT

To create the change required to build a brand, all of the following must be addressed:

- Corporate mission and vision – are they congruent with the brand essence and promise?
- Business-planning process – is it linked to the brand planning process?
- Corporate culture, values and behaviour – do they support the brand essence, promise and personality?
- Recruitment – are you screening people for congruence between their beliefs, values and personality and your brand's essence, promise and personality?
- Internal communication vehicles – are you using them to communicate brand positioning, strategies and priorities?
- Training and development – are you using these to increase understanding of brand positioning, strategies and priorities?

- Performance objectives (especially common objectives) – do they include brand objectives?
- Performance appraisal – do you provide feedback on how well individuals and groups are delivering against the brand promise?
- Rewards and recognition – do you reward and recognize people who have furthered important brand goals? Do you compensate people for achievement of brand objectives?
- Products and services – do they deliver against the brand promise?
- Operations, systems, and logistics – do they support delivery of the brand promise?

Brand marketing will not work (at least to its fullest potential) if it is confined to an advertising agency, public affairs department, or even a brand management function. This is especially true if the brand in question is the corporate brand. The CEO is the ultimate brand manager, and everyone throughout the organization must be a brand champion (which implies they all know the brand essence and promise). Indeed, the company should be organized to deliver optimally the brand promise, and the corporate culture must support the brand's promise. How can consumers know what your brand stands for if people in your organization do not? Does the person answering your free phone number know what the brand stands for? How about the in-store sales associate? The copywriter for your brand catalogue? The person developing a brand promotion? The people who design the brand's products?

Hiring employees whose personalities and values match those intended of the brand will ensure that the brand experience is consistently delivered as intended. Hiring employees who are category enthusiasts ensures knowledge, passion, credibility and the ability to communicate more easily with customers and potential customers. It also helps you tap into customer networks more easily. This is important across functions – from product development, sales and customer service to marketing research, quality control and senior management. For example, Oakley looks for employees who have a serious interest in sport. Southwest Airlines hires people for their sense of humour and positive attitude. Virgin Atlantic also hires people based on their congruence with company values.

At the Institute for International Research's The Branding Trilogy conference in Santa Barbara, California, Kristine Shattuck, Los Angeles Area Marketing Manager, Southwest Airlines put it well when she said, 'Enthusiastic employees spread enthusiasm to customers. Market to your employees as much as your customers. If your employees don't "get it", neither will your customers.'

You, your executive team, and all your organization's employees should share your passion about your brand each and every day. What story is uniquely your brand's own? Tell that story, and people will pass it on. As you know, 'word of mouth' marketing is one of the more powerful forms of marketing. The story could spread to a key decision maker or an important influencer.

Also investigate possible organizational misalignments. At Hallmark, a key brand objective was to differentiate the Hallmark brand of greeting cards from the Ambassador brand of greeting cards, but products for both brands were developed in the same business units. Those business units had profit and loss responsibility, controlled all of the product development resources and had sku (stock keeping unit) reduction goals that could not be accomplished except by combining skus across brands and removing the brand identity from the affected skus. That was a powerful incentive against brand differentiation.

Or consider the Hallmark licensing department. It had a strong incentive to licence the Hallmark name out to any organization that was willing to pay the appropriate royalties (whether or not the product category was right for the Hallmark brand). Why? Because it was not managed as a part of a strategic brand development group but rather as part of an independent division that was driven by revenue and profit generation goals. In both of these examples, the organizational design made it more difficult to achieve brand goals.

In both instances, education, persuasion, influencing and constant communication from the brand group was required to ensure brand goals were not completely compromised. Educating division heads and other executives was a critical component of this. If they understand the importance of brand stewardship, it makes the brand manager's job much easier.

Employee morale is a very important element in maintaining a strong brand. Employee morale affects everything from quality of front-line service and product defects to word of mouth negative comments about the company, some of which will eventually make it into the press (trade and general).

A very recent trend in some companies is to include the human resource function as a part (and in support) of the marketing function. Michael Porter's customer value chain concept is based on the thought that every activity a company performs should add to customer value, or it should be eliminated. If a company has chosen the right promises for its brands, the concept could be adapted to say that all company activities should contribute to the delivery of brand promises or be eliminated – this includes operations, logistics, marketing and sales, human resource management, organization design, technology development and procurement

Brands are typically a company's most valuable assets, along with its people. In fact, the value of the brand asset often exceeds a company's annual sales. However, in many companies, people view brand management functions and activities as 'overhead', implying they are expendable and non-value-added. (In contrast to this view, in the 1950s, Peter Drucker stated that 'marketing and innovation add value, everything else in the organization adds costs'. He assumed marketing was integrated throughout the enterprise.) Accounting systems that categorize brand spending as 'non-product' or 'non-direct' expenses often exacerbate the view of brand activities as 'overhead'. The long-term perspective of brand building also contributes to this view; a brand building (or diluting) activity typically does not produce visible results in the current quarter. The results are cumulative and are more visible over time.

If the brand is recognized for what it is – a very important asset that must be built, maintained and leveraged – then people will begin to view brand activities and spending very differently. This must begin with the CEO and the CFO, but it should be a view shared by all employees. The CFO can become one of the biggest brand supporters if he or she is aware of the financial value of the brand asset. This is why measuring the value of the brand asset is so important.

THE NEW BRAND MANAGEMENT PARADIGM

The most successful brand building organizations are creating a new brand management paradigm.

Table 12.1 *The new brand management paradigm*

Old paradigm	New paradigm
Individual product brands	Corporate brand
Business is defined as a product category (such as 'greeting cards').	Business is defined as the brand essence (such as 'caring shared').
Brand is managed by advertising department and agency.	Brand is managed by the CEO, a corporate officer responsible for brand equity management, and all employees in the organization.
	More and more companies are adopting what *BrandMarketing* has termed the 'Brand Czar' position. Kodak recently created a new vice president of brand and market development position; Gateway created a new vice president of brand management position; Compaq has a vice president for worldwide advertising and brand strategy; and ConAgra has a president of ConAgra brands.
Product management is the central focus of the organization.	Brand management is the central focus of the organization.
Brand management is treated as 'overhead' and brand marketing as an expense.	Brand management is a critical function performed by all employees, and brand marketing is an investment in the company's future.

The CFO is sceptical of the worth of the brand management function and brand spending.	The CFO knows the value of the brand as a financial asset and is one of the most outspoken supporters of brand management.
Brand marketing and brand identity standards and systems are aligned in support of the brand essence and promise.	Everything in the organization is aligned in support of the brand essence and promise, including the following: ● mission, vision and strategy; ● values and behaviours; ● communication; ● products and services; ● operations, systems and logistics.
Branding is often an afterthought ('Now what should we call this?').	No action is taken unless it supports or enhances the brand essence and promise.
Growth is product development or acquisition driven.	The brand essence and promise provide the direction, consumer permission and business incentive for all future growth.
The marketing department and agencies can accurately articulate the brand essence and promise.	All employees and business partners can accurately articulate the brand essence and promise.
Marketing department employees are compensated on performance against brand measures.	All employees are compensated on performance against brand measures.
Inwardly focused functional silos.	An integrated, market driven organization.

Increasingly, the brand is becoming the key source of differentiation that guides customer purchase choice. The brand is also the focal point around which an organization defines how it will uniquely deliver value to the customer for a profit. The brand embodies the 'heart and soul' of an organization. Its promise is delivered through its products, services and consumer communication – the total customer relationship and experience. If the brand promise is well conceived and consistently delivered through all business processes and customer contacts, the organization will grow and prosper.

Ultimately, you want to create a company full of brand maniacs, champions and evangelists. Not until this happens can you be sure that you have developed a brand-building organization.

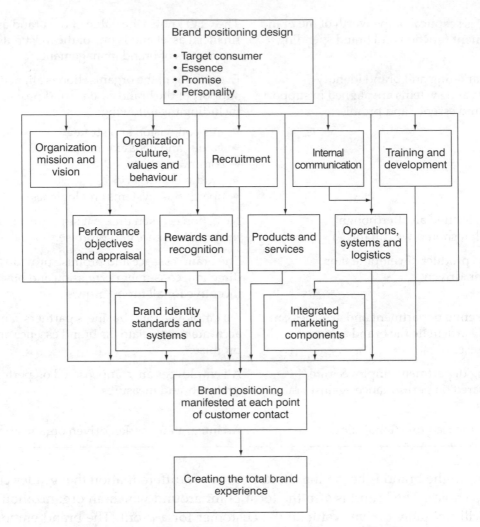

Figure 12.1 *Developing a brand-building organization*

CREATING A BRAND-BUILDING ORGANIZATION: OVERCOMING OBSTACLES

I have conducted numerous 'Creating a Brand-Building Organization' workshops in the last few years. The following are approaches that people in various organizations have found to be effective in overcoming some of the obstacles encountered in creating brand-building organizations:

Issue

How do you get corporate officers to support brand management initiatives when they do not understand the value of brand management or marketing?

Ideas

- Influence the leaders with books and speakers.
- Provide case studies of how brand management has worked in comparable companies and industries.
- Symbolically 'clean house' in the marketing department. Hire some new high profile marketers with a history of success.
- Understand operating units' objectives. Help units achieve their objectives through brand-enhancing initiatives. That is, tie what you do to others' objectives.
- Invite senior executives to help you solve brand management problems. Appeal to their egos and their propensity to mentor. (They will be much more bought in to the solution if they helped craft it.)
- Build momentum for brand-building initiatives from a grass-roots groundswell. This requires intensive communication and education. Start by identifying and influencing brand advocates throughout the organization.
- Work with HR to integrate a brand-building module into a variety of employee classes.
- To instil confidence, the marketing leaders should be optimistic, using words and phrases such as 'control', 'promising opportunity', and 'return'. (This has been validated as an effective technique by research conducted by Chris White at the University of Central Florida.[1]

Issue

How do you get corporate officers to act as brand champions when they are accountable for other corporate priorities?

Ideas

- Tie brand performance objectives to their compensation system.
- Give them bonuses based on achievement of brand goals.
- Educate them. Sell them.
- Include 'brand passion' as an executive hiring criterion.
- Figure out how the brand helps them.
- Schedule periodic meetings with them. Ask them how the brand management group can help them achieve their objectives.
- Figure out how brand actions can help them achieve their performance targets.

- Ask them for their help. Appeal to them as mentors. Ask for their sponsorship.
- Create (brand) councils of key decision makers and detractors.
- Make them the steering committee for your cross-functional brand team. Assign them specific roles as part of that steering committee.
- Ask your CEO to assign the corporate officers the role of brand coaches (assuming he or she is supportive of brand initiatives).
- Build brand allies before the meetings in which you present brand recommendations. Pre-sell all your initiatives. Uncover and address objections before the meeting.
- Interview key executives to identify what they have done to further the brand cause. Feature them and what they have done to further the brand in publications.
- Measure the brand's value as an asset. Enlist the support of the CFO.
- Facilitate exercises with them.

Issue

Once you have most of the brand pieces in place (brand promise and positioning, brand identity, etc), how do you translate all of that to a brand-building culture?

Ideas

- 'Walk the talk'. Challenge others to do so as well.
- Throw it back out to the organization to figure out. You don't have to know all the answers up front.
- Review the brand tenets with various groups. Ask them where your plans are lacking in helping you achieve brand goals.
- Develop a six-month plan including objectives, obstacles, messages and vehicles.
- Work closely with Corporate Communications to integrate brand-building education and messages into internal publications, videotapes and speeches.
- Volunteer to chair cross-functional task forces and management committees. Work brand-building topics into the agendas of those groups as appropriate. (Whoever controls meeting agendas largely controls the outcome of those meetings.)

Issue

Identify out-of-the-box tactics to ensure continued employee involvement in and support of brand initiatives.

Ideas

- Poster contest ('Communicate what the three brand tenets mean to you').
- Feature 12 of the posters on a 12-month calendar (or 52 of them on a 52-week calendar).

- Open houses (different areas showcase what they have done to promote brand initiatives).
- Promote (through internal publications or other means) 'the person on the street' who has helped build the brand.
- Name and recognize a 'brand champion of the month'.
- Conduct 'lunch and learn' sessions.
- Create brand 'certificates of appreciation'. Award them to people who have furthered brand causes.
- Catch people 'living the brand' and tell stories about them (in newsletters, in speeches, on the Intranet, etc).
- Capture on videos customer testimonials of how the brand promise was delivered.
- Post consumer letters highlighting how the brand promise was delivered against (or not) on the brand intranet site.
- Tie performance appraisals and compensation to delivery of the brand promise.
- Learn from 'best practice' companies. Share information with your peers at other companies.
- Ask this question on employee surveys: 'If you could only change one thing about the brand, what would you change and why?'
- Develop and publish brand performance measures.
- Incorporate brand goals in business plans.

Issue

If we believe front-line employees are 80 per cent of the way there in their understanding of the brand, what else should we ask them to know, say or do?

Ideas

- Validate your beliefs with research. Measure their understanding.
- Create an employee focus group. Run it by the people in the focus group (for ideas on what to do next).
- Ask them how they are going to 'live the brand'.
- Ask them what actions they are going to take to deliver against the brand promise.
- Instead of focusing on dissemination of information, focus on recognition for the appropriate behaviour.
- Apply the 'message pyramid'.
- Remember the 'rule of six' (you must communicate something at least six times before it registers with most people). It is unlikely that you have over-communicated this information.
- Focus on educating/communicating to 'new hires' (assuming a significant turnover rate from year-to-year).

- If front-line employees are at 80 per cent, what would it take them to get to 100 per cent? Brainstorm that question.
- Ask the following five questions: 1) Why are we doing this? 2) What are we going to look like? 3) What is my role? 4) How will you support me? 5) What's in it for me?

Issue

How do we convince geographically and functionally diverse groups to embrace the brand promise when we have little authority and can only use influencing skills?

Ideas

- Identify each stakeholder's burning issues and discover ways your brand initiatives can address them. Relate your brand programmes back to their issues.
- Sell your initiatives to top executives in other divisions and departments.
- Set up measures to highlight gaps.
- Manage by embarrassment. Make someone look like an idiot. (While this may not fit with every organization's culture, many organizations, including Microsoft, have found it to be an effective technique.)
- Identify influencers. Create a grass roots support for your initiatives.
- Network. Use networks.
- Identify people in the organization who 'get it' and have passion about the brand. Recruit, indoctrinate and use them.
- Highlight your brand's performance versus the competition (in newsletters, etc).
- Bring in outside, credible, objective voices who will reinforce your key points – brand executives at other companies, brand consultants, people who are known and trusted by your executive group.
- Build ownership through cross-functional teams.
- Flatter people. Play up to their egos.
- Widely distribute brand books.

Did you know...?

- The typical number one brand is worth 10 per cent more than the number two brand to consumers (range: 0 per cent to 35 per cent).

- Home Depot and Ralph Lauren use the same paint formula, but the Home Depot house brand charges $9.94 while Ralph Lauren charges $26.95. (The only differences between the two are packaging, price charged, and the brand.)

- GE receives a 26 per cent to 40 per cent price premium for its light bulbs, depending on the sku.[2]

- 42 ounces of Always Save Oatmeal is $1.69 while the same amount of Quaker Oats is $3.35. 32 ounces of Best Choice Ketchup is $1.29 while the same amount of Heinz is $2.05. 16 ounces of Best Choice spaghetti is $.89 while the same amount of Pata La Bella and De Cecco are $1.05 and $1.89 respectively.

Table 12.2   *Brand management checklist: developing a brand-building organization*

	Yes	No
Do the CEO and other corporate officers embrace the brand as a key corporate asset that must be built and leveraged?		
Is your CEO's primary perspective that of brand marketing (versus finance, operations or something else)?		
Has your CEO 'internalized' your brand's essence? Does he or she 'live' your brand's promise? Does he or she personally reinforce the brand's intended personality?		
Does your CEO have a long-term vision for the brand?		
Does the CFO understand that the brand is an important corporate asset?		
Have you calculated the value of your brand as a financial asset? Are all corporate officers aware of this value?		
Do people in your organization know the difference between brand management and product management?		
Does a brand management process drive product decisions (rather than a product management process driving brand decisions)?		
Are there brand evangelists in your organization? Are there brand champions in senior management? Are your employees brand zealots?		
Have you identified potential allies outside the brand management function who understand what you are trying to accomplish with the brand? Have you developed a plan to further indoctrinate them and to use them as brand advocates? Have you actively engaged them as brand advocates?		
Is there a formal process for managing your brands?		
Is there a person or group responsible for strategic oversight of your brands? Does this include oversight of individual sub-brands?		
Is someone held accountable for managing your brand's personality?		

Table 12.2   (*continued*)

	Yes	No
Do your senior managers own brand strategy (rather than a specific department or an ad agency owning it)?		
Do you manage your brands as a portfolio, versus allowing (or even encouraging) autonomy in the management of individual brands and sub-brands?		
Are differentiating features reserved for the brands whose promises they best reinforce? Are you confident that there is no pressure to copy one brand's best competitive features for the organization's other brands and sub-brands?		
In recruiting people for jobs in your organization, do you screen people for congruence between their beliefs, values and personality and your brand's essence, promise and personality?		
Do you have a comprehensive internal brand education and communication programme?		
Do you have a published glossary of brand terms to ensure everyone in your organization is using the same nomenclature and the same definitions?		
Can all employees accurately and consistently articulate your brand's essence and promise?		
Do you test employees for their knowledge of the brand essence and promise? Do you regularly ask them what they are doing to deliver against the promise?		
Are your suppliers and other business partners well versed in your brand's essence and promise?		
Do you have a method in place to indoctrinate new employees in your brand's essence and promise?		
Do you tell stories to 'drive home' your brand's promise and its importance to your company's future (in your internal communication)?		
Do your brand's essence and promise serve as rallying cries for your employees? Have you used the brand essence to galvanize and focus the activities of your organization's employees? Are your brand's essence and promise stated simply enough so that they are easy to remember?		
Do you tell your brand's story to as many people as you can each day (in your external communication)?		
Do you have a brand plan?		
Do your senior managers and corporate officers understand that designing your corporate brand (essence, promise, personality, etc) is inextricably linked with crafting your corporate mission and vision?		

Table 12.2   (*continued*)

	Yes	No
Is brand planning integrated as a key element of your business planning process?		
Does the brand promise drive all business decisions within your organization?		
Is 'impact on brand equity' an important criterion in the following decision-making processes: capital investment, budget allocation, business development/acquisition and cost reduction?		
Does every decision, action and communication produced by your organization reinforce your brand's essence, promise, personality and positioning? If not, can you identify each one that does not reinforce the brand's design and will you do something to correct it?		
Is there a process by which all marketing elements are integrated to deliver against the brand promise and key brand priorities?		
Are there formal processes that enable you to manage the brand across organizational boundaries?		
Do you constantly benchmark your brand practices against other companies to ensure you are incorporating best practices into your approach to brand management?		
Are you personally a student of brand management practices? Do you try to learn from the successes and failures of other brands?		
Do your organization's common measures include key brand measures?		
Are your compensation systems and career advancement policies tied to advancing the brand promise and achieving key brand goals?		
Do you offer special recognition for people who successfully further brand goals?		
Do you know what functions in your value chain contribute most to your consumer's experience of the brand? Do you have a process to focus organizational resources on those functions (and redirect them from other nonessential functions)?		
Are you redesigning your business processes and systems, networks of relationships, and customer service functions to better align with and support your brand's promise of differentiated consumer benefits?		
Does your organization structure support delivery of the brand promise?		
Does the corporate culture reinforce the brand promise?		

Table 12.2   (*continued*)

	Yes	No
Is there a spirit of open communication and cooperation between the brand management function and the rest of the organization (versus conflicting agendas, frequent misunderstandings, mistrust and a lack of cooperation)?		
Do people in your organization understand that brand building is a long-term exercise with cumulative results?		
Is your organization as focused on long-term brand building as it is on short-term sales promotion (in contrast to short-term performance goals largely superseding long-term brand building efforts)?		
Do you have a way of measuring return on marketing investment?		
Do you know if your brand keeps its promise at each point of contact it makes with consumers?		

NOTES

1   Source: *Marketing Managers' Interpretation of Marketing Information*, by Chris White, University of Central Florida, Marketing Science Institute, Report no 00–121.

2   Source: Jim Harmon, *General Electric: Creating a Global Brand Identity*, presentation at the Institute for International Research's Brand Masters Conference, December 1997, Atlanta, Georgia.

13

Integrated brand marketing

While brand identity management and advertising are two of the more important and visible components of brand management, I hope that by the time you have finished reading this book you will agree that brand management is much more holistic and interdependent than that.

For instance, a typical marketing budget is divided among the following activities: advertising, promotion, trade shows, lead generation, other sales support (collateral materials), Web site, Internet marketing, direct mail, telemarketing, publicity, brand identity management and market research. At Element K, we also devoted marketing resources to pricing strategy/management, product marketing, segment marketing, channel marketing and trade relations. If the company is a consumer products company, add packaging to that. If it has a retail component, add merchandising and possibly purchasing. Some organizations put sales under this umbrella as well. Do not forget about communicating with industry and financial analysts, too. Finally, add internal brand-building activities and brand management legal activities (trademarks, copyrights, etc), and you have a very complicated, interdependent set of activities which require skill-specific sub-disciplines and effective integrating mechanisms.

Not a day went by at Element K during which I did not try to integrate one or more of these activities with other ones. Consider just one marketing discipline: trade shows. Trade shows support product marketing plans and help generate sales leads, which go into the marketing database. Trade shows must also reinforce the brand promise and the most recent brand advertising campaign.

We invited current and potential customers to our trade show booth and events through direct mailings, e-mail blasts, trade magazine ad inserts and announcements on our Web site. We interacted with the trade press – maintaining relationships, providing company updates and pitching stories – and also used the shows to maintain relationships with industry analysts and business partners. We researched product innovations, potential partners and our competitors. We scheduled sales calls and demonstrated products to potential customers. We often timed new product announcements and press conferences to occur while the show was in session. We occassionally timed a local cause-related marketing activity to occur during the show to gain publicity in local newspapers. We frequently paid to sponsor the show in return for many items of value to a brand-building campaign: mailing lists, e-mail lists, a better booth floor position, workshop speaking slots, or having our logos plastered on trade show brochures, convention centre banners, cyber café computers, buses and a myriad of other things. Further, we usually decided to beef up our advertising and editorial presence in that month's issue of trade magazines. We sometimes placed ads on convention centre hotel room key cards or televisions. Once we even bought outdoor advertising along the route between the convention centre and the convention centre hotels. Meanwhile, we always kept in mind that each trade show must have a simple and coherent set of messages. And trade shows are just one marketing tactic in a brand-building campaign!

Figure 13.1 provides an overview of Element K's communication campaign architecture, including the role of each medium in achieving different marketing objectives.

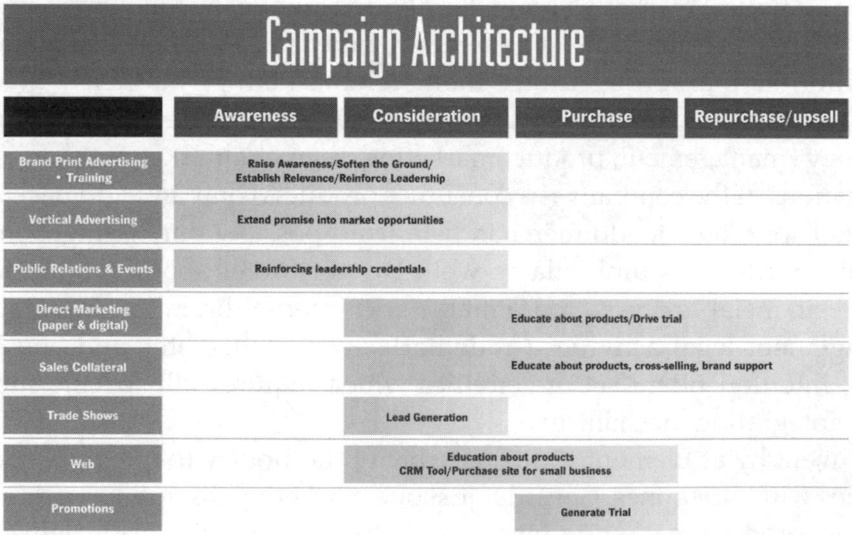

Figure 13.1 *Campaign architecture*

EFFECTIVE INTEGRATING MECHANISMS

When integrating your brand marketing efforts, here are some mechanisms you may find useful:

- A well-communicated brand positioning statement including the target customer and the brand essence, promise and personality.
- Conducting a brand positioning workshop with organization senior managers if necessary to build consensus.
- A brand marketing visionary at the top of at least the marketing organization (Marketing VP or Chief Marketing Officer), or better yet (from a marketer's perspective), the enterprise.
- As broad a span of control as possible for the chief marketing officer (encompassing as many of the disciplines listed above as possible) and frequent forums for him or her to communicate marketing issues and initiatives with other senior leaders of the organization.
- Specific brand management and marketing objectives (long term and short term).
- A brand marketing plan.
- Integrating brand plans with organization strategic plans.
- Product, programme and segment marketing plans (driven by or at least congruent with brand marketing plans).
- Marketing budgets allocated by market segment and sub-discipline (with 10–20 per cent of the overall budget held by the chief marketing officer for unforeseen opportunities).
- Integrated media plans.
- An intranet (or extranet) site devoted to the brand identity standards and systems (and any other published brand information of use to broad audiences).
- Digital brand asset management systems (to manage organizations with decentralized marketing control).
- A brand identity council comprising the following people: brand management personnel, general managers and creative directors from each of the organization's divisions.
- Frequent marketing update meetings for heads of each of the marketing sub-disciplines (for people to keep informed about what others are doing).
- Quarterly marketing planning sessions.
- At least biannual brand management forums or summits.
- Situating marketing people as close together as possible.
- Situating marketing people close to sales people.
- Situating marketing people close to product development people.
- Situating marketing people close to customer service people.
- Providing monthly or quarterly updates on progress against marketing objectives.
- Broadly disseminating brand management and marketing monthly reports.

- Carefully scripting the sales force on the brand story.
- Sending frequent marketing communications to the field sales force.
- Using as few advertising and other marketing agencies as possible. Some organizations will find that using a single full-service advertising/marketing agency will help to integrate their marketing effort with a single brand voice and visual style. Others will find that it is best to use multiple agencies with best-in-class services in specific areas: brand advertising, collateral materials, direct mail, public relations, and so on. Those that choose to do the latter put a greater burden on internal efforts to integrate brand marketing.
- Designating one internal copywriter and one internal graphic designer as keepers of the brand voice and visual style.
- Designating one brand management person as the ultimate enforcer of the brand identity standards. That person should be widely respected throughout the organization, possess outstanding interpersonal skills and be very assertive.
- Training every marketer to always ask, 'Have I reinforced the brand promise in this decision or activity?'
- The smaller the organization (especially those under 150 people), the easier it is to integrate marketing activities across the organization. The larger the organization, the more the integration will need to rely on formal processes and procedures.

Table 13.1 *Brand management checklist: integrated brand marketing*

	Yes	No
Does our brand always speak with one voice to our customers?		
Do we routinely integrate multiple marketing disciplines to achieve brand goals?		
Does everyone in our organization and do all of our business partners know our brand's essence, promise and personality?		
When we develop brand marketing programmes, do we start with the brand marketing objectives and brainstorm the most effective ways to achieve them (versus immediately applying a particular technique such as advertising or direct mail)?		
Do most of the marketing people in our organization know what most of the other marketing people are working on at any point in time?		
Do marketing people from various disciplines and divisions in our organization frequently collaborate and help one another?		
Are your sales promotions designed to help build the brand (or at least not to diminish it)?		
Is there a lot of cross-functional teamwork in your organization?		
Are people in your organization working against common goals?		

14

Creating the total brand experience

STARBUCKS

Ultimately, everything – products, services, retail environment, corporate culture, front line employees, marketing, and so on – must come together to create the total brand experience. Starbucks does this well. Not only is their product extraordinarily different from and better than a normal cup of coffee, but everything else they do also adds to the brand experience. Their stores feature the following carefully crafted components: the smell of fresh brewed coffee, exotic blends, exotic names (Venti Mocha Frappuccino®), piped-in jazz, comfortable wing chairs, a fireplace, live music, sophisticated sign graphics, and so on. And their employees (called 'partners'), receive extensive brand and customer service training and stock options to ensure the quality of the customer experience in the store. On their Web site, they devote space to the history and mystique of coffee brewing. Everything is designed to make you feel sophisticated without feeling intimidated. (Buy a cup of Starbuck's coffee and you are swept away from the ordinary for a while!)

SATURN

Saturn offers another example of a brand that carefully thought through the total brand experience. They extensively re-engineered their operations to radically alter the consumer car purchase experience (A 'different kind of (car) company'). To make the promise of 'salespeople as friends' real, it not only established a 'no haggle' pricing policy, it also put the following in place to ensure that salespeople would adhere to that policy:[1]

- restructured compensation packages that emphasized salary over sales commission;
- selling Saturn dealerships in groups by region to eliminate the incentive to pull business away from the Saturn dealership 'down the road' by price discounting;
- extensive salesperson training;
- communicating the approach to external audiences.

ADIRONDACK HAMLETS

I spend a lot of time in the Adirondack Park (in Northern New York State). There are dozens of hamlets scattered along the few main roads throughout the park, and these towns struggle with a seasonal tourist economy, long winters, stringent park regulations and the lack of an industrial base. To get tourists to stop in their hamlet (versus some other hamlet), many towns have adopted several techniques to make their hamlet more appealing:

- Most have adopted a brand identity system that incorporates a certain typestyle, a slogan (Keene Valley: Home of the Adirondack High Peaks) and an icon (Long Lake has adopted black bears, Raquette Lake a loon.

Figure 14.1   *The brand of Long Lake in the Adirondacks*

Figure 14.2   *The brand of Raquette Lake in the Adirondacks*

- Almost all have custom-made signs along the roads at the hamlet boundaries welcoming people into their hamlets and inviting them to return. Most of these signs are etched in wood with rustic touches reinforcing the 'Adirondack rustic style'.
- Many have added hanging flower baskets along the sidewalks in the hamlet centre.
- Most have tried to make the most of scenic vistas – mountain views, lake shores, and so on, removing obstructions and landscaping if necessary.

These hamlets have discovered that creating an identity, reinforcing the Adirondack rustic mystique, improving road-view aesthetics and leveraging the natural scenery improves the hamlet's tourist economy. These are good examples of enhancing the total brand experience.

HEMLOCK LODGE

To use another Adirondack example, I rent out my Adirondack home – Hemlock Lodge – occasionally throughout the year. I get many repeat customers from year to year, and they tell me that they really appreciate the attention to detail and the extra touches that improve the experience. For instance:

- Hemlock Lodge is a rustic log home with a loft, a great room, a central fireplace and rustic chandeliers. The house is situated to have a mountain view from the front porch and master bedroom.
- It is in a quiet, secluded setting, yet it is only minutes away from many attractions.
- I have decorated the house with rustic decor, from chainsaw-carved bears and loon decoys to rustic furniture and fixtures.
- There is an extensive library of maps, field guides, books on the Adirondacks, children's books, books about nature and the wilderness, classic literature, and so on.

- I have compiled a guide of all of the area's attractions.
- There are videotapes on various aspects of the Adirondacks and on the activities in which people are most likely to participate (fly fishing, skiing, hiking, kayaking, etc).
- I provide menus from area restaurants, restaurant reviews, and detailed directions to those restaurants that I recommend.
- I provide a list of useful Adirondack-related Web sites.
- I stock the house with pine-scented candles. (People consume the candles and firewood at an astounding rate – and obviously like to create the romantic atmosphere that firelight provides.)
- I have planted fragrant native trees, shrubs and other plants near the house (balsam fir, bayberry, wintergreen, etc).
- I maintain trails on the property, have planted wildflowers in the meadow in front of the house, and have placed benches strategically throughout the property.
- I have compiled a list of house eccentricities to address the questions that renters are most likely to ask during their stay.
- I provide a pre-trip information packet including directions to the house, an overview of area attractions, typical weather patterns by season, suggestions on what to bring, and other useful information.
- On the less-than-positive side, it has been difficult to eradicate the poison ivy (at least in an environmentally-friendly way) that grows naturally throughout the property. So I address this as best I can up front by warning people, providing articles covering the topic in depth, and providing preventative creams and soothing, anti-itch lotions.
- I am constantly enhancing the 'Hemlock Lodge experience' based on renter feedback, which they happily offer in a guest book I provide and which I politely solicit by e-mail after they have returned from their vacation.

So, by knowing what my renters (my customers) want and creating the experience that best delivers (and far exceeds) their hopes and expectations, I enjoy their return 'business' year after year.

TEN THOUSAND WAVES

Whenever I am in Santa Fe, I stay at Ten Thousand Waves (http://www.tenthousand-waves.com), a spa that is a case study in creating sensory experience. From its hillside setting, carefully designed layout, architecture, interior design, landscaping, use of water and gardens, fragrant trees, outdoor lanterns, shampoo (scented with real cedar), hand soap (scented with real coconut), in-room fireplaces, hot tubs, massage sessions, and so on, it addresses every human sense in a very sensual and spiritual way.

AUTOMOBILE MANUFACTURERS

Automobile manufacturers have become much better at creating the total brand experience, from the product to the purchase experience. Automobile design considers ergonomics and other human factors, textures, propensity of fabrics and other surfaces to maintain comfortable temperatures throughout the year, the 'feel' of knobs, buttons, and other controls, the look of the car itself (consider the PT Cruiser or the new VW Beetle), minimization of road noises, quality of stereo systems and radio reception, road handling and responsiveness to controls, and so on. And automobile manufacturers have adopted lessons from Saturn's purchase experience success.

MUSICAL GROUPS

Consider another example: musical groups as brands. Have you ever attended a concert that you will never forget? Was the music powerful? Did it speak to you in a way that is difficult to describe? Did the group establish a rapport with the audience that made every thing feel completely in sync? Did you find that you could not help but move to the rhythm of their beat? Was their show multi-sensory? Did they use lights and other special effects? Did their music evoke strong emotions? Did their music make you think about things differently? Did you completely lose track of time? Did you not want the concert to end? What if your brand could accomplish some of these same ends?

CREATING THE OPTIMAL BRAND EXPERIENCE

How do you create an optimal brand experience? First, ask the following questions:

- Will the experience impact all of the human senses: sight, sound, scent, taste and feel?
- How will it make people feel?
- Will people want to linger with your brand's products and services?
- Will people want to use the brand often? Will they want to return frequently (for applicable product/service categories)? Will they look forward to using the brand's products and services again?
- Does your brand reinforce something about who your customers are?
- Does your brand have a strong 'point of view'? Does it stand for something? Is it clear what it cares about?
- Is your brand exciting, soothing, exhilarating, fun, comforting, relaxing, stimulating, centring, calming, rejuvenating, etc?
- Will your brand conjure up images in your customers' minds? Will it evoke memories?

● Will your brand have the power to take people to 'a different place'? Can it put them 'in a different state of mind'? Will it have the power to change their mood?
● Will your brand make people feel as though they belong to something important or good or newsworthy?

CRISIS MANAGEMENT

While all organizations intend to create the best possible customer experiences, occasionally something real or perceived happens that produces just the opposite effect: a crisis. Every brand will experience a crisis at one time or another. The hallmark of a strong brand is how well it handles those crises.

The crisis could come as a result of something the company does (such as Exxon Valdez) or something that is foisted upon it (rumours that McDonald's hamburgers are made of worms). But, when a crisis occurs, it is time to enact a well-rehearsed crisis management plan. So think about a crisis management now (hopefully, long before any actual crisis), and begin with the following considerations:

● Steadily and consistently build brand goodwill over time.
● Identify and address potential problem areas ahead of any actual crises.
● Have a well-thought-through crisis (or emergency response) plan, including scenarios, step-by-step instructions on how to best address each scenario, approved spokespeople, contact information and key communication documents (fact sheets, backgrounders, press releases, bios, etc).
● Work with crisis management experts and your legal staff in developing those plans.
● Conduct crisis management drills at least once a year if not more often.
● Conduct a crisis vulnerability audit.
● During the crisis itself, follow these general rules:
  – Follow your crisis plan.
  – Identify your spokespeople.
  – Respond quickly.
  – Be honest. Don't deny or cover things up – ultimately, they will be exposed.
  – Accept responsibility as appropriate.
  – Share as much information as is possible and prudent.
  – Let people know what you are doing to manage the situation.
  – Show concern for those affected.
  – Let people know what you are doing to help people who are negatively impacted.
  – Explain what you are doing to cooperate with the authorities.
  – Let people know if neighbours or others are in danger and what they can do about it.

- Provide the media with telephone and Internet access and the other tools that they need to perform their jobs.
- Provide frequent updates to keep the communication lines open.
- Act with integrity, reinforcing the brand's personality.

If not handled well, a crisis can undo years of brand equity building. According to Bob Roemer – responsible for BP-Amoco's public and government affairs worldwide emergency response capabilities – the key to effective crisis management is to offer maximum information with minimum delay. If you do not have a well-rehearsed plan, you should work with your public affairs department and a PR agency to develop one.

Table 14.1   *Brand management checklist: creating the total brand experience*

	Yes	No
Have you designed (and implemented) the 'total customer experience' for your brand?		
Do you draw upon all of the human senses in creating your brand's customer experience?		
Does your brand evoke strong positive emotions?		
Does your brand make people feel good?		
Does your brand consistently exceed people's expectations?		
Does your brand create experiences that are memorable in the most positive sense?		
Do people want to linger with your brand's products and services?		
Do people look forward to interacting with your brand again and again?		
Does your brand steadily and consistently build goodwill over time?		
Do you have a written emergency response plan? Does it include a checklist of key operational and communication steps to be taken? Do you rehearse the plan at least once a year?		

NOTES

1   Source: Adam Morgan, *Eating the Big Fish*, p 140.

Section 4

Leveraging the brand

15

Brand extension

A brand may enter new product categories, new product formats within a category (line extension), or new markets or market segments. Examples of the latter include taking a brand currently targeted to women and extending it to the male market, and taking a brand that currently appeals to adults and extending it to the teen market.

Another example of extending a brand into new markets is extending it down from its current position to the value segment, or up from its current position to the premium segment. Often, to designate a premium version or offering, special words or phrases are used in association with the brand name – words such as gold, platinum, limited edition, signature collection, premier, elite, marquis, reserve, private, professional and executive class. But, in general, the more subtle the allusion to a brand's premium status, the more effective the approach.

The brand can be extended with or without using another associated brand. If another brand is used, it may be a sub-brand or a brand endorsed by the original brand. Another option is co-branding. Hallmark created the 'Confections' sub-brand to extend into gift candies but it did so in conjunction with Fannie Mae's Celebrated Collection (premium) sub-brand. The product is co-branded with each company's brand and sub-brand. Co-branding may be a faster way to enter a new category and gain credibility within it.

WAYS TO EXTEND THE BRAND

Regardless of the branding treatment, extensions can occur in the following ways:

- Manufacture the product (or supply the service) yourself.
- Acquire a company that makes the product (or supplies the service).
- Source the product or service from some other organization, but put your name on it.
- Licence your name for use by another company that makes the product or supplies the service. (Use brand licensing to extend the brand into new categories, expand the meaning of the brand, reinforce key brand associations, build your brand as a badge, or bring your brand to life in new ways. You should avoid licensing your brand where it does not make sense just to make a few extra revenue dollars. Where the licensing department resides in your organization structure will have a large impact on how well licensing is used to build (versus bleed) the brand.)
- Form an alliance or joint venture with another company to supply the product or service.

Obviously, the pros and cons of the various methods include speed to market, fit with core competencies, upside revenue and profit potential, asset risk, amount of control over the brand delivery, and the degree to which you are committed to the category in the long term.

BENEFITS OF BRAND EXTENSION

In addition to generating incremental revenue and profit for your brand, brand extensions can be beneficial in the following ways:

- helping to clarify and broaden brand meaning to consumers (for instance, extending Hallmark into candy and flowers may help redefine the brand, expanding it from 'greeting cards' to 'ways to show you care');
- reinforcing and building upon key brand associations;
- extending the brand's reach and relevance to new consumers;
- creating brand 'news' / 'buzz';
- laying the groundwork for future extensions.

Risks of brand extension include the following:

- creating confusion regarding brand meaning;
- tarnishing the quality image;
- conflicting with or counteracting key brand associations;
- creating new, undesired brand associations;

- 'turning off' current key consumer segments;
- if done in great excess with no focus, completely diluting brand meaning and overexposing the brand in the marketplace.

DANGERS OF EXTENDING THE BRAND INTO A NEW PRICE SEGMENT

One of the biggest dangers is a brand extension that repositions the parent brand in a negative light (like Bayer 'aspirin-free' products or 'fat free' Fig Newtons). One of the trickiest extensions is creating a 'value' version of the parent brand. Extending your brand up to a premium segment or down to a value segment has the greatest potential for negative impact, as a brand's quality and value perceptions are often central to its positioning. You do not want to create the perception that the original brand was overpriced.

Often the best solution is creating a new brand or sub-brand. If the market is moving away from your brand's position, it may be better in the long run, despite the cost, to create a new brand to meet and own the solution to the evolving needs of consumers. This is a more expensive approach with a higher probability of failure and is not a brand extension.

LINKING PREVIOUSLY UNLINKED BRANDS

If your company has just acquired another company or is considering entering a strategic alliance with another company, research is required to determine how, if at all, the brands should be linked: co-brand, parent brand/sub-brand, endorsed brand, one brand replaces the other, create a new brand, and so on. Understanding the impact of each branding approach on the essence, promise, personality and positioning of each brand involved, and the perceptions of the products and services sold under each brand name, should help you decide the best approach to take.

BRAND EXTENSIONS AND GLOBAL BRANDING

If you are in the process of building your brand globally, especially if your brand is in its infancy in some regions or countries, here is something else to watch out for with brand extensions. If a particular extension, especially one less central to the brand's promise, has a strong presence in a marketplace before you have a chance to establish the brand essence, promise and core meaning in that marketplace, it could be much more difficult to position the brand correctly. It would be better to withhold that extension from the marketplace until the core brand meaning is established there.

GENERIC NEW BUSINESS STRATEGIES

Generic approaches to new business strategy include the following:

- identifying gaps in your product/service portfolio (for the category as currently defined);
- identifying current consumers' unsatisfied needs;
- addressing emerging consumer needs;
- expanding the definition of your brand's category;
- exploiting an expanded brand identity;
- exploiting channel opportunities;
- applying new technologies;
- targeting new consumer groups.

When developing your growth strategies, you should clarify whether the growth will come primarily from existing customers, competitors' customers or non-users. The tactics will vary greatly for each.

BRAND EXTENSION STEPS

Brand extension work often starts with a brand asset study to identify the most promising avenues for brand extension (see Chapter 17, 'Brand research'). This is often followed by concept development and screening – from simple 'trigger' concepts (a simple several word concept description, often not even in sentence form) used in focus groups to 'ad form' concepts (a concept that is more fully developed to look like a full page print ad, typically with a couple of paragraphs of copy and a visual) tested quantitatively against a normative database. Next steps often include developing business and marketing plans (including pro forma financial statements) for the most promising concepts and then more formal funding reviews and approvals leading to prototyping and eventually market testing.

Did you know...?

- Typically, it costs between $75 and $100 million to launch a new (mass consumer) brand.
- The more extended a brand becomes, the more it needs sub-brands to aid with its extensions.

Table 15.1 *Brand management checklist: brand extension*

	Yes	No
Have you identified what your brand owns in the consumer's mind?		
Have you identified all areas in which the consumer gives your brand permission to operate?		
Do you have a clear understanding of whether your brand is over or under-extended?		
Have you identified all the ways your brand and others in its category have made compromises with the consumer? Have you found ways to redefine your business to break those compromises?		
Have you identified new categories for growth? Can you create new categories that meet previously unmet consumer needs?		
Have you targeted new market segments to which you would like your brand to appeal?		
Have you explored ways to make your brand more relevant to the next generation of consumers?		
Do you know what must be done to ensure the parent brand maintains a relationship with the consumer throughout his or her life (cradle-to-grave marketing)?		
Do you have a plan that specifies what categories your brand will enter next, in what order it will enter them and on what time-frame?		
Have you considered taking your brand global as an alternative growth strategy to brand extension?		
Do you have a way to screen all new brand extension proposals for their congruence with the brand promise and impact on brand equity?		
Are you sure that the brand's positive associations will not become negative when associated with a new product category?		
Have you thoroughly researched how proposed brand extensions might reposition the original brand in consumers' minds?		
Have you considered acquisition as a way to extend the brand?		
Do you have a brand licensing department? Does that department have strict guidelines for licensing out your brands in order to ensure brand image is not hurt and brand meaning is not diluted?		
Have you developed decision criteria to determine whether an extension: (a) uses an existing brand or (b) requires a new brand and, if (b), whether the new brand is: (c) a sub-brand or (d) an endorsed brand?		

Table 15.1 (*continued*)

	Yes	No
Do you have organizational mechanisms to screen, test and launch brand extensions?		
Do you test each new product or service for its impact on your brand's equity (quality, value, reinforcement of brand essence, promise and personality, etc)?		

16

Global branding

While many consumer goods markets in the West are stagnating, 65 per cent of the world's population is living in societies that are experiencing economic growth of 5 per cent or more a year. While the baby boom occurred between 1945 and 1960 in the United States, much of the rest of the world is still experiencing a baby boom that began in 1975. The average person has seen his or her standard of living double in the past 15 years, far surpassing that of the United States or Western Europe. Put very simply, the majority of the growth potential in consumer markets exists outside of the United States and Western Europe.[1]

BENEFITS OF GLOBAL BRANDING

In addition to taking advantage of the outstanding growth opportunities, the following drive the increasing interest in taking brands global:

- economies of scale (production and distribution);
- lower marketing costs;
- laying the groundwork for future extensions worldwide;
- maintaining consistent brand imagery;
- quicker identification and integration of innovations (discovered worldwide);
- pre-empting international competitors from entering domestic markets or locking you out of other geographic markets;

- increasing international media reach (especially with the explosion of the Internet) is an enabler;
- increases in international business and tourism are also enablers.

WHEN TO LEVERAGE A SINGLE BRAND GLOBALLY

A company is more likely to leverage a single brand globally if:

- it is already operating worldwide (one brand is more efficient);
- the brand is an extension of the owner and his or her personality;
- the brand's relationship to its country of origin creates positive associations (like a watch brand from Switzerland or a gourmet food brand from France).

GLOBAL BRAND CONSTANTS

At a minimum, when going global, the following elements should remain constant throughout the world:

- corporate brand;
- brand identity system (especially your logo);
- brand essence.

--- **Did you know...?** ---

Hewlett-Packard refers to the global brand constants and differences as Immutables and Adaptables.

GLOBAL BRAND VARIABLES

The following elements may differ from country to country:

- corporate slogan;
- products and services;
- product names;
- product features;

- positionings;
- marketing mixes (including pricing, distribution, media and advertising execution).

These differences will depend upon:

- language differences;
- different styles of communication;
- other cultural differences;
- differences in category and brand development;
- different consumption patterns;
- different competitive sets and marketplace conditions;
- different legal and regulatory environments;
- different national approaches to marketing (media, pricing, distribution, etc).

LANGUAGE TRANSLATION

A key question in global branding is this: do you translate the brand name into the local language or keep it in the original language? You should probably keep it in the original language if, one, there is no intrinsic meaning and it is easy to pronounce, or two, global awareness of the brand name is already high. You should consider translating the name into the local language if it is suggestive of a key benefit (that would be lost if the original name were used).

OTHER GLOBAL BRANDING QUESTIONS

Other key global branding questions:

- Have you identified the relative attractiveness of each market for your brand (and have you identified consistent criteria for doing so)?
- Have you conducted an attitude and usage study in each country whose market you are considering entering?
- Do you know the category and brand development indices in each country in which you operate?
- Do you have a global branding scorecard that can be applied country by country?
- Do you have agreement on which decisions are made centrally and which ones are made locally?

TAKING A BRAND GLOBAL: OTHER CONSIDERATIONS

Some considerations as you take a brand global:

- Because of the extended global baby boom, youth marketing is a huge opportunity. Brand names, designer labels and other forms of status will play well to the global youth market, in general.
- Global advertising needs to consider the fact that, for much of the world, the economy is booming and the context is unprecedented optimism. The tragic events of September 11 2001 notwithstanding, the economies of many nations continue this growth.
- The world's consumers are not naïve. Much of the world has access to English language television.
- Start marketing in countries before their spending power is fully realized. Due to media exposure, people are forming their brand opinions now.
- Representing male/female relationships appropriately will vary from society to society. Be sure that you fully understand the local cultures before attempting to do so.
- Using distributors is frequently a good way to break into foreign markets. It is critically important to carefully choose the right distributor when trying to enter a new market.

Ultimately, there is much to be gained by extending your brand globally. The saying 'think globally, act locally' makes much sense in this context. The key is determining what elements you will tailor for local markets. That depends upon a thorough understanding of the similarities and differences between the local markets you intend to serve.

Did you know...?

- 'Purchase intent' tends to be inflated for declining brands and understated for emerging brands.

- Advertising is often most effective in increasing share of market when brands are so similar that the advertising message is the primary source of differentiation.

LEVERAGING THE BRAND: HALLMARK CASE STUDY

In the early to mid-1990s, an ever-increasing share of greeting card sales in the United States occurred in the mass channels. Wal-Mart alone was projected to achieve a 20 per cent share of the total greeting card market by the year 2000. Three brands accounted for the vast majority of sales in these channels: American Greetings, Gibson and Ambassador – Hallmark's flanker brand. (The sale of Hallmark branded greeting cards accounted for no more than 20 per cent of the overall market. Hallmark branded products were sold primarily in Hallmark card shops and select chain drug stores. Hallmark's corporate share of greeting card sales was 39 per cent including all brands (Ambassador, Shoebox, etc).)

At the same time Ambassador brand sales were becoming an ever-increasing proportion of Hallmark's overall corporate sales, Ambassador's margins were eroding due to increased retailer leverage over manufacturers and heightened mass channel competition. This trend of a less and less profitable brand becoming a larger and larger share of corporate sales was not acceptable. We knew that more sophisticated contract negotiations and sales term innovations would not be enough to halt or reverse this negative trend. We had to do no less than change the rules of the game itself. After some thought, we knew our only hope was to unleash the power of the Hallmark brand in the mass channel. But that was tricky and unpopular as we did not want to undermine the success of the Hallmark card shops and chain drug stores – channels that were our 'cash cows' and to which we felt a strong loyalty.

We conducted the most extensive research in Hallmark's history to assess the impact of pursuing this strategy on Hallmark card shop and chain drug store sales, which turned out to be minimal. Nevertheless, prior to the launch of this strategy we fortified the viability of these two channels through extensive store consolidation, marketing, merchandising, systems and standards improvements, most notably through the development of the Hallmark Gold Crown programme. We also expended great efforts to quantify and communicate the equity and power of the Hallmark name to the mass channel retailers. In fact, one mass channel retailer believed in the power of the Hallmark brand so much that it refused to switch to one of our competitor's brands in return for $100 million in sales terms.

Some salient information may help you understand the strategy. Hallmark's primary competitors had significantly reduced their costs by reducing their internal marketing research and creative development capabilities. They leveraged Hallmark's resources in this area (Hallmark employed over 700 artists and writers and 70 marketing researchers at the time) through well-constructed systems of emulation. All mass channel (non-Hallmark) brands had raised prices faster than inflation for a number of years, due to the apparent lack of price sensitivity for greeting cards (until the major price thresholds of $2 and $3 were surpassed) and the pressures applied by retailers for ever increasing year-over-year sales productivity gains. In fact, while over 65 per cent of Hallmark branded cards were priced under $2, 89 per cent of competitive mass channel brand's cards were priced over $2. Competitors used their lower cost structures and higher product prices to fund ever-accelerating sales terms. They placed their bets on rich sales terms buying distribution with major mass retail chains, which was in fact occurring. (Greeting card manufacturers negotiate multiple year contracts with mass channel retailers in which they receive most or all of a retailer's business for a specified minimum floor space and number of stores for a specified period of time. In return for that privilege, they pay substantial sales terms.)

Despite the fact that mass channel share was increasingly based upon which brand could write the biggest cheque, Hallmark was betting on the fact that it could change the rules by introducing the power of brand equity to the mass channel. After all, Hallmark is the only greeting card brand widely recognized by consumers. (It had unaided top-of-mind awareness of nearly 90 per cent and Shoebox – a tiny little division of Hallmark – was the only other greeting card brand with significant top-of-mind awareness or preference.) Hallmark's product was also superior (validated by rigorous market research), and Hallmark products were priced lower than any other major competitive brand.

Compare this with what I was fond of saying about Hallmark's primary competitors, to rally the internal troops around this strategy, 'Would you rather be our competitors with overpriced, no name, inferior products?' If Hallmark could align consumer price perceptions with reality (Hallmark was perceived to be 'expensive' by consumers), I knew we could win with this strategy. Our competitors (both public companies, one of which consistently touted quarter over quarter revenue and profit increases) were locked into multiple year retailer contracts with very high sales terms. They would not be able to reduce prices without severely affecting their revenues, profits, and stock prices.

I could devote at least a whole chapter to the nuances of this strategy, but suffice it to say that Hallmark's static 39 per cent of the greeting card market share increased to 42 per cent with increased profitability in the first two years after we implemented this strategy. Since then, Hallmark's share has steadily grown to 55 per cent in a few short years. Unleashing the power of the Hallmark brand in the mass channel resulted in substantial market share and profitability gains for Hallmark without taking away from the success of the card shop and chain drug store channels. (Hallmark card shops achieved consistent month over month sales increases for at least three years during this period, validating my held belief that the added marketplace exposure to the Hallmark brand would have a positive impact on all channels carrying Hallmark products.)

Table 16.1 *Brand management checklist: global branding*

	Yes	No
Does your company operate as a global enterprise, versus a domestic company that sells its products internationally or that has separate international operations?		
Do you sell your brand in international markets?		
Do you believe global expansion of your brand will be a significant source of revenue growth for your organization for the next few years?		

Table 16.1 (*continued*)

	Yes	No
If you have grown internationally through acquisition, have you either (a) replaced the local brands you purchased with your global brand (if the local brands did not have strong brand awareness or loyalty) or (b) linked your corporate or parent brand name to the local brand name (if the local brands did have high awareness and loyalty)?		
Is your brand's market share as large or larger, on average, in international markets than it is in your domestic market?		
Is your brand's awareness as high, on average, in international markets as it is in your domestic market?		
Does your brand's essence remain the same throughout the world?		
Have you investigated the meaning of your brand's name (and other nomenclature), symbols, colours and other brand identity elements in each country in which your brand is sold?		
Does your brand's identity system work globally? Is it applied consistently throughout the world?		
Do you have agreement on which decisions are made centrally and which ones are made locally? Is there sound logic underlying that agreement?		
Have you identified the relative attractiveness of each market for your brand (and have you identified consistent criteria for doing so)?		
Have you conducted an attitude and usage study in each country whose market you are considering entering?		
Have you identified how each of the following vary from country to country (or from region to region): language, culture, consumption patterns, competitive set, marketplace conditions, legal environment, approaches to marketing?		
Do you know the category and brand development indices in each country in which you operate?		
Have you varied your approach to each of the following based on the above-mentioned national (or regional) differences: brand slogan, products and services, product names, product features, positionings, marketing mixes (pricing, distribution, media and advertising)?		
Have you made a conscious decision to either translate your brand name into the local language or keep it in the original language for each country in which your brand is sold?		
Do you have a global branding scorecard that can be applied country by country?		

Table 16.1 (*continued*)

	Yes	No
Are you organized so that your brand and its business are managed globally? If not, is there good communication and cooperation between your domestic and international brand management functions?		
If you use more than one advertising agency, do you coordinate the agencies' efforts to achieve an adequate level of consistency in communicating the brand's essence globally?		
Would you describe your brand as a 'global power brand'?		

NOTES

1   Source: *World Waves: Global trends for global brands*, Simon Silvester, Silvester Research [Online] www.silvester.com

Section 5

Brand metrics

17

Brand research

In previous chapters, I touched upon research that can help with brand positioning and advertising. In the next chapter, I will cover brand equity research in depth. In this chapter, I highlight a number of other research techniques that can be helpful to the brand management process, beginning with brand asset studies.

BRAND ASSET RESEARCH

Brand asset research is an important first step to brand extension. Brand asset research identifies and dimensionalizes a brand's meaning to consumers, including its elasticity across product and service categories. It identifies categories within which consumers give the brand permission to operate. (More often than you might expect, consumers will indicate that a brand offers products in a category that it does not. This clearly identifies 'low hanging (brand extension) fruit'.)

Typically, brand asset studies are conducted qualitatively (focus groups, mini-groups, one-on-one interviews, and so on) using the following techniques: word association, qualitative mapping, ranking various brands between contrasting viewpoints, brand extendibility probes, and (often in a second phase) identifying the appeal of various concepts as they relate to the brand in question. I have found that the best way to communicate the result is by mapping the categories, concepts and attributes as they relate to the core essence of the brand. (Think of a dartboard with the bull's eye being the brand's core essence. The concepts that are closer to the bull's eye are less risky brand extension opportunities. The ones further away risk diluting the brand's essence and have a greater chance of failure.

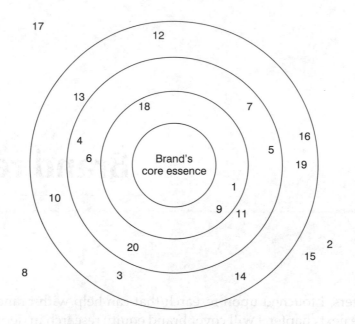

Figure 17.1 *Mapping brand extension opportunities*

BRAND ASSOCIATION MEASUREMENT[1]

It is important to measure associations both *from* (When I say 'Lexus,' what comes to mind?) and *to* (When I say 'luxury cars,' what comes to mind?) the brand. Qualitative research is an effective starting point if little is known. Specific qualitative techniques can be used to solicit associations. I cover Zaltman Metaphor Elicitation Technique (ZMET) and other projective techniques later in this chapter.

OTHER BRAND EXTENSION RESEARCH

After the brand asset study is complete, the next step in brand extension work typically is developing the most promising product concepts and then quantitatively screening them against the criteria of need/need intensity, uniqueness, market gap/dissatisfaction with current alternatives, and purchase intent. It is best if the results can be compared with a normative database for the brand and other companies in other industries. The final step, for those concepts that make it through the previous hurdles, is to create one or more test markets (taking the research in phases to reduce investment risk).

Successful brand extensions tend to have three characteristics:[2]

- Perceptual fit: the consumer must perceive the new item to be consistent with the parent brand.
- Benefit transfer: a benefit offered by the parent brand must be desired by consumers of products in the new category.
- Competitive leverage: the new items must stack up favourably to established items in the new category.

Therefore, an actionable quantitative brand extension research test should incorporate all three components. In particular, incorporating the competitive set for each concept is critical. Consumers evaluate new products in the real world in a competitive context, so they need to do the same in a research test.

OTHER USEFUL RESEARCH APPROACHES

The following are other useful research approaches.

Customer service testing

Customer service has a huge impact on brand perceptions. Do not take someone else's word that it is working. As a brand marketer, you should test your customer service approaches at least a couple of times a year. Test Web, telephone and in-person customer and technical support (as applicable). Look for these things:

- How quickly and easily were you able to get your question answered or problem solved?
- Is customer service available 24/7?
- How long were you put on hold, if at all?
- How many steps did you have to go through to get your answer?
- Did you have to communicate the same information more than once (name, account number, telephone number, etc)?
- How friendly and helpful was the human interaction?
- Were you treated like an intelligent adult?

Do you want to better understand the benefits your brand's product or service delivers? Do you want to discover ways to increase use of your brand's products and services? Try this: identify a group of very light users and ask them to use your product or service as frequently as your heaviest users do for an extended period of time (at least through several usage cycles). Identify a group of heavy users and ask them to refrain from using your product or service for the same period of time. Ask the latter group to articulate what they used in lieu of your product or service to accomplish the same result. Ask both groups to keep a journal of their thoughts and feelings as they use or refrain from using your product or service. Follow up with in-depth one-on-one interviews to better understand the role your brand's products and services play in their lives. I guarantee you this exercise will provide profound insight into the full potential for your brand's products and services.

The Zaltman Metaphor Elicitation Technique

An interesting new technique for discovering how consumers think about brands is the Zaltman Metaphor Elicitation Technique (ZMET), developed by Jerry Zaltman of Harvard Business School and Robin Higie Coulter of the University of Connecticut. The model combines neurobiology, psychoanalysis, linguistics and art theory to try to uncover the mental models that guide brand purchase behaviour. Study participants are asked to take photographs or collect pictures that say something about the brand in question. They return for one-on-one personal interviews which include story telling, sorting the pictures into what will become mental maps, answering a series of probing questions, creating collages that summarize their thoughts and creating a vignette that highlights important brand issues (among other possible exercises).

Other approaches to better understanding consumer behaviour include purchase diaries; spending time in participants' homes with them; shopping with participants; asking participants to spend a few weeks collecting photographs of whatever they would like, and later discussing the pictures in interviews; checking participants' cupboards, pantries and cabinets; and even analyzing household rubbish. Another approach is to create detailed identities for each of your target consumers and role-play each one for a day, including shopping for or using products in your category. Much of this is *ethnography*: putting yourself in the consumers' shoes by observing their brand shopping and usage patterns in real-life situations.

Most companies devote substantial marketing research resources to keeping in touch with their consumers, and yet the Internet provides for a 24/7 interaction with consumers through chat, message boards, discussion fora and other mechanisms (usenets or newsgroups and listservs). Smart companies will embrace these methods to keep in close contact with their consumers. These mechanisms are superior to most traditional research methods in the following ways:

- They provide for ongoing interactive dialogue.
- They allow the company to become aware of and address issues as they emerge.
- They can become a mechanism for creating a stronger bond between the consumer and the company.

Brand dimensioning

Martin Calle of One Calle has a technique he calls brand dimensioning. It is a six-week process which dissects participants' views of your brand on 3,000 'dimensions', or potential differentiating features, including some currently owned by the brand and many that may have been overlooked in the brand's design. He analyzes the participant data and recommends the combination of dimensions that he believes will solidly position your brand as a differentiated leader in its category.

Resonance

Steve Curtis, PhD, of Genoa Systems, uses a research method he calls 'resonance'. Resonance uncovers how consumers feel, how much they feel that way, and why they feel as they do. The rigorously quantified insights are based on the investigative sequence of helping the participant to relax, building the participant's self-esteem, and then asking him or her to visualize topics of interest to the marketer.

Projective techniques

Projective techniques can help you better understand brand personality. For instance, 'if the brand was an animal/car/person/sports team/occupation, what animal/car/person/sports team/occupation would it be and why?' Projective techniques also overcome some of the limitations of direct questioning:[3]

- People are not always conscious of their underlying motivations.
- People tell you what they think you want to hear.
- People are sometimes embarrassed to admit their real motivations, thinking that divulging them would reflect negatively on them.
- Most people think of themselves as being completely rational in their decision making, so they discount or dismiss non-rational reasons for their behaviours.

Other projective research techniques that help you get below the surface include:

- sentence completion;
- brand sorting (on a wide variety of dimensions);
- word association;
- collages;
- brand obituary/epitaph;
- brand press release/headline;
- consumer letters;

217

- brand time capsule;
- stereotypes;
- thought balloons;
- psychodrawing/modelling;
- role-playing and re-enactment.

I have also used the technique of providing participants with numerous pictures of a wide variety of people in a wide variety of settings. I ask which of those people would buy, receive as a gift, and use the brand, and which would not. I then ask them to explain their answers.

Another technique explores perceived differences between brands. Ask people to sort products (competitors' products and your products intermixed) into two piles: the 'brand in question' and 'not the brand in question'. (One version of this disguises the brand mark. The other one does not.) Once all the products have been sorted, probe why they thought the product either was or was not the brand in question. (As with the previous technique, if this exercise is done in focus groups, ask participants to write their answers down first so they are not biased by each other's answers. Collect all of the answer sheets at the end of the groups and compare the written responses to the group discussion.)

New logo research

When exploring new logo executions, the research may include any or all of the following components:

- **Logo imagery:** imagery evoked by various logo alternatives versus that evoked by the current logo (this usually includes the intended brand personality attributes and attributes such as 'boring').
- **Logo recognition:** each variation of the logo is 'mocked up' in its most likely usage environments (store marquis, product packaging, etc) and then people at various distances are asked about what they see. This measures visibility, recognition and the ability to break through visual clutter at various distances.
- **Logo recall:** one at a time, different logo alternatives and the current logo are mixed in with other companies' logos on a panel. People are allowed to view the panel for a few seconds. After that, the panel is covered or taken away and they must write down all of the brands that they remember seeing. Results are compared for each variation of the logo.
- **Logo preference:** each variation of the logo is featured on a card. People are given the deck of cards and asked to sort the logos/cards in order of preference. They are then asked to comment on why they ranked each logo variation the way they did.

Eye-tracking research is used to assess and enhance packaging, advertising, merchandising, brand identity and signage, direct marketing and Web design. By tracking eye movements, one can determine which messages or products a person saw and which ones he or she ignored.

A technique to better understand brand price premium includes exposing different groups of participants to a wide variety of products and brands within the category in question, each time with your brand mark and your competitors' brand marks applied to the products in different combinations. We compare the quality perceptions, associations, intent to purchase and price they would be willing to pay for the same products with different brand marks. A variation of this is to do the same with the products but without any brand marks, which highlights product (versus brand) preference.

Other useful research techniques are:

● Conjoint analysis: traditionally used for pricing research, conjoint analysis is very applicable for brand research as well. Respondents rate their buying intent for products comprised of various combinations of attributes (including product, service, sales terms, price and brand attributes). Brand name is one of the attributes. Not only is this an excellent approach to measure the overall equity of your brand name *vis-à-vis* competitors, but it also allows you to measure the interactions/relationships of your brand name with other attributes. Simulation exercises also allow you to project the impact on share of preference for various attribute combinations (what-if exercises).

● Corporate image tracking is an offshoot of brand image tracking, which measures changes in overall brand image on a variety of attributes. The premise is that consumers have experiences with your company and brands in a variety of ways, and it is important to quantify the frequency and impact of those different experiences on the overall brand/corporate image. For example, consumers interact with and experience the Hallmark name in many ways: shopping in Hallmark stores, buying and using Hallmark products, seeing television advertising, visiting the Web site, sponsorships and other public relations efforts, and most recently, viewing the Hallmark Channel on cable/satellite television. A research-tracking programme can measure the frequency of these various points of contact, as well as the satisfaction of those experiences and the subsequent impact on overall brand image.

● Electronic real time research (ERT) is qualitative research with some quantification of results. It is most often used for product research, but is adaptable to brand research. Perception Analyzer is one company that conducts this research:
  – to get immediate quantitative feedback on specific benefits or concepts;
  – to be able to instantaneously see that feedback by any chosen segmentation of the respondents;
  – to be able to ask the respondents questions based upon that feedback (for additional insights).

RESEARCH MANDATORIES

The first step in any research project should be to define the following to ensure that your research is actionable and provides the highest return on investment possible:

- objectives (both business and research);
- hypotheses;
- action standards.

There should be a predetermined feedback loop to identify whether the actions resulted in the intended outcome.

Online research resources

www.zoomerang.com – provides for simple online surveys.

www.qmrr.com/ – the Quirks.com Web site is your one-stop source for information on marketing research: everything from case studies of successful research projects and job postings, to the most comprehensive directories of custom research providers found anywhere.

www.imriresearch.com/www/gloss-en.htm: provides a comprehensive glossary of market research terms.

www.roper.com/ – RoperASW offers US and global research, syndicated and custom, quantitative and qualitative, to help clients gain a competitive advantage in:

- building great brands;
- creating strong customer loyalty;
- managing corporate reputation;
- increasing advertising effectiveness;
- mastering consumer trends.

www.gale.com/ – the Gale Group, a business unit of the Thomson Corporation, is a world leader in e-information publishing for libraries, schools and businesses. Best known for its accurate and authoritative reference content as well as its intelligent organization of full-text magazine and newspaper articles, the company creates and maintains more than 600 databases that are published online, in print and in microform.

Table 17.1 _Brand management checklist: brand research_

	Yes	No
Do you conduct research other than focus groups, satisfaction studies and attitude and usage studies?		
Have you conducted brand asset research? Have you been able to successfully extend your brand into new products or services based upon this research?		
Have you conducted brand equity research? Have you changed aspects of the brand based upon this research? Has this increased your brand's equity?		
Do you use online methods (chat rooms, discussion boards, etc) to stay in touch with your customers?		
Have you used a variety of projective research techniques to better understand your brand's associations and those of your competitors' brands?		
Have you ever used ethnographic research to better understand your customers?		
Do you measure the effectiveness of your advertising? Have you improved your advertising based upon this research?		
Do you conduct ongoing ad/brand tracker and corporate image studies? Have you researched the effectiveness of your brand's logo?		
Do you measure the effectiveness of your direct marketing? Do you measure the effectiveness of your online marketing? Have you been able to improve on both based upon this feedback?		
Do you keep track of the degree of commoditization within the categories in which your brand operates?*		
Do you create objectives, hypotheses, action standards and a feedback loop for all of your research?		
Do you believe your brand is winning in the marketplace based upon your brand research?		

* Determined by increased importance of price in the purchase decision, decreased perceptions of brand differentiation (including increased congruence between competitive brands' perceptual maps) and decreased preference for any brand in the category. Other supporting indicators: lower perceived brand innovation and vitality and higher perceived brand 'boringness' in general for all brands across the category.

NOTES

1   Courtesy of Dan Vandenberg, President of ConsumerVision, Inc. 'Naming Method' and 'Latency Method' are terms first used by Peter Farquhar.
2   Source: Dan Vandenberg, President of ConsumerVision, referencing Peter Farquhar's characterization of brand extension.
3   Source: Sharon Livingston's February 2 2002 e-newsletter, *Quantifying Emotional End Benefits,* and my experience in conducting hundreds of focus groups and other qualitative research.

18

Brand equity measurement

'You can't manage what you don't measure.' This is true of brand equity as well. Any strong brand equity measurement system will accomplish the following objectives:

- measure the brand's equity across a variety of dimensions at different points in time over time;
- provide diagnostic information on the reasons for the changes in brand equity;
- gauge and evaluate the brand's progress against goals;
- provide direction on how to improve brand equity;
- provide insight into the brand's positioning compared with its major competitors, including its strengths, weaknesses, opportunities and threats;
- provide direction on how to reposition the brand for maximum effect.

When I was named director of brand management and marketing at Hallmark, I was given two primary objectives: 1) to increase Hallmark market share and 2) to increase Hallmark brand equity. Market share is a relatively straightforward objective for which we already had metrics. Brand equity was much less well defined. I spent the better part of the next three years drawing upon the knowledge of various consultants, researchers and scholars, and dozens of different brand equity models, to define brand equity in a way that was useful to Hallmark. To be useful to Hallmark, it had to show us how to move people from high brand awareness to brand insistence. In fact, BrandForward's BrandInsistence brand equity measurement system grew its first roots at Hallmark. Since then, BrandForward has validated and refined this measurement system with scores of organizations across dozens of industries.

BRAND EQUITY MEASUREMENT SYSTEM COMPONENTS

Here are the components that this brand equity measurement system measures:

- brand awareness (first mention [top-of-mind unaided recall], total unaided recall);
- brand preference;
- brand usage;
- brand accessibility;
- brand value (quality and value perceptions and price sensitivity);
- brand relevant differentiation (open-ended question and perceptions on key attributes);
- brand emotional connection;
- brand loyalty (multiple behavioural and attitudinal measures including share of requirements / wallet);
- brand vitality;
- brand importance / rank in consideration set;
- brand imagery (against a standard battery of category-independent brand personality attributes (proven to drive brand insistence) and a customized battery of brand personality attributes for the particular organization and its product / service category).

MOST IMPORTANT BRAND EQUITY MEASURES

The most important brand equity measures are:

- Unaided brand awareness, especially first recall.
- Remembered / recalled brand experience.
- Knowledge of the brand's promise.
- Brand's position in the purchase consideration set.
- Brand's delivery against key benefits. (We have found two separate approaches to this to be insightful: mapping benefit importance against brand benefit delivery (scaled response) and an open-ended question, 'What makes brand XX different from other brands in the YY category?')
- Emotional connection to the brand.
- Price sensitivity.
- Relative accessibility.

SPECIFIC BRAND EQUITY MEASURES

These are specific questions/measures that help you manage a brand's equity:

Brand awareness

- What is the first brand that comes to mind when thinking about the xxx category?

Brand preference

- Which brand of [product category] do you prefer? (The incidence of those with no brand preference can also provide insights into the importance of brand in the category.)

Brand usage

- Which brand of [product category] do you most often use?

Brand accessibility

- widely available;
- easy to find and purchase.

Brand value

- quality perception;
- value perception;
- price sensitivity.

Brand relevant differentiation

- What makes brand xxx different from other brands in the yyy category?
- What one or two things make (category) brands different from one another?
- Which brand or brands of (product/service category) do you prefer when you are looking for the (relevant differentiated benefit)?
- Which brand of (category) best meets your needs? Why?
- How well does the xxx brand deliver against the yyy benefit (five-point scale)?

Brand emotional connection

- Your brand is almost like a friend to your customers.
- It stands for something important to them.
- It says something about who they are.
- It has never disappointed them.

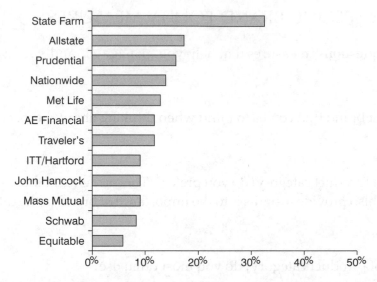

% strongly or somewhat agree; Q = has never disappointed me; base = aware of brand

Figure 18.1 *Brand emotional connection performance*

Brand loyalty

- Share of requirements / share of wallet.
- Share of last 10 purchases. (Constant sum questioning works best. Questions such as 'brand most often purchased' or 'brands bought in the past six months' almost always overstate purchases for well-known brands and understate purchases for low price brands.)
- Satisfaction.
- Repurchase intent.
- Willingness to recommend to a friend.
- Deal sensitivity.
- Switching propensity.

Brand vitality

- Do you hear more about the brand lately?
- Is the brand changing for the better?
- Which brand is reinventing the category?
- Which brand, in your opinion, will lead the industry four years from now?

Brand consideration set

- How many other brands in consideration set?

Ladder of the mind (consideration set continuum – seven-point scale)[1]

- I would never choose to buy this brand.

- I have never heard of this brand.

- I have heard of this brand but don't know much about it.

- Not one of my preferred brands but I would try it under certain circumstances.

- Not one of my preferred brands but from what I have heard about it recently I would like to try it/try it again.

- This is one of my preferred brands.

- This is the only brand I would ever consider buying.

Brand personality

- popular;
- trustworthy;
- unique;
- others: innovative, dependable, contemporary, old-fashioned, practical, boring, fun.

WHAT A ROBUST BRAND EQUITY MEASUREMENT SYSTEM MUST HAVE

A robust brand equity system should include all the measures listed above. It should be tailored to a particular company and industry. (At a minimum, the competitive set, personality attributes and category benefit structure will vary by industry. Ways of measuring value and loyalty typically also vary by industry.) The measurement system should also include behavioural and attitudinal measures, especially for brand loyalty. Through regression analysis and other techniques, the system should determine attitudinal measures that best predict brand loyalty and other desired behaviours (predictive modelling). The system should be capable of analyzing brand equity by category or customer segment if required. Comparing results of frequent users, occasional users and non-users is also very insightful. It is important to measure brand vitality, as purchase intent is overstated for well-known, well regarded older brands with waning differentiation (declining brands) and understated for newer brands with low awareness but high relevance and differentiation (emerging brands). Brand vitality can help adjust for this.

BrandForward's system also provides the following:

● A visual portrayal of positioning opportunities and vulnerabilities (mapping attribute/ benefit importance against brand delivery).

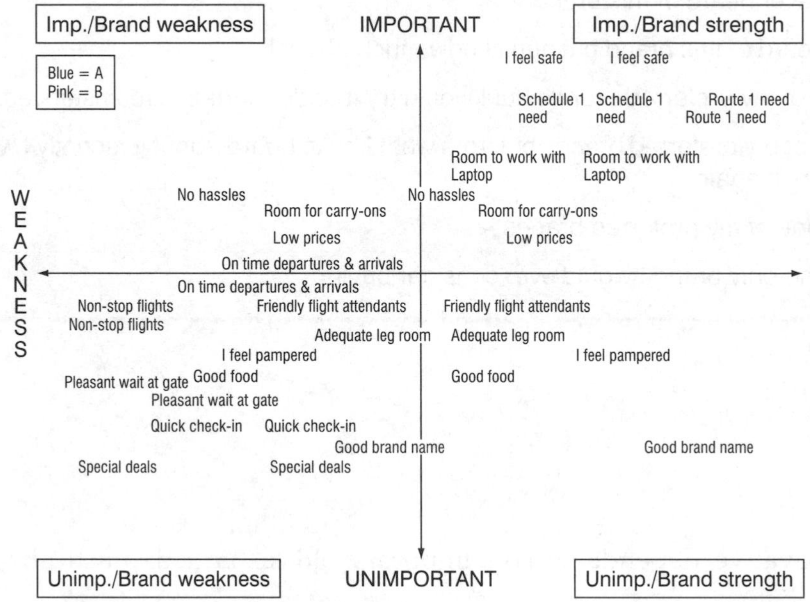

Figure 18.2 *Perceptual map: Airline brand A versus brand B*

● Comparisons to other industries (from a normative database) to identify additional opportunities and vulnerabilities.
● Identifying natural customer clusters.
● Demographic/lifestyle analysis and profiling.

COMMON BRAND EQUITY MEASUREMENT SYSTEM PROBLEMS

The most common brand equity measurement problems include the following:

● Too simplistic a system from which to manage brand equity. For instance, those omnibus studies which only measure two to four dimensions of brand equity such as awareness or favourability.
● No competitive comparisons are included in the measurement. (Many companies measure against themselves by, for instance, measuring customer satisfaction

improvements. A brand equity measurement system must include competitive comparisons. By definition, brands are positioned against other brands, and few customers compare you against yourself. Most customers compare you with other companies and brands. Competitive context is not only highly insightful – it is critical to managing your brand's equity.)

- The sample size is too small to provide for valid sub-group analysis.
- The sample size is too small to detect small changes in brand equity in the shorter term.
- Surveying customers too frequently. Typically, it is sufficient to measure brand equity once a year unless one of the following conditions exist:
  - the brand is new;
  - you have repositioned the brand or otherwise altered the brand communication or delivery in a major way.
- Using the organization's own customer and/or prospect list so that brand awareness, usage and other measures are not projectable to the general population.
- The survey is designed in a way that biases the unaided brand awareness question – rendering the results of that question invalid.
- Some organizations we have worked with could not identify a primary product category or set of competitors due to the uniqueness of their brand or the lack of a brand unifying principle. This eliminated some of the most important brand equity measures (top-of-mind awareness, brand differentiation, etc) from the measurement system (and usually led to a brand positioning project for us).
- Not including a tailored set of brand/category benefit statements in the study. These must come from a rigorous understanding of the category benefit structure, typically identified by prior qualitative customer research dedicated to the purpose of identifying that structure.
- Confusing other studies with a brand equity measurement system. Most typically, people have believed the following to be brand equity measurement systems (or viable substitutes for them): customer satisfaction studies, attitude and usage studies, corporate image studies.

ASSESSING THE EFFECTIVENESS OF AN ORGANIZATION'S BRAND EQUITY MEASUREMENT SYSTEM

We have found that brand equity measurement systems are most effective when clients can answer each of the following questions affirmatively:

- Do you have a profound understanding of your brand's consumers?
- Do you know what drives your brand's equity?
- Have you established and validated equity measures for your brand?

- Have you set objectives against these measures?
- Do key decision makers regularly see results against these objectives?
- Are people held accountable for achieving brand objectives?

BRAND EQUITY SHOULD NOT BE MEASURED JUST FOR CUSTOMERS

Businesses should also monitor their brand equity with the following groups (in addition to their customers):

- industry analysts;
- financial analysts;
- employees;
- business partners.

BRAND EQUITY MEASUREMENT: INSURANCE INDUSTRY CASE STUDY

In late 1999, BrandForward conducted a comprehensive brand equity study of the insurance industry. Our findings in that industry have implications for many industries. Here is what we found:

- While there are over 100 insurance brands whose names people have heard of, few achieve widespread top-of-mind awareness (first recall).
- The insurance industry is highly fragmented with a low dominance of usage and preference by a few brands.
- Very few companies are aggressively claiming relevant differentiating benefits in consumer communication. The few that are, rapidly gain market share (witness GEICO which is claiming price/value leadership in auto insurance with substantial advertising support).
- Prices/rates are cited as one of the top differentiating benefits, suggesting that the category is commodity-like for many consumers.
- While behavioural loyalty is high, attitudinal loyalty is much lower, indicating a consumer's propensity to switch companies when the switching becomes easier (something the Internet might facilitate).
- Emotional connection to insurance brands is very low. Less than one in five consumers say that their insurance brand has never disappointed them. (The top brand on this measure disappointed two-thirds of its customers at some time. All brands below the top eight on this measure disappointed over 90 per cent of their customers.)

- Our analysis of the most powerful differentiating benefits indicates that many of them lie with the way in which insurance agents/representatives and the claims adjusters interact with customers.
- Our data would indicate that the industry is ripe for consolidation or strong niche marketing.
- Three opportunity areas emerged for insurance companies:
  - reinventing the process by which they interact with their consumers;
  - claiming a highly relevant, unique point of difference (focusing on a product category, a consumer benefit or both);
  - increasing emotional connection with their consumers.

The study provides the following lessons that are applicable to other industries:

- Strong, recognizable brand names and logos are important, but the brands behind those trademarks must stand for something unique and important in consumers' eyes. What does your brand stand for?
- When price becomes the major point of difference in an industry, consolidation will occur. The companies that are most likely to succeed in this environment (other than the acquirers) are those that aggressively take ownership of relevant points of difference and redesign themselves to consistently deliver against those points of difference.
- The importance of the customer points of contact to strong brands cannot be underestimated. Aligning these with your brand's promise is critical. This may require redesign of your hiring, training, performance management, recognition and rewards, and other HR practices. It may also require a redesign of your customer service processes.
- Companies that are market driven, truly caring about their consumers and constantly changing their products and services to meet changing consumer needs, will succeed at the expense of companies that are purely sales driven.

——— Did you know...? ———

Allan L Baldinger and Joel Robinson of the NPD Group conducted a major study to better understand the link between attitude and behaviour in brand loyalty. They found the following:

- The larger the brand, the larger the group of consumers whose attitudes towards the brand are stronger than their behaviour ('prospects') and the larger the group of consumers whose attitudes towards the brand are weaker than their behaviour ('vulnerables').

- Brands that have more 'prospects' than 'vulnerables' tend to increase market share; brands that have more 'vulnerables' than 'prospects' tend to lose market share. A key characteristic of a healthy brand is that it has more 'prospects' than 'vulnerables'.

- Healthy brands would do well to focus on trial-generating strategies because the attitudinal commitment of their buyers, both current and new, will be strong.

- Unhealthy brands would do well to fix image problems and strive for improvements in key attribute ratings among their current loyal consumers. This would lead to an emphasis on retention strategies through communications and product offerings.

Baldinger and Robinson also discovered a surprisingly low year-to-year retention rate (approximately 50 per cent) among consumers who were highly loyal (behaviourally) to brands.[2]

BRAND BUILDING AND MARKETING ARE INVESTMENTS WITH A TANGIBLE RETURN

I am tired of hearing some businesspeople say that there is no way to correlate business results with marketing expenditures, implying that marketing is an expense with no corresponding return. Some other businesspeople are slightly more charitable, and say that there is no way to measure direct results. This is wrong – at least for direct response marketing, including direct response marketing via the Internet. (Many direct marketing Web sites even offer free direct marketing ROI calculators.) For other types of marketing, this is partially wrong.

There are a few important components to measuring the results of marketing programmes: 1) being clear about the programme's objectives upfront; 2) being sure that there are ways to measure results against the objectives; 3) measuring those results; and 4) evaluating the programme's results against the objectives. This is a closed-loop system.

It is also important to keep in mind that there are marketing programmes with long-term results such as brand building, and there are marketing programmes with short-term results such as direct response marketing and sales promotion. You must be clear about which ones each marketing investment is intended to achieve.

Table 18.1 *Types of marketing investment*

Type of marketing investment	Brand building	Direct response marketing, sales promotion, and other shorter-term marketing expenditures
Primary result	Creation of leverageable asset	Short-term increase in sales
Indirect impact on business	Decreased price sensitivity, increased customer loyalty, increased revenues, increased share of market, increased ability to hire and retain quality employees, increased stock price, increased company value, increased ability to grow into new product and service categories, increased ability to mobilize the organization around a vision	NA
Measurement	Financial: asset value Non-financial: awareness, relevant differentiation, preference, loyalty *et al*	Programme ROI

MEASURING MARKETING ROI

There are many useful models for estimating the impact of various revenue drivers on total revenues. One of the more widely used models is as follows:

The total customer base (number of people)
x (multiplied times) the average number of purchase transactions per person (per time period)
x (multiplied times) the average unit sales per transaction
x (multiplied times) the average price per unit
x (multiplied times) the per cent of those transactions received by your brand
= (equals) your sales (per time period).

You can design your marketing programmes to affect any combination of these factors, and you can measure the level of investment required to get the results through each of these levers:

● You can introduce your products to new audiences.
● You can encourage customers to upgrade their products or services or to purchase additional products and services.

- You can entice them to make more frequent purchases.
- You can increase the amount that they pay for the products and services.
- Your can encourage them to rely upon your brand for a greater proportion of their purchases.

Given the right data, it becomes trivial to estimate the return to your company from increasing your market share by one share point, gaining one more customer, or retaining a current customer's business for another year.

I will take another example: lead generation. If you code ads and direct mail pieces, you will be able to determine which marketing programmes resulted in leads, which of those leads were qualified, which of those qualified leads were translated into sales by your sales force, and how much revenue each of those successful leads returned. You can relate this to the marketing investment required to generate those leads. Now you have calculated return on marketing investment.

Many marketing tactics achieve numerous objectives. For instance, banner ads have been shown to increase brand awareness and reinforce a brand's positioning, while also generating sales leads or transactions (depending on what is on the other side of the 'click-through'). Trade shows also achieve multiple ends. Through its post-show research, Element K had found that shows increased brand awareness and preference and the prospect's propensity to purchase its products. They also increased current customer attitudinal loyalty. They generated qualified sales leads as well. Be careful to evaluate marketing tactics that achieve multiple ends against all of those ends – not just one.

On a macro basis, you can measure the effectiveness of marketing expenditures by comparing increases in total marketing expenditures to increases in sales for a specified period of time (quarter-over-quarter, year-over-year, etc). Two cautions are necessary with this approach, however. First, a complex combination of variables affects sales. Not all of the credit (positive or negative) can be attributed to marketing actions. The general economy, sales tactics, and other executive-level decisions can also impact sales in significant ways. Second, remember that some of your marketing programmes, including most brand-building programmes, are designed to affect a longer-term cumulative result not measurable in the short term.

THE IMPORTANCE OF INVESTING IN THE BRAND ASSET

A number of recent studies have shown that the percentage of a company's value that is unaccounted for by tangible assets has increased significantly. From 50 per cent to 90 per cent of a company's total value is now attributable to factors other than tangible assets. In a 1996 study, the Cap Gemini Ernst & Young Center for Business Innovation (CGI) discovered that non-financial assets account for 35 per cent of institutional investors' valuation of a company. In its 2000 *Measuring the Future: The value creation index* report, CGI reported that, after rigorous research, they discovered 50 per cent of a traditional company's value and 90 per cent of an e-commerce company's value resulted from nine factors. The following value drivers seem to be common across most industries:[3]

- innovation/R&D;
- quality of management;
- employee quality/satisfaction;
- brand investment;
- product/service quality.

'Neel Foster, a board member at the Financial Accounting Standards Board [said], 'As we move into more of an information age and service-based economy, the importance of soft assets is becoming more relevant to valuing some companies than brick and mortar. A lot of companies don't even have brick and mortar.'[4] An increasing number of methods have emerged to measure non-financial business drivers, from economic value added and the balanced scorecard to value-based management and the more recent value creation index (from CGI). Wharton accounting professors recently conducted a study across 317 companies and discovered that 36 per cent of the companies sampled used non-financial measures to determine executive incentive compensation.[5]

Building brand awareness, differentiation and emotional connection together with the appropriate pricing and distribution strategies results in brand preference, purchase, repeat purchase and, eventually, loyalty. I have also indicated that an increasing body of evidence links brand-building activities with a wide range of long-term benefits, from decreased price sensitivity and increased customer loyalty to increased stock price and shareholder value.

Sometimes, the results of brand building programmes are obvious, especially for new brands. When I arrived at Element K, Element K was a newly created brand. People in the e-learning industry had not heard of Element K. Our sales force found it difficult to gain the attention of potential buyers, we were not on industry analysts' 'radars', we did not receive coverage in trade magazine articles, people passed by our trade show booth, and we got few calls from conference companies. After a year of focused and relentless brand-building efforts, prospects come to us (we were on their 'short lists'), we were in all of the industry analysts' reports, our president wrote a column for one of the major trade publications, we sponsored a major user conference in parallel with one of the most important industry trade shows, we received a continuous stream of invitations to participate in conferences and other industry events, companies approached us about business partnerships, our employees were sought after as industry experts, and our competitors talked about us. In this case, the results of our brand-building efforts were obvious and did not require the validation of formal brand equity measures or the corresponding revenue increases (both of which we also had).

You can measure and manage the non-financial impact of your brand through a brand equity measurement system (covered earlier in this chapter). You can also measure the financial value of your brand as an asset. Activity based costing (ABC), discounted cash flow (DCF) and economic value added (EVA) have made brand valuation possible: as have a myriad of more recent customer purchase tracking techniques.[6] Interbrand (www.inter-brand.com) has a depth of experience in brand valuation. Don E Schultz, PhD, Professor of Integrated Marketing Communications at Northwestern University and President of Agora Inc, has studied and applied the concepts of brand valuation and return on marketing investment in depth. Both would be good resources for people with a further interest on this topic.

BRAND BUILDING AND MARKETING AS INVESTMENTS: A SUMMARY

- Brand building is an investment that results in a significant leverageable asset.
- Other shorter-term marketing actions exist for the sole purpose of increasing sales.
- You can measure the asset value of brands.
- You can also measure the non-financial aspects of brands that drive positive financial consequences in the long term, such as awareness, relevant differentiation and loyalty.
- You can and should measure ROI for other shorter-term marketing programmes.
- Brands are a primary source of value creation for organizations.
- While some business people (typically finance and operations types) may view marketing as an expense without significant corresponding benefits, this is untrue. Marketing is one of the most important investments a company can make.

The implication of this is, do not look first to marketing (and employee training, for that matter) when expenses need to be trimmed to achieve short-term goals. This will only hamper value creation and revenue growth in the long term.

Marketing is a fundamental driver of organizational success. Together, brand building, marketing and sales strategies and tactics create, build and sustain a company's revenues. To ensure positive results, you must understand and track how each marketing programme impacts sales in the short term and the long term. In many instances, you will be able to track and measure the specific short-term impact of specific programmes. In others, especially for longer-term brand-building programmes, you will have to track and measure indirect business drivers – brand awareness, attitudinal loyalty and so on – and validate how each of these affects revenue gains in the long run. Formal marketing (and brand) plans and metrics will help you achieve this end. And don't forget – a brand is an asset, and one of the most important assets in creating long-term value for organizations. Build the brand, sustain it, and leverage it.

Table 18.2 *Brand management checklist: brand equity measurement*

	Yes	No
Do you know what drives your brand's equity?		
Have you established and validated equity measures for your brand?		
Are your measures projective and actionable?		
Have you established targets against those brand equity measures? Do you actively manage against those targets?		
Do you measure your brand's equity at least once a year?		
Are people held accountable for achieving brand equity objectives and targets?		
Is senior management regularly updated on performance against brand equity objectives and targets?		
Do you measure each of the following brand equity dimensions: awareness, accessibility/convenience, value, relevant differentiation, emotional connection, preference, usage, vitality, loyalty and key associations?		
Do you also measure your primary competitors against the same brand equity dimensions?		
Do you know if competitors are making inroads on key associations that you intend your brand to own?		
Do you measure behavioural *and* attitudinal aspects of brand loyalty?		
Do you measure repeat purchase rates? Do you measure consumer brand advocacy?		
Can you translate consumer loyalty to purchase probability?		
Do you measure your brand's price premium (with consumers and the trade)?		
Do you measure its time/convenience premium?		
Do you measure 'intent to purchase'?		
Do you measure your brand's rank in the consideration set?		
Do you measure your brand's 'share of dollar'/'share of requirements'?		
Do you measure your brand's share of market?		
For products sold at retail: do you measure retail sales productivity/turns for your brand versus competitive brands?		
Is your brand equity system sensitive enough to measure changes in your brand's equity over time?		

Table 18.2   *continued*

	Yes	No
Does the system provide diagnostics on why the equity is increasing or decreasing?		
Does the system provide insights into positioning threats and opportunities?		
Do you track changes in consumers' ability to accurately play back key brand positioning points?		
Do you have a plan (and measurement targets) for the brand associations you want to increase and decrease?		
Do you use the system to actively manage your brand's equity?		
Has your brand's equity been increasing over time?		
Is your brand perceived to be authentic? Is it perceived to have integrity?		
Is your brand likable? Is it confident?		
Do you know if your brand is perceived to be an up-and-comer (rather than on the decline)? Do you measure brand vitality?		
If your brand is venerated and dominant in the market, would you be able to tell if it was in danger of becoming generic? If it was, are you aware of the steps that can be taken to avoid that outcome?		
Have you measured the financial value of your brand asset? Have you shared that with your organization to reinforce that your brand is an asset that should be actively managed and leveraged?*		

*Interbrand does this well and still features 'The world's most valuable brands' on its site at http://www.interbrand.com/features_effect.asp?id=48. *Financial World* also has historically featured top public companies' brand asset values.

NOTES

1   Source: Martin Stolzenberg, President, Stolzenberg Consulting, and Peggy Lebenson, Senior Vice President, Data Development Corporation, transcript proceedings, Tracking the obvious: new ways of looking at old problems.

2   Source: Allan L Baldinger and Joel Rubinson, *Brand Loyalty: The link between attitude and behavior* [Online] http://www.npd.com/corp/newsletters/product_brandbbldrjar.htm

3   Source: *Measuring the Future: The value creation index*, Cap Gemini Ernst & Young Center for Business Innovation, 2000.

4   Source: Michael Baltes, Measuring non-financial assets, *Wharton Alumni Magazine* Winter 1997 [Online: http://www.cfigroup.com/nonfinl.html].

5   Source: Michael Baltes, Measuring non-financial assets .

6   Source: Don E Schultz, PhD, *Managing and Measuring Brand Value*, white paper.

Section 6

Other brand management considerations

19

How organization age and size affect brand management issues

Brand management issues differ significantly based on the age and size of the organization. A key role of brand management is to create and reinforce an identity that promises relevant points of difference to consumers. Smaller, younger organizations have an advantage in this area for a number of reasons (outlined in Table 19.1).

Table 19.1 *Branding differences between small, younger and larger, older organizations*

	Smaller, younger organizations	Larger, older organizations
Leadership	An entrepreneur with a vision and passion.	A seasoned executive with experience in running large, complex enterprises.
Size	A small number of people who work closely together and often share the entrepreneur's vision and passion.	A large number of people in different divisions and departments with different functional backgrounds and allegiances, often very much decentralized.
Business scope	Usually focused on one core product or product category.	Usually offering a wide variety of products and product lines, many times in multiple business categories and even in different industries.

Table 19.1 *continued*

	Smaller, younger organizations	Larger, older organizations
Brand structure	Usually one brand.	Often very complex including multiple brands, sub-brands, endorsed brands, etc.
Organization infrastructure	Rapidly being built to support the entrepreneur's vision.	Many assets, systems, processes, organizational levels, etc. Very difficult to change.
Corporate culture	Usually strong based upon the entrepreneur's personality. May evolve as new top managers are added.	May be very strong based upon the legacy of a strong founder or a current strong leader. Companies that have long and rich histories often have entrenched cultures.
Marketplace	The business category is often in its infancy with many positioning possibilities for a new company.	Industry is often mature or maturing, sometimes declining. Competitors are much more entrenched with few, if any, viable marketplace positions not taken. (Recently deregulated industries provide notable exceptions.)
Decision making	Usually very quick with fewer decision makers.	Depending on the organization design, the decision-making process can be very cumbersome.
Financial resources	Often scarce as the organization is growing rapidly and reinvesting all available cash flow. May be less scarce after an IPO.	Usually substantial including cash flow and borrowing capacity.
Primary marketing method	Publicity.	Advertising.
Brand identity	Often evolving, but easier to encode in standards and systems (because the organization is starting with 'a clean slate').	Often strong and entrenched, but more difficult to codify due to the scope and complexity of the enterprise and the inconsistencies that have arisen over time.
Brand awareness and esteem	Usually low or non-existent.	Often high.
Brand differentiation	Often very high, but not always. (If its differentiation is not high, the organization may go out of business or be a takeover target.)	Usually declines over time as more and more competitors enter the market or achieve parity on what were differentiating benefits.

According to Al Ries and Laura Ries' (1998) book, *The 22 Immutable Laws of Branding*, the first two laws of branding are as follows:

The law of expansion: the power of a brand is inversely proportional to its scope.

The law of contradiction: A brand becomes stronger when you narrow its focus.

Clearly these first two laws favour smaller, younger organizations.

Brand identity firms will tell you that often they can create much stronger brand identities for smaller, younger companies because those companies have fewer constraints (existing logos, store décor and signing), more focused businesses and stronger business visions. They also have a more coordinated marketing function (often a department with just a few people). Conversely, large organizations usually have separate product development, advertising, promotion, public relations, sales and marketing research departments (to name a few).

Some people will tell you that the best promise a large organization's brand can make is to be 'the quality, innovation leader in (insert the company's business category)'. They say that organizational brands of large enterprises offer authority and assurance *period*. Yet some of the most successful organizational brands have more focused (consumer-benefit based) brand essences. For instance, Disney promises 'fun family entertainment', Nike promises 'genuine athletic performance', and Hallmark promises 'caring shared'. All three are distinctive yet broad enough to make multiple product categories possible. Consider all the businesses that Disney is in. And Hallmark, too, has much growth left (despite a mature greeting card category) and could offer gift confectionery and flowers, and even 'love boat' cruises.

BRAND PROBLEMS: SMALL VERSUS LARGE COMPANIES

Table 19.2 gives a summary of the most likely brand problems of small and large organizations:

Table 19.2 *The most likely brand problems of smaller, younger and larger, older organizations*

Smaller, younger organizations	Larger, older organizations
Lack of funds	Current leadership team (including CEO) does not know what distinctive, compelling value their organization brings to the marketplace
Lack of time	Original marketplace position is no longer distinctive or compelling

Table 19.2 (*continued*)

Smaller, younger organizations	Larger, older organizations
Little or no marketplace awareness of the brand	The brand structure has become too complicated and unclear
(Sometimes) do not fully understand who is buying their products and services and for what reasons	The brand identity standards and systems have fallen into disuse
Often lack brand management and marketing expertise	The organizational infrastructure and institutionalized bureaucracy work against a reinvigorated brand position
	Marketing functions are not integrated
	The organization has become too big and decentralized to create a consistent brand voice

For smaller, younger organizations, key brand activities include developing a strong brand identity, building brand awareness through publicity (see box 'The value of publicity'), and other less expensive means, and sometimes, better understanding their consumers through marketing research (such as attitude and usage studies and focus groups). Building 'trust' through consultative selling, legendary service, customer testimonials, guarantees and other approaches is also very important.

Because they must build their brands quickly with limited funds, they often resort to breakthrough ideas, out-of-the-box marketing tactics, strong differentiation, thought leadership and the element of surprise to pierce the marketplace clutter (versus the steady, consistent leadership messages and other brand-building tactics more typically employed by larger, more established brands).[1] In taking these risks smaller, younger organizations have much more to gain and far less to lose than their larger, older counterparts.

For larger, older organizations, the brand management job is much more complex. The most important task is to get the senior leadership team to agree to a distinctive, compelling marketplace positioning for the brand. Often the brand needs to be repositioned. Often, too, the brand identity standards and systems need to be overhauled (and the brand hierarchy simplified). Frequently, major organizational design changes are required. The necessary changes may be as wide-reaching as rethinking the business portfolio itself. Clearly, brand management needs vary with organization age and size.

The value of publicity

At the Institute for International Research's The Branding Trilogy conference in Santa Barbara, California, Jill Vollmer, Vice President of Brand Marketing for Mondera.com, said, 'Publicity has helped us achieve five times the ad value of media placement for every $1 spent. If you consider that the message is coming from a third party (not paid, but endorsed), the additional credibility may result in 10 times the value'.

Table 19.3 *Brand management checklist: how organization age and size affect brand management issues*

	Yes	No
Do you know what your organization's number one brand management priority is?		
Given your organization's age and size, do you know what its most likely brand management issues are?		
If you work for a smaller organization with a relatively young brand, have you addressed the following: (a) building brand awareness quickly and aggressively, (b) pursuing breakthrough ideas, strategies and tactics to do so, (c) fully understanding your customer's neattitudes, needs and behaviours, (d) identifying relevant and compelling points of difference to break through the market place clutter and (e) establishing 'trust' through outstanding service, guarantees, customer testimonials and other vehicles?		
If you work for a larger organization with an older and more established brand, have you addressed the following: (a) lack of a unifying brand vision, (b) lack of innovation, (c) lack of compelling differentiating benefits, (d) overly complicated brand architecture and (e) inconsistent brand identity and communication?		

NOTES

1   Source: Birk, Tom (2001) Small Wonder: Joining CP&B from Arnold changed more than my wardrobe, *Adweek*.

20

Legal issues in brand management

I am not a lawyer and this is not legal advice. This chapter is meant merely to consider legal issues in brand management. When actually dealing with any specific issues in this area, please consult with lawyers who have an expertise in intellectual property law.

This chapter generally considers US law, and readers in other countries should be aware that there are likely to be differences in their local laws.

While the best defence against copycat competitors is to stay ahead of them with a continuous stream of innovative, highly differentiated, and superior products and services, it is equally important to seek as much legal protection as possible for your brand.

TRADEMARK LAW

As a brand steward, you must be aware of the laws under which legal protection is available. First, trademark law protects a brand's identity. That is, it protects names, titles, taglines, slogans, logos, other designs, product shapes, sounds, smells, colours, or any other features that distinguish one source of products or services from another. Trademarks that protect services are often called service marks ('SM'). There are also 'collective membership marks' (Boy Scouts of America) and 'certification marks' (UL approved).

'™' indicates an unregistered trademark.

'SM' indicates an unregistered service mark.

® indicates a registered trademark.

© represents copyrighted material.

   Harley-Davidson filed to federally register the sound of its motorcycle engines, Dirt Devil vacuum cleaners are strongly associated with the colour red, and Taco Bell owns the Chihuahua icon.

Trademarks, like brands, build in strength over time. The test for trademark infringement is 'confusing similarity'. Put another way, if the average consumer believes both products to have come from the same source, there is infringement. Obviously, the more a consumer is familiar with a particular brand, the more defensible its mark. That is why it behoves a company to do the following:

- Choose a distinctive mark, including a 'coined' name. As I mentioned in the brand identity chapter, brand names range from generic and descriptive to suggestive and arbitrary or fanciful ('coined'). Obviously it takes longer to build meaning for 'coined' names, but they are also more distinctive and easiest to protect legally. Kodak, Xerox, and Exxon fall into this category. Suggestive marks are the next most protectable. Examples include Coppertone, Duracell, and Lestoil. Descriptive marks are not protectable unless the brand creates a secondary meaning for the word. Examples include Weight Watchers, Rollerblade, and Wite-out. Generic marks, such as Shredded Wheat and Super Glue, are not protectable at all.
- Avoid geographic names as a part of its mark – they can be the basis of trademark refusal.
- Register the mark.
- Be consistent in its use of the mark.
- Create strong trade dress (mentioned below).
- Widely advertise and distribute its trademarked products.
- Do all of this over a long period of time.

Because the strength of a mark is dependent upon consumers' familiarity with it, it is much easier for a competitor to neutralize your mark soon after it has been introduced than after it has been in use for a long period of time.

Courts use the following tests to determine infringement:

- Strength of the trademark claiming infringement.
- Similarity of the two marks.
- Evidence of consumer confusion.
- Care a consumer takes in comparing products.
- Intent of the organization in using the potentially infringing mark. Some drug and grocery stores have used generic brands that emulate a leading brand's package shape, colours, typestyle, formulation, and so on, side by side with the leading brand to imply that there are no differences between the two, encouraging consumers to purchase the lower priced generic item. In this situation, there is clearly intent to emulate the leading brand and reduce the perceived differentiation and value advantage of that brand, but it is not clear that there is intent to deliberately cause confusion as to source.
- Relatedness of the two businesses.
- Overlap between communication and distribution channels.

By using the mark in association with your products and services over time, you gain trademark protection. Registering your mark (marks can be registered at the state and federal levels) provides additional protection. While common law and federal trademark statute protect an unregistered mark, registering your mark transfers the burden of proof to the second comer in challenging a mark's registration. With federal registration, you can sue infringers in federal courts. Also, after five years of registration, the mark becomes uncontestable. Federal trademark registrations last 10 years and can be renewed every 10 years *ad infinitum*.

You can acquire trademark rights in one of two ways. To acquire trademark rights based on use in commerce, you must be the first person or organization that uses the mark in conjunction with the products or services for which trademark protection is sought. To acquire the mark base upon intent to use, you must apply to register the mark through the United States Patent and Trademark office (or your national equivalent).

Before choosing a trademark, first conduct a simple search to weed out marks that are not available. This search can be done online for free. (See 'Online resources' at the end of this chapter.) After that, for the remaining candidates, conduct a full search through a law firm specializing in trademark law or an experienced trademark search firm.

Strong brands run the danger of becoming category descriptors. Always use trademarks as adjectives, not verb or nouns. If your brand is in danger of becoming a category descriptor, consider talking about your brand in the following way: 'Jell-O® gelatin,' 'Kleenex® facial tissue' and 'Xerox® photocopier' to differentiate the brand from the category.

TRADE DRESS

Trade dress is a second form of legal protection for a brand. Trade dress is a brand's distinctive aesthetic design features (package or product design). To be protectable, trade dress must be non-functional and distinctive (or have acquired a 'secondary meaning', that is, source-identifying characteristics). The more non-functional differentiating features one can build into a product and its packaging, the more likely it will be that infringement can be proved.

It is easy for a competitor to say, 'I developed this very similar product independently' when it is fairly generic (such as a birthday card with a floral design that says simply, 'Happy birthday'). It is more difficult to convince a courtroom of that when your product has many of the same random non-functional elements as a competitor's products (a line of cards of an unusual size that open from the top with rounded edges printed on green tinted recycled paper, all at 99 cents and all addressing the theme of friendship). For a competitor to develop a similar line of cards with similar features independently is highly unlikely. It points to copying.

To protect its trademarks and trade dress, a company must constantly be watchful for and strenuously defend against infringement. For instance, Apple has filed several lawsuits to defend its iMac against knock-offs. Trademark rights can be enforced through lawsuits at a state or federal level. Proving infringement requires proof that the infringer had second use of the mark and that the second user's mark is confusingly similar to the senior party's mark.

When launching brand extensions, companies should be careful to maintain the same brand identity and trade dress in those new items. If the brand's name and logo are the only common elements across all of a brand's products, it weakens the power of the other trade dress elements to differentiate and legally protect the mark.

COPYRIGHT LAW

While organizations do not often pursue this protection, logos are typically protectable by copyright law. Make sure your organization, and not an outside person or agency, owns the copyright to your brand's logo. Advertising/marketing agencies will often include an assignment of rights, titles and interests (including copyright interests) to their clients in their letters of agreement. While trademark infringement requires proof of 'confusing similarity', copyright infringement requires proof of 'substantial similarity'.

Online legal interpretation is evolving, but in general, organizations whose brands are strong and well known ('famous brands') can legally defend their names and other marks against unauthorized use in domain names and <META> tags. (Playboy (unsuccessfully) and Estee Lauder (successfully) sued other sites for using their brand's names or slogans in their site's meta-tags.)

Other online legal issues include the following:

- cybersquatting – people who register and warehouse domain names that are another party's marks;
- for-pay search engines selling marks as keywords to businesses that do not own the marks;
- spammers who use other marks' e-mail addresses as return addresses for their solicitations.

SPECIAL PROBLEMS: ORGANIZATIONS THAT LICENSE AND FRANCHISE THEIR MARKS

Organizations that license and franchise their marks encounter added challenges to protecting their marks. License and franchise agreements should be drafted to provide maximum control over the mark and to minimize the mark owner's exposure to liability. Further, every effort should be made to establish processes to review, approve and monitor use of the mark by licensees and franchisees.

TRADE SECRETS

Do not overlook trade secrets as a form of protection. Trade secrets are simply information, techniques, procedures, codes, patterns, plans, processes, formula, prototypes, and so on, that are developed confidentially and that are kept confidential. The Coca-Cola syrup formulation is an example of a trade secret. (The added value of this approach from a brand perspective is that it often creates a mystique that has its own cachet.)

Sometimes it is better to keep something a trade secret than to patent it. In some industries, companies routinely watch for competitors' new patents and then try to design around them. Non-compete and nondisclosure agreements are important, but not infallible, in protecting trade secrets. The US Economic Espionage Act of 1996 protects trade secrets against theft. Information is legally considered to be a trade secret if an organization can show that it took reasonable measure to keep the information secret and that there is economic value to the information not being made public.

Did you know...?

Coca-Cola's syrup formula is kept in a bank vault in Atlanta, and only Coca-Cola's board of directors has the power to request the vault to be opened. Only two anonymous employees know the formula and they are not allowed to fly together on the same plane.[1]

A business can protect its trade secrets in the following ways:

- Share confidential information only on a 'need to know' basis.
- Mark all confidential documents 'Confidential – no copies allowed'. For added security, number each copy and keep a log of which numbered copy was given to which employee.
- Require all those (employees, suppliers, customers, other business partners) who might come in contact with trade secrets to sign confidentiality and non-disclosure agreements.
- Require employees to sign non-compete agreements, prohibiting them from working for competitors for a period of time after their employment with you.
- Educate employees about the treatment of proprietary information during and after their employment with you.
- Carefully orchestrate employee terminations so that the employee is not able to take proprietary information with him or her.
- Develop, communicate and enforce security processes – from building security to paper document and computer security.
- Make extensive use of shredders.
- Be especially careful of contract workers. Provide them with a company computer so they do not have to use their own on the job.

Did you know...?

Perceptions of your product or service's performance has a significant impact on your brand's equity.

Source: *They Said My Brand Was Popular – So What?*, Nigel S Hollis (1996), Group Research and Development Director, Millward Brown International. Validated by several other sources.

FALSE OR DECEPTIVE ADVERTISING

False or deceptive advertising is another legal consideration in brand management. Advertising is considered to be false or misleading if it *could* mislead consumers about a product's place of origin, nature, quality or maker. It is not necessary to prove actual deception. Advertisers must be accurate about material aspects of their products or services and those of their competitors (in comparative advertising) to avoid prosecution.[2] The Federal Trade Commission looks for the following when investigating complaints:

- What are the expressed or implied claims? What was said and what was not said?
- Are the claims material? That is, do they say something about the product's functions, features, performance, effectiveness, maker, price, safety, etc?
- Does the advertiser have evidence to support the claims?
- Could the ad as a whole mislead a consumer acting reasonably under the circumstances?

False advertising claims can be brought before the following entities for resolution:[3]

- the organization against which the claim is made;
- state or local consumer protection offices;
- the National Advertising Division of the Better Business Bureau;
- the Federal Trade Commission;
- industry self-regulating bodies;
- advertising regulatory bodies.

Online resources for legal issues in brand management

www.uspto.gov/web/menu/tm.html – United States Patent and Trademark Office

www.tmarksman.com/tminfo.htm – trademarks for small businesses

www.copylaw.com/new_articles/trademrk.html – *Trademark Basics* by attorney Lloyd J. Jassin

http://copylaw.com/new_articles/tradedress.html – *Trade Dress Protection: How to tell a book by its cover* by Attorney Lloyd J.Jassin

www.oliveandolive.com/primer.htm – *Patents, Trademarks, Copyrights and Trade Secrets: A primer for business executives, entrepreneurs and research administrators*, Olive and Olive, Pennsylvania.

www.tomwbell.com/writings/FullVTD.html – *Virtual Trade Dress: A very real problem* by Tom W Bell

www.tmexpress.com – TradeMark Express®

www.ipcenter.com/ – Intellectual Property Center

www.aipla.org/ – American Intellectual Property Law Association

www.intelproplaw.com/News/ – Recent Intellectual Property News

www.micropatent.com – MicroPatent

www.inta.org/ – International Trademark Association

Table 20.1 *Brand management checklist: legal issues in brand management*

	Yes	No
Do you know that coined names and fanciful or arbitrary marks are the most protectable by law?		
Is your trademark distinctive?		
Have you completed a full trademark search for any new brand name you are considering using? Have you completed this search in all countries in which the brand might operate?		
Have you registered your trademark at a federal level and in all countries in which your brand will operate?		
Have you marketed your brand in all 50 US states? (The first organization to use a particular name in a specific geographic area has 'priority of use' protection in that area under common law.)		
Have you searched to ensure that the brand name you are considering is available as an Internet domain name? Have you registered that domain name? Have you registered typical variations of that domain name? Have you registered that domain name as '.com', '.org', '.net', etc?		
Do you know the difference between trademarks with a ™ and an ®?		
Do you use the ™ and ® symbols when appropriate?		
Do you always use your brand name as an adjective (versus as a noun)? If you are concerned that your brand name may become a category generic descriptor, are you using the following wording in all of your brand communication: '[brand name] brand [product category descriptor]'?		
Do you design your brand's trade dress to have as many arbitrary design elements as possible so that you are more likely to win a trademark infringement legal battle with your competitors?		
Does your brand identity system include as many elements as possible (beyond name and logo)? (Examples: visual style, brand voice, colours, icons, typography, slogan, mnemonic devices.)		
Do you retain experts to help you protect your brand mark online?		
Did you know that trademark protection is enhanced through proper use and can be lost through improper use?		
Did you know you can sue another company for using your brand's name or slogan in its site's meta-tags?		
Did you know that using another organization's well-known mark as a domain name is also illegal, even if used associated with an unrelated product or service category?		

Table 20.1 (*continued*)

	Yes	No
Do you aggressively pursue those who are using your brand mark improperly or illegally?		
Do you have strong brand identity standards and systems that are available to all employees and vendors? Have you trained all people who might use the trademark in its proper use?		
Are you very careful to whom you license your trademark? Do you have processes in place to monitor their use of your mark and to immediately stop (or correct) their use of your mark if they are using it improperly?		
Are you very cautious about creating registered users of your mark internationally? (They will have rights to your mark forever, even after you have severed a business relationship with them.)		
Are you also protecting your intellectual properties through patents, copyrights and trade secrets?		
Have you maintained thorough records of trademark development and use?		
Have you kept your Web site's log files to validate that your brand has been operating in all 50 US states and in many foreign countries?		
Did you know that people can legally use your brand mark if the following three conditions are met: 1) it is a necessary use; 2) the use is limiting; and 3) there was no consumer deception? (For instance, a watch repairman who only repairs Timex watches can say in advertising copy (or on the side of his building) that 'I repair Timex watches' even if he is not employed or licensed by Timex to do so. This, however, does not give him the right to use the Timex logo improperly.)		
Did you know that under the US Trademark Dilution Act of 1995, you can now stop others from using your trademark if it weakens, blurs or tarnishes the mark?		
Did you know that you can take action against a competitor for false or misleading advertising claims? Do you know the process you must follow and what you must prove?		
Did you know that, as a manufacturer, you can lawfully set resale prices? Saturn and Coach both do this. (While this is possible in the United States, it is a very complex area of law that should not be pursued without thoughtful legal advice.)		
Do you know a successful intellectual property attorney? Is that person available to help you with your legal issues?		

NOTES

1 Source: Stephen Fishman and Rich Stim, _Trade Secret Basics_ [Online] www.nolo.com
2 Source: American Bar Association, _False Advertising_ [Online] http://nbc-2.findlaw.com/ newcontent/consumerlaw/chp5_a.html
3 Source: American Bar Association, _False Advertising_.

Section 7

Brand management:
a summary

21

Common brand problems

Awareness of the problems and pitfalls brands can encounter is an important step in maintaining a strong, healthy brand.

Problem number 1: the cumulative result of gradually and incrementally decreasing product or service quality to reduce costs

Analysis: there is the old story about each new brand manager of a coffee brand improving brand profitability and his or her promotion potential by slightly reducing the ratio of premium Brazilian coffee beans to the less expensive African beans. Each time, consumer research indicates no discernible difference in taste or preference, but one day the company discovers that its coffee brand share has significantly eroded. Brand quality erosion may not be discernible in the short term, but over time it will negatively affect a brand's market share. **Manage brands for the long term.**

Problem number 2: the cumulative effect of raising product or service prices at a rate greater than inflation over time (inviting low-end market segments and competitors)

Analysis: this is the other side of a brand's value equation: price. Consider what has happened in several industries in which companies have raised prices faster than inflation over time. Remember Marlboro's Black Friday? Would Malt-o-Meal exist if cereal companies had not raised their prices as much as they had? And would discount card stores like Factory Card Outlet have grown from zero share of the greeting card market to over 20 per cent within a few years if greeting card companies had not raised card prices to well over $2 or $3 in the same time period? **Make sure your brand delivers good value to the consumer.** Even if price sensitivity studies show you can raise prices more, consider the long-term consequences. If you 'push the envelope' on price, you will invite two outcomes: one, consumers leaving your category, and two, new competition.

Problem number 3: focus on short-term profitability at the expense of long-term revenue growth

Analysis: this may be the underlying cause of the previous two problems. This problem is driven by the organization's reward systems. If brand managers and general managers are compensated and promoted on delivering quarterly or annual financial results without a focus on longer-term business growth, this is sure to occur. This problem is most acute in publicly held companies that are pressured to deliver quarterly financial results. The solution is to **create a balanced scorecard that integrates growth objectives into common and individual performance measures.**

Problem number 4: limiting the brand to one channel of distribution or aligning the brand too closely with a declining channel of trade

Analysis: have you heard much about Tupperware lately? While that brand was one of the pioneers of the network marketing approach, it has not extended its distribution much beyond that. In contrast, Rubbermaid branded products are available in many popular distribution channels. **Do not ever become too dependent on one channel of trade. Always look for the best new opportunities for distributing your products or services.**

Problem number 5: reducing or eliminating brand advertising

Analysis: when it is time to 'tighten the organizational belt', advertising is always a likely source of savings. The budget is usually big enough to contribute significantly to cost savings and it is often difficult to tell advertising's return on investment. Finally, even if there is an ill effect, the brand will not immediately suffer from an equity withdrawal. (Or so goes the all too common logic.) But actually, recent studies have shown there is a positive correlation between advertising spending and revenues, earnings, market share and stock price. Tod Johnson of the NPD Group (which has studied customer purchase behaviour since 1978) indicates that a decline in brand loyalty has two causes. One is erratic advertising or advertising that does not keep pace with the competition. The other is cannibalization caused by brand extensions.[1] **Set specific objectives for your advertising and track results against those objectives. Copy test all of your ads to make sure**

they are effective. And, finally, constantly and vigilantly sell the importance of advertising to key internal decision makers.

Problem number 6: applying branding decisions at the end of the product development process ('Now, what will we name this?') versus treating brand management as the key driver of all of your enterprise's activities

Analysis: you are probably working for a manufacturing company that really does not understand brand management and marketing. They design, manufacture and sell products and services. They do not market brands, or if they do, they leave that function to the advertising or communications department or to the advertising agency. A brand is a source of a promise to the consumer. Everything a company does should support that promise. **Start with the target consumer and the brand design (essence, promise, personality and positioning) and then decide what the products and services will be.** (This may be an organization design and staffing competency issue.)

Problem number 7: confusing brand management with product management

Analysis: these are not the same. Brands, if well managed, should have a much longer life than individual products and even product categories. **Brand management is much more holistic than product management, encompassing all of the marketing elements and many of an organization's other functions.** Consumers do not develop relationships with products nor are they loyal to products. Brands and what they stand for establish the emotional connection with consumers. As Jim Speros of Ernst & Young put it, 'Products are manufactured in factories... brands are created in the mind of the consumer'. (If need be, pass this book around to those who are most in need of enlightenment!)

Problem number 8: defining your brand too narrowly, especially as a product category (for instance, 'greeting cards' versus 'caring shared')

Analysis: one of the key advantages of a strong brand is its ability to be extended into new product and service categories. It is a growth engine for your organization. It helps you transcend specific product categories and formats that may become obsolete. **Define your brand's essence and promise in terms of what key benefits your brand delivers to consumers (independent of the specific product or service). Then continue to find new ways to deliver against that essence and promise.** GE successfully broadened its frame of reference by moving from 'General Electric: Better living through electricity' to 'GE: We bring good things to life'.

I consider one of my most important successes as the 'brand guy' at Hallmark was to change our leaders' perceptions of Hallmark as a greeting card company/brand to a 'caring shared' company/brand, paving the way for us to launch gift confectionery, flowers and other products to sustain our growth into the next decade. I did not want to see us make the same mistake that Smith-Corona did (defining itself as a product, typewriters, versus a consumer benefit, word processing).

Problem number 9: failure to extend the brand into new product categories when the core category is in decline

Analysis: 'It is our core category. It is our "cash cow". We must focus all of our resources on preserving it.' Sound familiar? It is one thing to prematurely walk away from your core category. It is yet another to myopically focus all of your organizational resources on a flat or declining category in the misguided hope that you may be able to revive it, especially if you are not trying to radically redefine or re-engineer it. **Try and try again, but also know when it is time to 'quit' (that is, when it is time to do no more than maintain and 'milk' the core category and reinvest the profits in new, more promising ventures).** Often, realistic financial projections are the best 'wake-up' call in these situations.

Problem number 10: over-extending your brand into different categories and markets so as to completely blur the brand's meaning and points of distinction

Analysis: you can always make more money in the short term by licensing your brand out for use on a variety of products or by extending your brand into a myriad of new categories. The long-term effect of this, however, is detrimental. People will no longer be able to tell what your brand stands for. It will lose its meaning and its point of difference. **Extend your brand based on a clear understanding of its essence, promise and personality. And make sure your consumers 'get it'.**

Problem number 11: frequently changing your brand's positioning and message

Analysis: new brand managers and marketing executives often feel as though they need to make a name for themselves to continue to climb the corporate ladder. Do not succumb to the temptation of doing this by changing the advertising campaign or the brand slogan, especially if the current ones are working well or have not been in place long enough to assess their effectiveness. **Consistent communication over time is what builds a brand.** After all, Hallmark has used its 'When you care enough to send the very best' slogan since

1944; the Marlboro Man has been Marlboro's icon since 1955; Absolut Vodka has featured its bottle's shape in consumer communication since 1978; and GE has been using its 'We bring good things to life' slogan since 1979. If you do make changes, make them gradually in an integrated fashion based on sound consumer research.

Problem number 12: creating brands or sub-brands for internal or trade reasons, rather than to address distinct consumer needs

Analysis: there is nothing more inefficient or wasteful than creating a new brand or sub-brand for a purpose other than meeting a different consumer need. **Brands and sub-brands should exist to address different consumers and consumer need segments.** It is expensive to launch a new brand (and very expensive to maintain multiple brands that meet similar consumer needs; it also adds unnecessary complexity to your organization). Worst of all, it dilutes the position of your original brand. This problem often results from egos and organization structure. People head up divisions or business units that deliver specific products or services. They create a name and identity to put on business cards and to rally their employees around, whether the products or services are similar to products or services other divisions create or not. (This has resulted in the following printer lines for Hewlett Packard: DeskJet, OfficeJet, OfficeJet Pro, LaserJet, DesignJet, DeskWriter, and PhotoSmart. It is unlikely that the consumer understands many of these distinctions. He or she is likely to think of them all as Hewlett Packard printers.)

Sometimes, companies create separate brands or sub-brands for trade reasons – for instance, to offer something different to speciality stores versus mass channels of distribution. (Hallmark created the Expressions from Hallmark brand to offer mass channel stores while speciality stores continued to carry the Hallmark brand. These two brands do not meet different consumer needs and I am not sure consumers perceive differences between the two.) This problem can also result from mergers and acquisitions in which the brands are neither rationalized nor strategically managed after the enterprises are combined. (WorldCom runs this risk with its MCI, 10–10–321, 1–800-Collect, 10–10–220, Skytel, and other brands.)

Problem number 13: launching sub-brands that inadvertently reposition the parent brand in a negative light

Analysis: what does Miller Lite say about Miller High Life? What do Bayer aspirin-free products say about Bayer aspirin? What do fat-free Fig Newtons say about Fig Newtons? **Make sure you know what you are doing when you create a new sub-brand, and be sure to test its impact on the parent brand.**

Problem number 14: overexposing the brand to the point that it becomes uncool

Analysis: occasionally, a brand can become so ubiquitous through aggressive marketing and distribution that it seems to be everywhere. While brand awareness soars, the brand loses any uniqueness or mystique that it once had. The brand seems to no longer make a unique statement about the individual who uses it. It becomes common. People tire of it. This is particularly true if the brand is mostly hype and logo and identity with no strong underlying idea or compelling point of difference. Nike has struggled with this. Its abundant success has also been its downfall (while Nike does stand for something, its overexposure made it too common). **The lesson here: focus more on the core consumer and maintaining relevant product/service differentiation and less on brand and logo ubiquity.**

Problem number 15: well known, high-profile brands are often targeted by special interest groups who want to make public statements about their causes

Analysis: high-profile brands are prone to being knocked off their pedestals by environmental, human rights, equal rights and other activists, and by anti-big-business groups. Nike, Wal-Mart, and McDonald's have struggled with this issue, as has the Boy Scouts of America. Nike has struggled with opposition to its campus sponsorships and concerns about its alleged use of third world 'sweat shops'. Wal-Mart is seen as all-powerful and monolithic, and is often accused of putting long-standing local 'mom and pop' stores out of business through monopolistic practices. People are concerned about Wal-Mart's alleged use of third world 'sweat shops', too. McDonald's is now struggling with a number of revelations from the recently published book *Fast Food Nation: The dark side of the all-American meal*. The Boy Scouts of America is a target because of its squeaky clean, wholesome image, and its recently highlighted position on homosexuality. **Lesson: if your brand is well known: 1) identify possible exposures (through internal muckraking) and rectify them if at all possible; and 2) develop public relations and crisis management plans to address the exposures.**

Problem number 16: treating brand management primarily as 'logo cops'

Analysis: often the current power structure within an organization will try to put a new brand management function in this 'box', either out of ignorance or as a way to minimize or negate a power shift. As I hope you have discovered by now, the brand management function has responsibilities far beyond brand identity management. It is multi-faceted, affecting all of marketing and much of the rest of the enterprise. For this reason, **it is important that the brand management function exists at a high level in the organization**

structure. It is also important that the organization's senior executives understand and support this scope of responsibility.

Problem number 17: viewing brand equity management as a communications exercise, but ignoring it in other business processes and points of contact with the consumer

Analysis: too often, organizations relegate brand management to a specific department (advertising, marketing, brand management, etc) or agency. Brand management is an organization-wide process, especially if the brand is a corporate brand. **The brand promise must be delivered at each point of contact with the consumer, including customer service lines and retail sales associates. For the brand promise to be clear to your consumers, it must be well understood by everyone in your organization from the CEO to the receptionist.** It must be manifest not only in consumer communication, but also when and wherever the brand name and logo are used. There is a recent trend to design the total enterprise in support of the brand promise, including putting mechanisms in place to develop a brand building culture.

Problem number 18: not delivering against the communicated brand promise

Analysis: again, this is a symptom of viewing brand management as a communications exercise. As mentioned earlier, United Airlines' 1997 advertising campaign, 'United Airlines rising' backfired on them. While they were trying to communicate that their service was rising to meet consumers' expectations, their flight attendants were involved in a labour dispute, and threatening CHAOS ('Creating Havoc Around Our System') and their customer relations department was so unresponsive to complaints that it prompted a disgruntled customer to create the Web site www.untied.com, featuring United Airlines passenger complaints.

The lesson here: the communicated promise must be delivered in product, service and the total customer experience. Internal brand strategy education and communication may be necessary to ensure all employees are helping the brand deliver its promise. Tying employee compensation to delivery against the brand promise will also help to ensure the promise is delivered.

Problem number 19: not linking brand planning to the business' strategic planning process

Analysis: a brand plan is useless if it is not an integral part of the organization's business planning process. And if you aspire to be a market driven organization, the brand plan should drive the business planning process. **Redesign your processes to ensure these two are integrally linked.**

Problem number 20: licensing the brand name out to whoever will pay for it

Analysis: while this will generate additional revenues and profits in the short term, it is an unwise practice in the long term. You should use brand licensing to:

- extend the brand into new categories;
- expand the meaning of the brand;
- reinforce key brand associations;
- build your brand as a badge;
- bring your brand to life in new ways.

You should avoid licensing your brand just for short-term gain where it does not make sense. Where the licensing department resides in your organization and what its objectives are will have a large impact on how well licensing is used to build (versus bleed) the brand.

Problem number 21: trying to be the best at something, especially core category benefits, rather than owning something different

Analysis: being the best is not a point of difference if being good is 'good enough' for consumers. In industries that have focused on customer satisfaction (such as the automobile industry), standards have risen to the point that all options satisfactorily meet customer needs. In those industries, brands must find new points of difference if they are to maintain consumer loyalty.

Problem number 22: trying to own what have become cost-of-entry benefits, and not owning any differentiating benefits

Analysis: this is similar to the previous problem. **It is not sufficient to claim leadership of a benefit that consumers expect of all brands in the category.** An airline cannot win in the marketplace by trying to own 'safety'. A very high level of safety is a given in that industry. An airline might win, however, by exclusively guaranteeing on-time departures and arrivals (if that were possible) or by offering first class service throughout the plane (Midwest Express).

Interestingly, from airline industry laddering studies, we find that consumers want a few key things from airlines: safety, the desired routing, desired departure and arrival times, and, given these things, the lowest price. It is not surprising that most airlines serve only peanuts, pretzels, or other snacks (and are largely undifferentiated in any substantive ways), but three highly successful airlines have emerged in the United States based upon further differentiation: Midwest Express, known as 'The best care in the air' (offering first class accommodations and treatment throughout the plane), Southwest Airlines (offering an inexpensive but highly reliable trip with a casual, fun atmosphere), and more recently, Jet Blue (featuring a fleet of brand new planes with roomy leather seats and free individual television viewing (24 channels) at each seat).

Problem number 23: focusing too much on product attributes and not enough on brand benefits in consumer communication

Analysis: you will have to decide on the right combination of attributes, benefits, consequences and basic human values your brand claims to possess or address. Typically, the further up the need hierarchy your brand climbs, the more difficult it is for competitors to make similar claims (or to emulate what your brand delivers).

Problem number 24: trying to make too many points in your brand communication rather than focusing on the one or two most compelling points of difference

Analysis: the effectiveness of brand communication diminishes in direct proportion to the number of points you attempt to make in your communication. Regarding brand communication, more is not better. I see this problem most often in companies with a very junior marketing staff or in companies in which marketing is practised by non-marketers (engineers, doctors, lawyers, and so on). Ask these questions of each marketing piece you produce. Does it quickly and clearly communication the most compelling reasons to choose our brand over the competitive alternatives? And is it convincing?

Problem number 25: for market leader: following challengers because it is easier and produces more immediate results, rather than creating new ways to meet consumer needs

Analysis: this is an easy trap to fall into: if you are ahead, just match the competition to stay ahead – that way they can never catch up. That is a fairly common sailboat-racing tactic. The problem with this strategy is that you begin to play by your competitor's rules. **It is easier to win at your own game than at someone else's. It may be a more natural reaction to match competitive moves, but as you are doing that, you are distracted from doing what you do best – playing your own game. And, remember, other competitors that are playing by different rules may not be far behind.**

Problem number 26: not applying the latest product and service innovations to your flagship brand because it is getting too old and stodgy (a self-fulfilling prophecy)

Analysis: it is a tragedy to walk away from a brand into which you have invested millions of dollars over time. **It is better to reposition, revitalize, and extend an aging brand than to ignore it.** You should carefully monitor consumer opinion to ensure the brand is perceived as relevant and vital. Also, track the brand's consumers to make sure they are not a shrinking or aging group. Often, new sub-brands can make the parent brand more relevant to new consumer segments.

Problem number 27: no central control of the brand portfolio (so that each brand team is free to apply the best differentiating features of one brand to each of the others in the portfolio)

Analysis: certain attributes, features and benefits should be off limits to certain brands within your portfolio. When the business is organized and run by product category or channel of trade (as opposed to brand), there is more pressure to apply the best ideas to all brands regardless of each brand's positioning or intended point of difference. If the business is organized by brand and most people understand brand concepts, this is less likely to happen.

Procter & Gamble might offer several different brands of detergent, but each has a distinct point of difference. One might make clothes whiter, one might work best in cold water, one might take out tough stains, one might be gentle on clothes, one might be hypoallergenic, and so on. Since Procter & Gamble manages by brand, they really understand that points of difference are central to a brand's success, whereas somewhere else (a company organized around product development, run by engineers, etc), people might feel more pressured to add the best features they come up with to all their products.

A highly placed brand management group or council should have the authority to ensure that brand teams, product development teams, business units, divisions and subsidiaries do not blur the lines between your organization's brands because of a 'silo' or short term approach to the business.

Problem number 28: no brand identity standards and systems

Analysis: a brand should be presented consistently across all applications: name, logo, personality, visual style, icons, and so on. The only way to ensure this is with comprehensive brand identity standards and systems that are well understood and easy to use. Standards manuals are a minimum requirement. With the advent of digital technology, CD ROMs and an intranet site should also be considered. Think of your brand as a person. Does it present itself consistently in all situations or does it seem to have 'multiple personalities'?

Problem number 29: marketing is divided into functional 'silos' (advertising, promotion, brand management, product development, publicity, and so on) with no integrating mechanism

Analysis: reorganization and process redesign are the answers to this problem. **Marketing must be approached in an integrated fashion.**

Problem number 30: defining your target consumer too broadly (for instance, women aged 18–65)

Analysis: by definition, a brand cannot be all things to all people. A brand promises relevant differentiated benefits to a target consumer. Increasingly, companies are focusing on brand usage over penetration. That is, they are getting a larger portion of a smaller group's business by offering more products and services that deliver against the brand promise. This helps to build loyalty. This is in lieu of trying to attract additional consumers to the brand. **It is a well-known fact that it costs seven times more to gain a new consumer that it does to get a current consumer to make an incremental purchase. Corporate parent brands can achieve increased targeting through well-targeted sub-brands.**

Problem number 31: not really understanding the consumer, and his or her needs and motivations

Analysis: this is the 'kiss of death' for a brand. A brand only exists to uniquely meet consumer needs. **An important part of any business is staying in touch with consumers, understanding what they need and why they are buying the business's products and services.** Your research should include ongoing market research (of consumers and competitors) and ongoing brand equity monitoring. In-depth qualitative research will give you a better understanding of consumer needs and motivations. This includes ethnography (putting yourself in consumers' shoes by observing their brand shopping and usage patterns in real-life situations) and projective techniques ('If the brand were an 'animal/car/person, what animal/car/person would it be?'), among other types of research. Very successful companies, such as Harley-Davidson, experience the brand right along with their consumers.

Problem number 32: unsuccessfully extending the brand up to a premium segment or down to a value segment

Analysis: while some companies have successfully employed this tactic to grow (Honda slowly extended from lawn mower engines to Honda Accords, yet it created the Acura brand for its highest-end cars), it can be very tricky to execute successfully. **Know what**

impact price segment extensions will have on your core brand. Conduct extensive consumer research before and throughout the process. There are many sub-brand and message subtleties that may be required to support such a move. Price affects quality perceptions and is an important brand-positioning cue.

Problem number 33: choosing generic (non-proprietary) brand names

Analysis: while it might be tempting to choose a name that describes your product or service, it is a mistake. The name can soon become confused with that of every other brand that takes a similar approach, or worse yet, it can link the brand to an outdated product or technology. Consider brands that include 'sys' or 'tech' in their names. Is it easy to tell them apart? In retrospect, how about the wisdom of the 'Cellular One' name now that PCS and other technologies have emerged? **Own a name that is suggestive of a timeless consumer benefit (Aris Vision Institute – for laser eye surgery) or one that is 'coined' and whose meaning you can define through consumer communication (Kodak or Xerox).**

Problem number 34: not keeping up with the industry on product or service innovation

Analysis: no matter how much of a market share advantage or leadership legacy you have, you should not rest on your laurels. The marketplace is too competitive for you not to constantly reinvent yourself. Maintain a large pool of resources to invest in new ideas. Award the resources based on projected incremental sales and return on investment. Even pursue new business approaches that could make your current core business obsolete. If you do not, someone else will. Think about the impact of digital technology on Kodak's chemical based photography leadership. Consider Encyclopedia Britannica's entry into interactive software (which sells for a fraction of the cost of their traditional hardcover bound volumes).

Problem number 35: spending too much money on trade deals and sales promotion at the expense of brand building

Analysis: brands shift some leverage back to the manufacturer from the retailer. (This is one relationship the manufacturer can own with the consumer.) Brands also combat category commoditization and the resulting downward pressure on price. Is your sales organization bigger and more powerful than your brand management and marketing organization? Do you know how much you are spending on trade deals and price promotions? Is it more than you are spending on brand building? **It is difficult, but essential, to move from a sales 'push' to a marketing 'pull' organization if you are to maintain a competitive differential and a price premium.**

Problem number 36: no person or department has responsibility for the brand: it lacks internal mindshare, supervision and management

Analysis: fortunately, fewer and fewer organizations experience this problem these days. At a minimum, most have assigned a brand manager or a brand management department. After having read this book, it should be clear that **the complexity of the brand management task makes it very difficult to develop a powerful brand in the absence of a brand management mind-set and function.**

Problem number 37: well thought-out marketing decisions are second guessed by non-marketers who think marketing is a matter of opinion rather than an art and a science for which experience matters

Analysis: when people without marketing experience, insight or appreciation are in positions to evaluate, review and approve marketing decisions, this often leads to sub-optimal or ineffective marketing. I have witnessed many well thought-out plans or campaigns undermined by people in authority who would have done better to hire and empower the best marketers rather than try to second-guess every marketing action. Most marketers would never claim to know how to perform surgery, write a legal brief, design software or reconcile journal entries. Yet many doctors, lawyers, engineers, accountants and others think they can produce a better ad or develop a better marketing campaign. **Just because marketing seems less than 'black and white' and is not always measurable on a quarterly basis does not mean that experience does not count.**

Problem number 38: decisions that adversely affect the brand are made outside of the brand management context

Analysis: when making decisions (ranging from mergers and acquisitions, product extensions and cost cutting, to outsourcing critical customer services, producing private label products to fill production capacity, and offering price discounts to meet quarterly revenue goals), always consider the impact on the brand. Corporate executives, general managers, engineers, production managers, salespeople, and others frequently do not consider the impact on brand strategy or equity in such decision making. This highlights the importance of the CEO assuming the role of chief brand champion. It also underlines the importance of creating a brand-building organization.

Problem number 39: senior managers do not understand what the brand stands for

Analysis: this could well be the most pervasive and detrimental problem of all. The consumer will never be able to understand what the brand stands for and what its points of difference are if your management team does not. It would benefit you to gain the CEO's support to involve the management team in a process of defining what the brand stands for, including its target consumer, essence, promise, personality and marketplace positioning. A particularly important part of that exercise is to gain insight and consensus on the brand's most compelling point of difference. **Managing the transformation of your entire management team into well informed brand champions may be a difficult process to manage, but the investment of time and effort will be well worth it.**

Problem number 40: quarter-over-quarter revenue and profit pressures gradually undermine the brand

Analysis: constant market pressures to increase revenues and profits cause a myriad of problems (see problems 1–3 and 10). One of the biggest problems is putting pressure on the brand to extend into more and more market segments to broaden its appeal and to provide for more revenue growth. This eventually comes at the expense of the meaning of the brand itself. Witness Volvo. It had a very clear point of difference – family safety – until it created the 850 GLT, which was intended to extend the brand into younger and older childless markets. Volvo promoted this car as a fun car to drive – not necessarily a safe car for the family. Its styling erred from the boxy, armour/safety-implied styling of typical Volvos. The car's success has been underwhelming, precisely because it is incongruent with the brand's image. The degree to which the 850 GLT is successful is the degree to which it will blur Volvo's primary point of difference in the marketplace. **If a company must grow to keep Wall Street happy (as all public companies must do), then it should consider one of two approaches: 1) introduce new products and services that deliver against the brand's essence and promise (a family-safe ride in Volvo's case); or 2) bite the marketing bullet and launch new brands.**

─────────────── **Did you know...?** ───────────────

In his white paper, *Communication as Value Builder*, Dr David Jensen, Senior Vice President with Ketchum in Atlanta, cites a 1998 study by the Wirthlin Group, which concludes that companies with good reputations are:

- seven times more likely to command premium prices for their products and services;

- five times more likely to have their stock recommended;

- four times more likely to be recommended as a good place to work;

- three times more likely to be recommended as a joint venture partner;

- one and a half times more likely to receive the benefit of the doubt.

NOTES

1   Source: David N Martin, *Be the Brand*, New Marketplace, Richmond, Virginia, 2000, p 44.

22

Keys to success in brand building: a summary

As I think about the most important things that can be said about brand management, the following come to mind:

THE BOTTOM LINE: WHY BRAND MANAGEMENT IS ESSENTIAL

Brands deliver the following key benefits to organizations:

- Increased revenues and market share.
- Decreased price sensitivity (or the ability to charge price premiums to consumers and the trade).
- Increased customer loyalty.
- For manufacturers, additional leverage over retailers.
- Increased profitability.
- Increased stock price and shareholder value.
- Increased clarity of vision.
- Increased ability to mobilize an organization's people and focus its activities.
- Ability to attract and retain high quality employees.
- A strong, well positioned brand extends the life of your organization indefinitely by providing independence from a particular product category, increasing flexibility for

future growth (through extension) and, therefore, increasing the ability to expand into new product and service categories and alter the product and service mix to keep up with marketplace demands. Without a strong brand, your organization's lifespan will be tied to the lifespan of the products it manufactures or the services it provides.

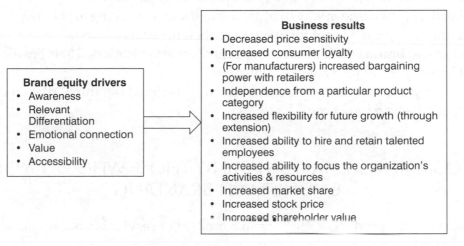

Business results
- Decreased price sensitivity
- Increased consumer loyalty
- (For manufacturers) increased bargaining power with retailers
- Independence from a particular product category
- Increased flexibility for future growth (through extension)
- Increased ability to hire and retain talented employees
- Increased ability to focus the organization's activities & resources
- Increased market share
- Increased stock price
- Increased shareholder value

Brand equity drivers
- Awareness
- Relevant Differentiation
- Emotional connection
- Value
- Accessibility

Figure 22.1 *The importance of a strong brand*

BRAND POSITIONING/DESIGN IS EXTREMELY IMPORTANT

You must define the target consumer, essence, promise, personality and positioning for your brand.

BRAND INSISTENCE DRIVERS

- The goal of brand equity building is to move consumers from brand awareness to brand insistence.
- Awareness, relevant differentiation, emotional connection, value and accessibility drive brand insistence.
- Creating awareness is the first step in building a strong brand.
- Strive to maximize brand impressions and accessibility.
- Overexposing a brand will accelerate its death.

FOCUS AND DIFFERENTIATION: THE TWO MOST IMPORTANT CONCEPTS IN BRAND DESIGN

- The more specific your brand's promise, the stronger your brand's equity will be.
- Ideally, the brand tells a story that is unique to its organization.
- Differentiate your brand in ways that are relevant and compelling to your target consumer.
- By definition, a brand is not for everyone – therein lies its power.
- Number two brands must never try to emulate market leaders. Their power (as is true of all brands) lies in relevant differentiation.
- Whenever possible, a brand should try to own the 'next big thing' (the emerging key relevant differentiating benefit).

COMMON MISTAKES MADE BY THOSE WHO DO NOT UNDERSTAND BRANDING

- A brand is not a product or service and a product or service is not a brand.
- Brand management is not product management.
- Brand management is much more than advertising or brand identity management.

A brand is the personification of a product, service or organization. It is also the source of a relationship with customers. Like a person, it must have human qualities and possess a soul.

- Think of a brand as a person – possessing core values and a personality.
- The brand is the source of the organization's relationship with people.
- Strive to create an emotional connection with your consumer.
- The most successful brands tap into deeply felt human needs.
- A brand must have a heart and a soul.
- A brand must be trustworthy. It must earn people's trust.
- A brand must be courageous. It must unwaveringly stand for something.
- A brand must possess integrity, that is, it must deliver what it promises – always.
- A brand must be authentic, not manufactured.
- A brand must win people's hearts. It must endear itself to consumers.
- A brand gets credit for attempting to do what is right.

OTHER IMPORTANT BRAND ATTRIBUTES

- A brand must deliver a good value.
- A brand must be accessible and convenient.

You must focus the organization on delivering the brand promise – brand management is much more than marketing (aka making the brand promise real).

- Branding is not an afterthought; rather it is the core value of the organization.
- Have a singular focus on delivering the brand promise.
- The brand's products and services must deliver upon the brand's promise.
- Focus everything your organization does on delivering the brand promise.
- An organization must manifest its brand's essence, promise and personality at each point of contact it makes with people.
- Carefully manage all the points of contact you make with the consumer.
- An organization's culture must reinforce its brand's essence, promise and personality.
- To be truly successful, a brand must be based upon the enlightened vision of a strong leader and a relentless employee passion to better meet the needs of the customer.
- Do not forget to hire, train, motivate and compensate front line employees to deliver the brand's essence, promise and personality.
- The brand's essence, promise and personality must drive organization decision making and resource allocation.
- Ultimately, you want to use brand identity systems, advertising, packaging, retail environment, services, the Internet and other delivery mechanisms to 'bring your brand to life'.

Brand management and marketing start with a profound understanding of the customer.

- A brand must be based upon a profound understanding of the target consumer and the marketplace in which he or she lives.
- Have a profound understanding of your consumer and his or her values, attitudes, motivations and behaviours (purchase and usage).
- Understanding the target consumer's hopes and fears is essential to designing a strong brand.

THE IMPORTANCE OF CHOOSING THE RIGHT BRAND BENEFITS

Ideally, a brand should own benefits that are: 1) highly important to the target consumer; 2) a core competency of the delivering organization; and 3) not being addressed by the brand's competitors.

- A brand must engage people on an emotional and sensory level.
- It is much more powerful and sustainable for a brand to own emotional, experiential and self-expressive benefits than it is for it to own functional benefits.
- Competitors cannot easily emulate brand benefits that are based upon your organization's core values.

To be truly successful, a brand must be based upon the enlightened vision of a strong leader and a relentless employee passion to better meet the needs of the customer (or, brand as an internal rallying cry).

- Strategic vision is an essential component of strong brands.
- Brand management must be owned at the highest level of the organization – and throughout the organization.
- Brand management is a much less difficult task if the CEO has internalized the brand's essence, promise and vision.
- It is certainly as important (if not more so) to indoctrinate employees about what the brand stands for as it is to do so for external audiences.
- The brand can become the mobilizing influence and rallying cry within an organization.
- The brand's vision should inspire and empower people.
- The most successful brands possess passion. Its leaders are 'hungry' with 'fire in their bellies'.
- Everyone in the organization must truly believe in and 'live' the brand.
- Convert everyone in your organization (and suppliers and retailers) into evangelists for your brand.
- Story telling is an important part of brand building.
- Your organization must have a clear vision of how your brand uniquely adds value in the marketplace. People in the organization must share a vision of what the brand stands for.
- When employees sincerely believe that their brand stands for something that makes a difference in the world, the brand becomes unstoppable.

Use as wide an array of brand identity elements as possible for maximum effect.

- In today's multimedia environment, an organization must use all of the components of a brand identity system for greatest effect – brand name, logo, icon, typography, colours, tag lines, attitude, voice, visual style, scent, sound, motion/animation, and so on.
- Your brand's identity system should be multi-faceted, going well beyond name, logo and slogan to include personality, voice and visual style, among other elements.

- Consistent execution of brand identity is crucial. Think of your brand as a person. It should exhibit consistent behaviours, not multiple personalities.

Miscellaneous

- Direct marketing, the Internet and direct experiential interaction with consumers will become increasing important in building strong brands.
- Organizations that recognize that their people and brands are their most important assets will be more successful than those that do not.

THE IMPORTANCE OF SUPERIOR PRODUCTS AND SERVICES TO STRONG BRANDS

- Brands are meaningless if not delivered upon by superior products and services.
- Find a way to have your brand redefine quality within its product category.
- A brand must be kept vital and relevant. It requires constant innovation, communication and promotion.
- Understand all the compromises your brand (and every brand in your category) makes with consumers. Break those compromises to 'leapfrog' the competition.
- Value-generating innovation may be the most powerful engine for brand growth. Products, services, innovation and the customer experience are all integral elements of a strong brand.

CREATE A TOTAL BRAND EXPERIENCE FOR YOUR CUSTOMERS

Always give your customers something new to discover about your brand.

THE FUTURE OF BRANDS: CO-CREATING PRODUCTS, SERVICES AND EXPERIENCES WITH CUSTOMERS

- Communicate with the consumer whenever and wherever you can.
- Maintain a constant and intimate dialogue with your customer.
- The most powerful brands in the long run are those that are co-created by the consumer and the marketer; those that are a result of ongoing dialogue.
- Brands that align themselves with communities and, more powerfully, create communities will thrive.
- Brands that share values with consumers will survive.

CELEBRATION OF THE BRAND MANAGER – IT IS AN UNDERRATED, DIFFICULT, BUT INTRINSICALLY REWARDING JOB

Brand management is an art and a science. It requires in-depth consumer research, thorough analysis, creativity, sound judgement and strategic vision. Due to its complexity and its need to touch all aspects of the business, brand management is not easy. But it can be very rewarding.

WAXING PHILOSOPHICAL: BRAND MANAGEMENT AT ITS BEST

At its worst, the organizational brand is a name and a logo that is inconsistently applied to an unrelated set of products and services. It is overused and means nothing, and it reminds people of the worst of an over-commercial society. It feels cold and seems exploitative. It is perceived to be a vestige of a past era.

At its best, brand management aligns organizations with value-adding activities. It keeps organizations focused on meeting real human needs in compelling new ways. And, at its best, the organizational brand defines how the organization best meets its customers' needs in unique and compelling ways. It serves as the organization's unifying principle and rallying cry; it infuses the organization with a set of values and a personality; and it holds an organization's employees to a consistent set of behaviours. The organizational brand stands for something. It establishes trust and a certain level of assurance; it makes it possible for people to establish relationships with the organization; and it creates expectations that must be fulfilled. The brand can bring an organization to life in a very real way.

In the end, brand management is all about meeting people's physical, emotional, spiritual, intellectual and other needs in unique ways. It is the application of free enterprise to the timely and timeless needs of mankind.

I wish you a brand at its best. May you unleash your brand's power and transform your organization through branding.

Did you know...?

- Generating trial is frequently the focus of smaller brands, while large brands tend to focus on maintaining (and building) loyalty.[1]

- For a new brand, it is important to track the number of stores deciding to sell the product, while for a mature brand, it is more important to look at the number of stores delisting the product.[2]

- For a fast-growing brand, the number of new loyal customers is important, but for an established brand it is the number of lost loyal customers that is the telling indicator.[3]

● In a major brand loyalty study, the researches found that two thirds of the time, when people who were more attitudinally loyal than behaviourally loyal to the brand ('prospects') outnumbered those who were less attitudinally loyal than behaviourally loyal to the brand ('vulnerables'), the brand's market share increased. Market share decreased when the opposite was true. That is why it is important to measure both attitudinal and behavioural loyalty.

NOTES

1   Source: Allan L. Baldinger and Joel Robinson, *Brand Loyalty: The link between attitude and behavior*, NPD Group.
2   Source: Lars Finskud, *Bringing Discipline to Brand Value Management*.
3   Source: Lars Finskud, *Bringing Discipline to Brand Value Management*.

23

Brand management and marketing resources

www.brandera.com/ – BrandEra.com, the Marketer's Marketplace, serves as the business-to-business destination for the marketing communications industry. It brings professionals with marketing needs together with suppliers of creative solutions. It offers timely news articles, a Request for Proposals Exchange, and searchable online portfolios for freelancers (photographers, illustrators, graphic designers, multimedia artist, art directors and copy-writers). There are also comprehensive ad agency listings, a fully searchable resource centre and industry directory, job classifieds, an online collaborative tool, and more.

www.clickz.com/ – Comprehensive archive of articles on all aspects of marketing.

www.webmarketingtoday.com/webmarket/branding.htm – Web Marketing Info Center: Branding on the Web – features a comprehensive archive of articles.

http://marketing.about.com/?once=true&pid=2737&cob=home – About Marketing: articles, forums, chat and more.

www.marketingprofs.com – MarketingProfs.com: marketing know-how from professors and professionals.

www.mad.co.uk/bs/ – mad.co.uk is an invaluable resource for marketing, media, new media, advertising and design professionals.

www.admedia.org/internet/home.html – Internet advertising resource guide.

www.iab.net/ – Founded in 1996, the Interactive Advertising Bureau is the industry's leading interactive advertising association. Its activities include evaluating and recommending guidelines and best practices, fielding research to document the effectiveness of interactive media, and educating the advertising industry about the use of interactive advertising and marketing. Membership includes companies that are actively engaged in the sale of interactive advertising and marketing.

www.interactivehq.org/ – the Association for Interactive Media (AIM) is the largest trade association in the world devoted to helping companies that use the Internet and interactive media to reach their respective marketplaces with maximum effectiveness. AIM, an independent subsidiary of the Direct Marketing Association, serves diverse corporate interests from e-mail marketing, e-tailing, online marketing, content provision, e-commerce, market research, broadband access and the rollout of interactive television.

www.forrester.com/ – As leading analysts of emerging technology, Forrester set the standard in business and technology research by staying ahead of market trends and technology change. They predict industry behaviour, rank winners and losers, project future market growth, and provide prescriptive guidance about what actions to take – and when.

www.harrisinteractive.com – Harris Interactive is a worldwide market research and consulting firm, best known for The Harris Poll® and its pioneering use of the Internet to conduct scientifically accurate market research. Headquartered in the United States, with offices in the United Kingdom, Japan and a global network of local market and opinion research firms, the company conducts international research with fluency in multiple languages.

www.dynamiclogic.com/ – Dynamic Logic is a leading online research company specializing in measuring online advertising effectiveness Beyond the Click™. Their AdIndex product provides online advertisers, ad agencies and publishers with feedback regarding the branding effectiveness of their specific online advertising campaigns.

www.eyetracking.com – Eye Tracking, Inc. delivers high quality eye-tracking services to your visual products. They offer you:

- real-time videos that show where users are looking;
- detailed graphical and statistical reports;
- next day results.

www.eyewonder.com/ – EyeWonder's EYERIS™ technology allows you to deliver your streaming video and audio to the widest audience possible.

www.grafiksolutionz.com – Founded in Woodland Hills, California, Grafik Solutionz Intl Co (GSICO) has been the primary source for corporate logos and trademarks for advertising and promotional use since 1994. They stock over 45,000 logos and trademarks from a variety of categories, and their library is growing every day. Individual logos and marks may be purchased for same day e-mail delivery. They can also track down a logo for you if they do not have it in stock, usually within 24 hours.

www.ahaa.org – Association of Hispanic Advertising Agencies (AHAA): listing of the largest Hispanic agencies.
www.awool.com/awoolhis.html – Hispanic Marketing Resources.
www.intes.com/marketing/marketingscience.html – *Marketing Science Journal* (published by the Institute for Operations Research and the Management Science).

BRAND RELATED PUBLICATIONS

http://bubl.ac.uk/journals/bus/ – Abstracts from marketing journals.
www.adage.com – *AdvertisingAge*.
www.marketingpower.com – American Marketing Association.
http://brandmarketing.com – *Brand Marketing*.
www.mad.co.uk/bs/ – *Brand Strategy*.
www.brandweek.com – *Brand Week*.
www.arfsite.org/Webpages/JAR_pages/jarhome.htm – *Journal of Advertising Research*.
www.mcb.co.uk/forums/market.htm – links to several (mostly European) marketing journals.
www.mcb.co.uk/jpbm.htm – *Journal of Product and Brand Management*.
www.salesandmarketing.com – *Sales and Marketing Management*.

MARKETING RESEARCH

www.warc.com – World Advertising Research Center.
www.casro.org – Council of American Survey Research Organizations.

--- **Did you know...?** ---

- It costs seven times more to get a new consumer for the brand than it does to get a current consumer to make an incremental purchase.

- In some sectors, an increase in the consumer base by just one per cent is otherwise equivalent to a 10 per cent cost reduction.[1]

- Depending on the category, a 5 per cent increase in customer loyalty will lift the lifetime profits per customer by up to 95 per cent.[2]

- Increasingly, brands are shifting their focus from penetration to usage. Greater success comes from getting a larger portion of a smaller segment's business (versus getting more consumers to buy your brand). This can be accomplished in many ways, including offering more and different products and services that deliver against your brand's promise.

NOTES

1   Source: Robert Passikoff, PhD, president of Brand Keys, Inc.
2   Source: Robert Passikoff, PhD, president of Brand Keys, Inc. Larry Light indicates that, on average, a 5 per cent increase in loyalty results in a 25 per cent increase in profitability.

24

Brand audits

A brand audit provides an analysis of an organization's brand and its brand management and marketing effectiveness. It assesses a brand's strengths, weaknesses, opportunities and threats. It identifies brand growth opportunities, including those achieved by brand repositioning and brand extension. The audit should result in recommendations to improve brand equity, brand positioning, and brand management and marketing effectiveness.

The following are typical components of a brand audit:

Strategy review

- business plans;
- marketing plans;
- brand positioning statement;
- brand plans;
- creative (or agency) briefs;
- media plans.

Marketing research review

- brand positioning research;
- brand asset studies;
- brand equity measurement system (awareness, preference, usage, value, accessibility, relevance differentication, vitality, emotional connection, loyalty, associations, personality);

- brand extension research;
- product/service concept testing;
- logo recall and recognition testing.

Communications review

- advertising and promotion materials;
- other brand marketing elements: pricing, packaging, merchandising, distribution, direct marketing, sponsorships, flagship stores, etc;
- press kit;
- press releases;
- sales collateral materials;
- business cards, letterheads, etc;
- Web site;
- intranet site;
- employee training programmes;
- manager training;
- sales force training.

External information source review

- competitors' press releases, advertising and promotion;
- industry analyst reports;
- customer comments;
- business partner comments;
- marketing vendor interviews.

Employee interviews

- corporate officer interviews;
- marketing employee interviews;
- sales force interviews;
- front-line customer contact interviews;
- general employee interviews.

Human resource systems review

- organization charts;
- department mission/vision statements;
- department objectives;
- common objectives;

- recruiting criteria;
- individual competency dictionary;
- succession planning criteria;
- planning and resource allocation systems/processes.

Proprietary brand research (performed by the auditing company, if required)

- brand asset research;
- brand equity research;
- brand positioning research (qualitative and quantitative).

A qualified brand audit company will investigate the following areas of brand management:

Brand research

- Does this company have a deep understanding of its consumers' values, attitudes, needs, desires, hopes, aspirations, fears and concerns?
- Has this company rigorously analyzed its competition?
- Which of the following types of brand research has the company conducted: brand positioning qualitative and quantitative, brand asset studies, brand equity measurement and monitoring, brand extension, logo recall and recognition?
- How robust is each of these research studies?
- How are the company and each of its competitors positioned in the marketplace?

Brand strategy

- Is there a marketing plan?
- Is there a brand plan?
- Are those plans aligned with and integrated into company business plans?
- Does the company have a future vision and a well thought out plan to get there?
- Is it clear which marketing objectives, actions and vehicles will provide the greatest leverage in achieving the long-term vision?

Brand positioning

- Is there a brand positioning statement? Does it include the following: target consumer, differentiating brand benefit, brand essence, brand personality?
- Do most employees know the brand's positioning (verbatim or paraphrased)?
- Was the brand's key differentiating benefit based on an analysis of consumer needs, organizational strengths (core competencies), and competitive weaknesses?

- Does the brand own a benefit that is highly differentiated, compelling and believable?
- What are the brand's strengths, weaknesses, opportunities and threats?

Brand identity standards and systems

- How robust is the company's brand identity system?
- How easy is it for the company's employees and business partners to use?
- What brand identity controls does the company have in place?
- Is the company's brand architecture simple and understandable?
- Which of the following brand identity components does the company use in its system: name, logo, icon, tag line, type style, colours, shapes, symbols, visual style, mnemonic (sound) device, brand voice, music, animation, etc?
- Does the company have co-branding standards?
- How accurately and consistently have these standards been applied across all internal and external communications?

Brand advertising

- Do the ads break through the marketplace clutter?
- Do they powerfully communicate the brand's promise and personality?
- Do they include the 'reasons why' (differentiating benefit proof points)?
- Do they connect with the target consumer on an emotional level?
- Do they tap into the consumers' beliefs, values, aspirations, hopes and fears?
- Do they include components that are 'ownable'?

Organization design and internal brand building

- Is the company market driven or does it have a traditional manufacturing company design?
- Does the company's culture support the brand's essence, promise and personality?
- Is the company's marketing function centralized or distributed?
- What mechanisms has the company put in place to integrate its marketing?
- Are all of the required marketing functions present?
- Are brand objectives integrated into company and common objectives?
- Do the company's recruiting, training, performance management, compensation, succession planning, business planning, budgeting, resource allocation and other systems support brand building? Are they designed to help the company deliver upon its brand's promise?
- Does the company screen job applicants for their alignment with the brand's essence, promise and personality?
- Is the organization a 'learning organization'?

Brand extension

● What are the brand's assets?
● Is the brand over or under-extended (or both)?
● What are the most promising areas for brand extension?
● What processes does the organization have in place for brand extension? How does it safeguard against inappropriate extension?

Marketing employee competency

● How competent are the company's marketers?
● Which skill sets do they possess and which ones are missing?
● Has the company augmented missing internal skill sets with external sources?
● What are its external marketing vendors' strengths and weaknesses?
● Do the company's marketing employees (and its senior managers and all of its employees) exhibit a marketing mind-set? That is, do they profoundly understand its customers and sincerely and passionately strive to meet their wants and needs?

Brand auditors should assess the strength of an organization's mission and vision and the strength of its brand's essence, promise and personality (especially in relationship to the organization's stakeholders' perceptions of the organization). As part of the process, the auditor should investigate how congruently each of the following groups or sources articulate or manifest these organizational and brand attributes:

● its leaders;
● its official documents;
● its internal and external communications;
● its marketers;
● its salespeople;
● its customer service employees;
● its other employees;
● its business partners;
● each and every point of contact the brand makes with its clients/customers.

Ideally, the company performing the audit will have broad and deep experience (as line managers and as consultants) in each of the following areas:

● brand research;
● brand strategy and positioning;
● brand identity standards and systems;

- brand advertising;
- organization design.

Audits will vary from company to company based upon the company's unique needs, organizational complexity, marketing competency, and other factors. Given the large amount of work, to complete the audit in a reasonable period of time, the audit team should consist of at least three people. The more marketing experience each team member has, the better.

Audit costs may vary from a low of $150,000 to more than $1,000,000 depending on the global reach of the business, complexity of the brand and product structure, amount of proprietary research required, project's duration, number of people assigned, audit firm's profit margin and billing rate, and so on. If an audit company provides an estimate much lower than that, it indicates a lack of understanding of the scope and complexity of this type of project.

The project may last anywhere from a month (fast track with concentrated interviews and little to no additional research) to six months. Weaknesses to look out for in self-proclaimed brand auditors are:

- strong in other areas of marketing (advertising, promotion, etc), but not brand management;
- primary foci are brand research, strategy and positioning, but little knowledge of how to design an organization to deliver upon the brand promise;
- strong knowledge of brand management but little understanding of organization design;
- lack brand research experience.

A brand audit should identify strengths, weaknesses, opportunities and threats in the following areas:

- brand strategy and positioning;
- brand equity;
- leveraging the brand for business growth;
- capacity of the organization to manage and market the brand effectively;
- alignment of the organization's structure and systems to deliver upon the brand's promise.

BOTTOM LINE QUESTIONS (THAT A STRONG BRAND AUDITOR WILL ATTEMPT TO ANSWER)

- Does this company have a profound understanding of its consumers?
- Is the brand well positioned in its marketplace? Does it own a relevant and compelling point of difference?
- Do the leaders of this company have a vision for their brand(s)?
- Is this company's marketing staff competent?
- Is the organization mobilized to deliver upon its brand's promise?
- Does the corporate culture reinforce the brand essence, promise and personality?
- Are the brand identity standards and systems simple, robust and powerful?
- Does this organization accurately and consistently reinforce its brand's identity and positioning in internal and external communication?
- Does the brand create an emotional connection with its consumers?

Campbell's Soup

In early 2000 at my local grocery store, a can of Always Save cream of chicken soup was 66 cents, a can of Best Choice cream of chicken soup was 89 cents, and a can of Campbell's cream of chicken soup was $1.03. Which brand accounted for 8 out of 10 cans of soup purchased in the United States at the time? Campbell's. That's the power of brand equity!

Interestingly, more recently Progresso has significantly eroded Campbell's market share, not by undercutting their prices, but rather by building a differentiated, higher quality, higher priced soup brand. Progresso is successfully attempting to reposition Campbell's as a mediocre condensed soup more suitable for children.

The quick brand health assessment or, you know your brand is winning in the marketplace when...)

- The brand is mentioned to customers and potential customers, and they brim with enthusiasm in their response.

- Employees are enthusiastic and consistent in recounting what makes their brand special.

- The brand's market share is increasing.

- Competitors always mention your brand as a point of reference.

- The press can't seem to write enough about your brand.

- The CEO has a strong vision for the organization and its brand. He or she talks more about the vision than financial targets.

- The organization's leaders always seem to 'talk the brand' *and* 'walk the brand talk'.

Did you know…?

That any of the following can and have been branded:

- products and services;
- companies;
- professional service firms;
- restaurants;
- elementary schools and high schools;
- municipalities;
- states;
- regions;
- software;
- musical groups;
- other performing arts groups;
- summer camps;
- musicians;
- authors;
- other individuals.

References and further reading

Aaker, David A (1995) *Building Strong Brands*, Free Press, New York

Aaker, David A (1991) *Managing Brand Equity*, Free Press, New York

Aaker, David A and Brown, Phillip (1972) 'Evaluating Vehicle Source Effects', *Journal of Advertising Research*, 12, 11–16

Aaker, David A and Joachimsthaler, Erich (2000) *Brand Leadership*, Free Press, New York

American Productivity & Quality Center and American Marketing Association (1998) *Brand Building & Communication Consortium Benchmarking Study*, American Productivity & Quality Center and American Marketing Association, presented in Houston, TX

Anthony-Rodriques, Kelly (1998) *Brand Management: From print to broadcast on the Web*, Seybold San Francisco/Publishing 1998 Web Publishing Conference, September 1

Baldinger, Allan L and Rubinson, Joel, *Brand Loyalty: The link between attitude and behavior*, NPD Group

Baltes, Michael [accessed 11/30/01] Measuring non-financial assets, *Wharton Alumni Magazine* [Online] www.cfigroup.com/nonfinl.html

Barwise, Patrick (1997) Editorial: brands in a digital world, *Journal of Brand Management*, **4** (4) (Spring)

Bell, Tom [accessed 6/21/01] *Virtual Trade Dress: A very real problem* [Online] www.tombell.com

Bettles, Jennie [accessed 10/23/99] *Branding Amid the Noise*, article on ClickZ Network [Online] www.searchz.com

Blair, Margaret Henderson (2000) An empirical investigation of advertising wearin and wearout, *Journal of Advertising Research*, **40** (6 November/December), pp 95–100

Blankenship, A B _et al_ (1998) _State of the Art Marketing Research_, NTC Business Books, Lincolnwood, Illinois

Blattberg, Robert C, Getz, Gary and Thomas, Jacquelyn S (2001) _Customer Equity: Building and managing relationships as valuable assets_, Harvard Business School Press, Boston

Boyce, Rick [accessed January 26 1998] _Brand Building With Internet Media_, AdTech Report no 8 [Online] www.o-a.com

Brand Management: From print to broadcast to the Web, Seybold San Francisco/Publishing '98 Web Publishing Conference, September 1 1998

Brandenburger, Adam M, Nalebuff, Barry J and Brandenberger, Ada (1997) _Co-opetition: 1. A Revolutionary Mindset That Redefines Competition and Cooperation; 2. The Game Theory Strategy That's Changing the Game of Business_, Ada Brandenberger

Bruzzone, Donald E and Tallyn, Deborah J (1996) Linking tracking to pretesting with an 'arm', _Advertising Research Foundation Advertising and Brand Tracking Workshop_, November 12–13 pp 169–77

Buckingham, Richard A (2001) _12 Tools for Building Lifetime Business Relationships_, Kiplinger Books, Washington

Building Your Brand Online [accessed 10/22/99] Advantage Internet [Online] www.aibn.com/brandbuild.html

Business Wire Business Editors (2000a) 5 common myths about trademarks; don't get burned by trademark ignorance, _Business Wire_, February 9

Business Wire Business Editors (2000b) Harley-Davidson declares victory in the court of public opinion – drops federal trademark application, _Business Wire_, June 20

Cannon, Hugh M (2001) Addressing new media with conventional media planning, _Journal of Interactive Advertising_, **1** (2), Spring [Online] http://jiad.org/vol1/no2/cannon/ 8/11/01

Cap Gemini Ernst & Young Center for Business Innovation (2000) _Measuring the Future: The value creation index_, Cap Gemini Ernst & Young Center for Business Innovation [Online] http://www.cbi.cgey.com/research/index html

Carbone, Lewis P (1998) Total customer experience drives value, _American Management Association International_, July/August, pp 62–63

Chassaing, Thierry, Edelman, David C and Segal, Lynn (1998) _Customer Retention: Beyond bribes and golden handcuffs_, Boston Consulting Group pamphlet

Cialdini, Robert B, PhD (1993) _Influence: The Psychology of Persuasion_, Quill, William Morrow, New York

Clancy, Kevin J and Krieg, Peter C (2000) _Counter-Intuitive Marketing: Achieve great results using uncommon sense_, Free Press, New York

Clancy, Kevin J and Shulman, Robert S (1994) _Marketing Myths that are Killing Business: The cure for death wish marketing_, McGraw-Hill, New York

Conference Board (1998a) _Managing Reputation With Image and Brands_, Conference Board

Conference Board (1998b) _Managing the Corporate Brand_, Conference Board

Cristol, Steven M and Johnson, Bob (1997) *Building Brand Equity on the World Wide Web*, Summary of a Presentation to the Business Week Corporate Branding Symposium, Chicago, June 17 [Online] www.haas.berkeley.edu/wba268/brandweb.htm

Cult Brands [accessed 4/12/01] www.Forbes.com

Czerniawski, Richard D and Maloney, Michael W (1999) *Creating Brand Loyalty: The management of power positioning and really great advertising*, AMACOM, New York

Davis, Scott M (2000) *Brand Asset Management: Driving profitable revenue growth through your brands* Jossey-Bass, San Francisco

Dawson, Ross (2000) *Developing Knowledge-Based Client Relationships: the future of professional services*, Butterworth-Heinemann, Oxford

Durgee, Jeffery F (1986) Depth interview techniques for creative advertising, *Journal of Advertising Research*, **25** (6), pp 29–37

Ehrenberg, Andrew (1997) Description and prescription, *Journal of Advertising Research* (November/December) pp 17–22

Ehrenberg, Andrew, Barnard, Neil and Scriven, John (1997) Differentiation or salience, *Journal of Advertising Research* (November/December), pp 7–14

Ellwood, Iain (2000) *The Essential Brand Book: Over 100 techniques to increase brand value*, Kogan Page, London

Erdem, Tulin (1998) An empirical analysis of umbrella branding, *Journal of Marketing Research*, 35 (August), pp 339–51

Ericson, Paul, Gorgman, Randy and Verma, Mike (2001) How to get in the news, *In the News – Media Relations: Ad Council Academy of Rochester: Enhancing Professional Know-How*[SM], Advertising Council of Rochester, New York

Ericsson Connexion (1998) Brand building on the web, *Ericsson Connexion* no 4 (December)

Farquhar, Peter H , Han, Julia Y and Ijiri, Yuji (1992) Brands on the balance sheet: brand values belong in financial statements, recognized measurement standards are all that business needs, *Marketing Management* (Winter) pp 16–22

Finskud, Lars (1998) Bringing discipline to brand value management, *Brand Valuations*, Financial Times Retail & Consumer Publishing

Fischler, Robert [accessed 10/23/99], *Round-Up At The Branding Ranch*, ClickZ Network [Online] www.searchz.com

Fishman, Stephen and Stim, Rich [accessed 6/26/01] *Trade Secret Basics* [Online] www.nolo.com

Flowers, Jim [accessed 8/4/01] *Ideation: It's more than just brainstorming* [Online] www.bsu.edu/classes/flowers2/beyond htm

Gad, Thomas (2001) *4-D Branding: Cracking the corporate code of the network economy*, Financial Times/Prentice Hall, London

Gelb, Gabriel M [accessed 9/25/01] *The Nuts and Bolts of Business-to-Business Marketing Research*, CRM University Learning Center [Online] www.techmar.com/u_busmktresearchbma.asp

Georgiou, Paul and Miller, Stephen (1996) 10 years of advertising tracking, *Rent-A-Car Business Advertising Research Foundation Advertising and Brand Tracking Workshop*, November 12–13, pp 1–12

Gladwell, Malcolm (2000) *The Tipping Point: How little things can make a big difference*, Little, Brown, Boston

Gobé, Marc (2001) *Emotional Branding: The new paradigm for connecting brands to people*, Allworth Press, New York

Gordon, Ian H (1998) *Relationship Marketing: New strategies, techniques and technologies to win the customers you want and keep them forever*, John Wiley, New York

Gregory, James R with Wiechmann, Jack G (1997) *Leveraging the Corporate Brand*, NTC Business Books, Lincolnwood, Illinois

Guide to Consumer Law: False advertising [accessed 6/21/01] [Online] http://nbc-2.findlaw.com

Haigh, David (1997) Brand valuation or brand monitoring? That is the question, *Journal of Brand Management*, **4** (5) pp 311–19

Hankinson, Philippa and Hankinson, Graham (1999) Managing successful brands: an empirical study which compares the corporate cultures of companies managing the world's top 100 brands with those managing outsider brands, *Journal of Marketing Management*, **15** (1–3) (January–April) pp 135–55

Harding, Carlos and Le Brigand, Patrick (1996) Brand tracking is good, but is it good enough? *Advertising Research Foundation Advertising and Brand Tracking Workshop*, November 12–13, pp 92–104

Hebard, Amy J and Rubinson, Joel (1996) Value and loyalty measurement at AT&T, *Advertising Research Foundation Advertising and Brand Tracking Workshop*, November 12–13, pp 47–71

Hester, Edward L (1995) *Successful Marketing Research: The complete guide to getting and using essential information about your customers and competitors*, John Wiley, New York

Hill, Sam and Lederer, Chris (2001) *The Infinite Asset: Managing brands to build new value*, Harvard Business School Press, Boston

Hit-ranking search engine hits [Online] www.iglou.com

Hollis, Nigel S (1996) They said my brand was popular – so what? *Advertising Research Foundation Advertising and Brand Tracking Workshop*, November 12–13, pp 105–22

How Search Engines Rank Web Pages [accessed 10/30/99] [Online] www.searchenginewatch.com

Hutchinson, Alan [accessed 11/29/01] *Use Return on Investment for Quantifying Marketing Results*, MarketWare Technologies [Online] http://www.mrlweb.com/roi.html

Ind, Nicholas (2001) *Living the Brand: How to transform every member of your organization into a brand champion*, Kogan Page, London

Jassin, Lloyd J [accessed 6/21/01] *Trade Dress Protection: How to tell a book by its cover* [Online] www.CopyLaw.com

Jassin, Lloyd L [accessed 6/21/01] *Trademark Basics* [Online] www.CopyLaw.com

Javed, Naseem (1993) *Naming For Power: Creating successful names for the business world*, Linkbridge, New York

Jensen, David (2001) *Communication as Value Builder*, Ketchum white paper

Jensen, Rolf (1999) *The Dream Society: How the coming shift from information to imagination will transform your business*, McGraw-Hill, New York

Joachimsthaler, Erich and Aaker, David A (1997) Building brands without mass media, *Harvard Business Review* (January–February) pp 39–50

Jobst, Joseph [accessed 10/23/99] Branding on the net *Global Internet Marketing News* [Online]

John, Deborah Roedder, Loken, Barbara and Joiner, Christopher (1998) The negative impact of extensions: can flagship products be diluted? *Journal of Marketing*, **62** (January) pp 19–32

Kalin, Sari (2001) Brand new branding: forget what you knew about branding, the web changes everything. Four experts explain how and why, *Darwin*, pp 62–68

Kalra, Ajay and Goodstein, Ronald C (1998) The impact of advertising positioning strategies on consumer price sensitivity, *Journal of Marketing Research*, **35** (May) pp 210–24

Kania, Deborah [accessed 10/23/99] *Branding.com*, ClickZ Network [Online] www.searchz. com

Kapferer, Jean-Noel (1997) *Strategic Brand Management*, Kogan Page, London

Keller, Kevin Lane (1998) *Strategic Brand Management*, Prentice Hall, New Jersey

Keller, Kevin Lane (1999) Brand mantras: rationale, criteria and examples, *Journal of Marketing Management*, **15** (1–3) (January–April) pp 43–51

Keller, Kevin Lane, Heckler, Susan E and Houston, Michael J (1998) The effects of brand name suggestiveness on advertising recall, *Journal of Marketing*, **62** (January) pp 48–57

Klein, Naomi (1999) *No Logo: Taking aim at the brand bullies*, Picador, New York

Knapp, Duane E (2000) *The Brand Mindset: How companies like Starbucks, Whirlpool, and Hallmark became genuine brands and other secrets of branding success*, McGraw-Hill, New York

Lindstrom, Martin (2001) *Clicks, Bricks & Brands: The marriage of online and offline brands*, Kogan Page, London

Lindstrom, Martin [accessed 10/23/99] *Offline Versus Online Brands – The winners and losers* [Online] www.searchz.com

Longman, Kenneth A (1997) If not effective frequency, then what? *Journal of Advertising Research*, (July/August) pp 44–50

Mabley, Kevin [accessed 10/23/99] *Branding Matters, But Lesser-Known Causes Can Prevail* [Online] www.cyberdialogue.com

MacRae, Chris (1996) *The Brand Chartering Handbook: How brand organizations learn 'living scripts'*, Addison-Wesley, Harlow

MacRae, Chris (1999) Brand reality, editorial, *Journal of Marketing Management*, **15** (1–3) (January–April) pp 1–24

Martin, David N (1989) *Romancing The Brand: The power of advertising and how to use it*, American Management Association, New York

Martin, David N (2000) *Be the Brand: How to find a powerful identity and use it to drive sales*, New Marketplace/Oaklea Press, Richmond, Virginia

McEwen, Rob (1998) Brand interaction: the oft-neglected element of online branding, *Web Commerce Today*, **15** (October 15)

McEwen, Rob [accessed 10/23/99] *The Little Things That Make A Difference* [Online] ClickZ Network, www.searchz.com

Mei-Pochtler, Antonella and Airey, Philip *The Brandnet Company*, Boston Consulting Group pamphlet

Michaels, Nancy and Karpowicz, Debbi J (2000) *Off-The-Wall Marketing Ideas: Jumpstart your sales without busting your budget*, Adams Media Corporation, Holbrook, Massachusetts

Mitchell, Alan (1999) Out of the shadows, *Journal of Marketing Management*, **15** (1–3) (January–April) pp 25–42

Moore, James (1999) *The Death of Competition: Leadership and strategy in the age of business ecosystems*, Wiley, New York

Morgan, Adam (1999) *Eating the Big Fish: How challenger brands can compete against brand leaders*, John Wiley, New York

Morgan, Anderson & Company (1997) *How Marketers Are Refocusing To Protect and Enhance Their Companies' Brand Assets: Organizing for the betterment of the brand*, White Paper no 5, Morgan, Anderson & Company, New York

Moskin, Jonathon E (1997) Innovation is key to fending off copycats, *Advertising Age* (May 26) p 24

Murphy, William [accessed 6/26/01] *Implementing a Plan to Protect Your Company's Trade Secrets* [Online] www.alllaw.com/articles/intellectual_property/article7.asp

Nagle, Thomas T and Holden, Reed K (1995) *The Strategy and Tactics of Pricing: A guide to profitable decision making,* Prentice Hall, Upper Saddle River, NJ

Ogilvy, David (1985) *Ogilvy On Advertising,* Vintage, New York

Olive & Olive [accessed 6/26/01] *Patents, Trademarks, Copyrights and Trade Secrets: A primer for business executives, entrepreneurs, and research administrators*, Olive & Olive, Pennsylvania [Online] www.oliveandolive.com

Osborne, Dawn, *Trade Marks on the Internet: Not just a matter of domain names and meta tags*, INT Media Group [Online] www.domainnotes.com

Pecaut, David *Brand Renaissance*, Boston Consulting Group pamphlet

Peters, Tom (1997) *The Circle of Innovation*, Alfred A Knopf, New York

Pine, B Joseph II, and Gilmore, James H (1998) Welcome to the experience economy, *Harvard Business Review* (July–August)

Poffenberger, Albert T (1925) *Psychology in Advertising*, A W Shaw, Chicago

Pratkanis, Anthony and Aronson, Elliot (2000) *Age of Propaganda: The everyday use and abuse of persuasion*, W H Freeman, New York

Quek, Patrick (1999) *Return on Marketing Dollars* (November) [Online] www.hotel-online.com/Neo/Trends/PKF/Special/MarketingDollars_Nov99.html

Rabuck, Michael J and Rosenberg, Karl E (1997) Some observations on advertising for large brands, *Journal of Advertising Research* (May/June) pp 17–25

Ries, Al and Ries, Laura (1998) *The 22 Immutable Laws of Branding: How to build a product or service into a world-class brand*, HarperCollins, New York

Ries, Al and Ries, Laura (2000) *The 11 Immutable Laws of Internet Branding,* HarperCollins, New York

Ries, Al and Trout, Jack (1993) *The 22 Immutable Laws of Marketing: Violate them at your own risk!* HarperCollins, New York

Rivkin & Associates [accessed 6/26/01] Naming Strategies: 33 tips & tactics for generating names, *Naming Newsletter,* Rivkin & Associates [Online] www.namingnewsletter.com

Rivkin & Associates [accessed 6/26/01] Tips & tactics: 10 dos and don'ts for smart naming, *Naming Newsletter,* Rivkin & Associates [Online] www.namingnewsletter.com

Rosen, Emanuel (2000) *The Anatomy of Buzz: How to create word of mouth marketing,* Doubleday, New York

Saatchi & Saatchi Strategic Planning (2001) *From Transactions to Relationships: A relationship-building model of communication*, Saatchi & Saatchi Strategic Planning

Sapherstein, Michael B (1998) *The Trademark Registrability of the Harley-Davidson Roar: A multimedia analysis* (October 11) [Online] http://infoeagle.bc.edu/bc_org/avp/law/st_org/iptf/articles/content/1998101101 html

Schlosser, Eric (2002*) Fast Food Nation: The dark side of the all-American meal*, HarperCollins, New York

Schmitt, Bernd and Simonson, Alex (1997) *Marketing Aesthetics,* Free Press, New York

Schultz, Don and Gronstedt, Anders (1997) Making Marcom an investment: market-driven accounting system splits spending into business-building and brand-building activities, *Marketing Management*, pp 41–49

Schultz, Don E and Bailey, Scott (2000) Customer/brand loyalty in an interactive market-place, *Journal of Advertising Research* (May–June) pp 41–52

Schultz, Don E, Tannenbaum, Stanley I and Lauterborn, Robert F (1995) *Integrated Marketing Communications*, NTC Business Books, Illinois

Settle, Robert B and Alreck, Pamela L (1986) *Why They Buy: American consumers inside and out,* John Wiley, New York

Sheldon & Mak [accessed 6/26/01] *How Distinctive is It?… The inherently distinctive test as applied to trademarks*, Sheldon & Mak Service Marks and Product Designs [Online] www.usip.com/articles/inherent.htm

Shultz, Don E and Walters, Jeffrey S (1997) *Measuring Brand Communication*, ROI Association of National Advertisers [Online] www e-ratings.at/pubs/ci/2001/q2/features/measuring.htm

Silverstein, Michael (1998) *Creating a Flawless Brand Experience*, Boston Consulting Group pamphlet

Silvester, Simon *World Waves: Global trends for global brands*, Silvester Research Ltd [Online] www.silvester.com

Simon, Carol J and Sullivan, Mary W (1993) The measurement and determinants of brand equity: a financial approach, *Marketing Science*, **12** (1) (Winter) pp 28–52

Spoelstra, Jon (2001) *Marketing Outrageously: How to increase your revenues by staggering amounts!* Bard Press, Austin, Texas

Stalk, George, Jr, Pecaut, David K and Burnett, Benjamin (1996) Breaking compromises, breakaway growth, *Harvard Business Review* (September–October) pp 131–39

Stewart, David and Furse, David H (1988a) Analysis of the impact of executional factors in advertising performance, *Journal of Advertising Research*, **27** (6 December 1987/January 1988), pp 45–50

Stewart, David and Furse, David H (1988b) Analysis of the impact of executional factors in advertising performance, *Journal of Advertising Research*, **40** (6 November/December), pp 85–88

Stimulating Creativity in Computer Mediated Learning: Individual and collaborative approaches [accessed 8/4/01] [Online] http://home.okstate.edu/homepages.nsf/toc/EPSY5720cm119

Stolzenberg, Martin and Lebenson, Peggy (1996) Tracking the obvious: new ways of looking at old problems, *Advertising Research Foundation Advertising and Brand Tracking Workshop*, November 12–13, pp 148–68

Sulham, Priscilla L (1999) Trademark infringement: take steps to protect company brand online, *American City Business Journals*, July 16, 1999 print edition of the *Puget Sound Business Journal* [Online] http://seattle.bcentral.com/seattle/stories/1999/07/19/focus12.htm

Sullivan, Luke (1998) *Hey Whipple, Squeeze This: A guide to great ads*, John Wiley, New York

Sutherland, Max and Sylvester, Alice K (2000) *Advertising and the Mind of the Consumer: What works, what doesn't and why*, St Leonards, NSW

Sutherland, Max and Holden, Stephen (1997) Slipstream marketing, *Journal of Brand Management*, **4** (6) pp 401–06

Tchong, Michael (1998) Branding on the Web, *ICONOCLAST: Business 2 0's Newsletter for Internet Marketing Executives* (August 12)

Temporal, Paul (2001) *Branding in Asia: The creation, development and management of Asian brands for the global market*, John Wiley, Singapore

Temporal, Paul and Trott, Martin (2001) *Romancing the Customer: Maximizing brand value through powerful relationship management*, John Wiley, New York

Thomas L Harris/Impulse PR (1999) *The Basic Heuristics of Directed Creativity*, Thomas L Harris/Impulse PR Client Survey [Online] www.directedcreativity.com/pages/Heuristics.html

Tilley, Catherine (1999) Built-in branding: how to engineer a leadership brand, *Journal of Marketing Management*, **15** (1–3) (January–April) pp 181–91

Travis, Daryl (2000) *Emotional Branding: How successful brands gain the irrational edge,* Prima Venture, Roseville, California

Trout, Jack (2001) *Big Brands Big Trouble: Lessons learned the hard way,* John Wiley, New York

Trout, Jack with Rivkin, Steve (1997) *The New Positioning: The latest on the world's #1 business strategy,* McGraw-Hill, New York

Upshaw, Lynn B (1995) *Building Brand Identity: A strategy for success in a hostile marketplace,* John Wiley, New York

Verbeke, Willem, Ferris, Paul and Thurik, Roy (1997) The acid test of brand loyalty: consumer response to out-of-stocks for their favourite brands, *Journal of Brand Management,* **5** (1) pp 43–52

Wansink, Brian (1997) Making old brands new, *American Demographics* (December) pp 53–58

Weilbacher, William M (1995) *Brand Marketing,* NTC Business Books, Lincolnwood, Illinois

What Makes A Name Good for Protecting Brands and Corporate Identities [accessed 6/26/01] [Online] www.redpatent.com

Williams, Roy H (1999) *Secret Formulas of the Wizard of Ads,* Bard Press, Austin, Texas

Wong, Thomas (2000) *101 Ways to Boost Your Web Traffic: Internet promotion made easier,* Intesync, Union City, California

Brand management quiz

QUESTIONS

1. Can you name three individuals who have successfully branded themselves?
2. Can you describe their brands' essences?
3. Can you identify their target audiences?
4. Can you name three commodities that have been successfully branded?
5. What created the perceived differences between each of those brands and the commodity?
6. What industry is currently trying to transform itself from commodity status through branding?
7. What are some of the ways in which electric utility companies can differentiate themselves?
8. What major brands built their businesses with little or no advertising?
9. Of 25 top brands in 25 different product categories in 1923, how many are still category leaders today?
10. As consumer satisfaction increases in a product category, does consumer loyalty increase or decrease? Why? If you could only use one of the two measures (consumer satisfaction or consumer loyalty), which would you use?
11. If a consumer has a high repeat purchase rate, is he or she necessarily a loyal consumer?
12. Are the heaviest purchasers the most loyal?
13. Give a few examples of 'ingredient branding', branded components of other brands' products or services.
14. Name four or more brands that have become (or run the risk of becoming) category generic descriptors.

15. Which is the most predictive of brand market share? (a) brand loyalty, (b) brand value, (c) brand penetration, (d) brand awareness, or (e) brand differentiation?

ANSWERS

1. Madonna, Dennis Rodman, Martha Stewart, Stephen King, Isaac Asimov, Deepak Chopra, MD, and Marilyn Manson, to name a few.
2. Hint: Create a two-to-three word phrase that captures the 'heart and soul' of each individual.
3. Hint: Create a two sentence description of the type of person who would most appreciate (that is, derive functional, emotional, experiential or self-expressive benefits from) each individual.
4. Bottled water, vodka, chicken, bananas.
5. Hint: (a) What makes you choose one brand over another in the category: consistent quality, taste, health concerns, making a personal statement? (b) What communicates these attributes: brand name, packaging, label, advertising?
6. Electric utilities.
7. Bundled services, environmental/social responsibility, customer service, energy reduction consulting, add-on services, and so on. (Nicor has chosen 'unconditional primal warmth' as its point of difference.)
8. Harley-Davidson, Body Shop, Starbucks, Compaq, Wal-Mart, Haagen-Dazs, Palm Pilot, Hotmail, Trivial Pursuit, ICQ.
9. 20.
10. (a) Decrease, (b) because, as satisfaction increases, most options eventually exceed consumers' requirements. When that happens, consumers become indifferent between brands. (c) Consumer loyalty.
11. No, not necessarily. His or her behavior could be driven by a purchaser frequency program that does not create sustained (or attitudinal) loyalty. The reverse, however, is true. Loyalty should result in high repeat purchase rates.
12. Not necessarily. Often, the most enthusiastic category purchasers buy the product – regardless of brand – whenever and wherever they find it.
13. Dolby, NutraSweet, Intel, Kevlar, Lycra, Nylon, Gore-Tex and Culligan (Culligan water filtration systems are sold within GE appliances).
14. Aspirin, Cellophane, Escalator, Styrofoam, Kleenex, Shredded Wheat, Thermos, Band-Aid, Scotch Tape, Super Glue, Chap Stick, Wite-out, Beer Nuts, Jello, Rollerblade, Bungee Xerox and Palm Pilot.

15. (c). Brand penetration is the most predictive of brand market share. It does not guarantee profitable market share, however. For instance, if it is achieved by 'buying' distribution (by paying retailers high sales terms), it will result in high market share at reduced profit margins. For profitable market share gains, one must focus on all of the drivers of customer brand insistence: awareness, accessibility, value, relevant differentiation and emotional connection.

Index

Visit Kogan Page on-line

Comprehensive information on
Kogan Page titles

Features include

- complete catalogue listings,
  including book reviews and
  descriptions

- special monthly promotions

- information on NEW titles and
  BESTSELLING titles

- a secure shopping basket facility
  for on-line ordering

PLUS everything you need to know about
KOGAN PAGE

http://www.kogan-page.co.uk

Praise for *The Brand Management Checklist*

'*The Brand Management Checklist* is an asset for the beginner and veteran brand builder alike. No matter what size your organization or how great your brand expertise, this book can provide a point of reference and new insights.'

Elizabeth A Hunter, Senior Brand Specialist, Bank of America

'Finally, a road map for the often treacherous journey of building and maintaining great brands. This is an indispensable tool for all marketers. *The Brand Management Checklist* is the essential toolkit for today's (and tomorrow's) brand marketers.'

Jim Harman, Manager, Corporate Advertising, General Electric

'A comprehensive guide unlike any other on the market today. Apply what you learn to your brand building activities and watch the value of your brand and bottom line increase.'

Amy Kelm, Worldwide Consumer Brand Development Manager, Hewlett-Packard

'Brad VanAuken has delivered one of the best brand education and reference tools I have come across. This book will always be within arms' length from my working area for assistance in brand savvy throughout every workday.'

Carole L Sustak, Manager, Marketing Strategy & Branding, AAA National

'Many books have been written about branding in the last 15 years. Many are short and focus on only a few aspects of the complex process of building and nurturing a brand. With *The Brand Management Checklist*, Brad VanAuken has pulled it all together in one of the most comprehensive books ever written on the subject. If you work in marketing, read it. If not, make sure your marketing team has.'

Ron Dix , Senior Vice President, Marketing and Sales, Bush Brothers & Company

'The checklists are an incredibly effective way for any marketer to evaluate and grade their brand's current marketing performance. *The Brand Management Checklist* should really be named *Brands for Dummies*. I'm definitely going to keep this one around and I only wish that I had found it years ago.'

Dan Hucko, Vice President, Corporate Communications and Investor Relations, Harris Interactive Inc

'Brad VanAuken's practical, step-by-step guide to brand management and marketing resonates with experience and insight. Excellent refresher for the most seasoned marketer and a great introduction for those new to the field. I'm keeping a copy on my desk and giving one to everyone in our advertising agency.'

Sharon Napier, President, Wolf Group

'This book surprised me. It's found a newly practical and authoritative way to describe how to do branding. In this, it is quite unlike any of the other 100 plus books on brand that I have read.'

Chris Macrae , Chief Brand Officer, valuetrue.com and author of *World Class Brands* and *Brand Chartering Handbook*

'*The Brand Management Checklist* will be the definitive work on the subject for years to come. All that's needed now is for business men and women with creativity and depth to read it, and work with it. When that happens, Brad VanAuken will have done the marketplace a great service.'

Peter Holloran, President, Cognitive Marketing Inc

'Thank you for your insight. Your book is concise and is an excellent teaching tool for the first-time and experienced brand manager.'

Ernie Avellana, Vice President of Marketing, Control Diabetes Services, a subsidiary of Eli Lilly & Company

'I've referred to the draft copy you sent in December so much that it's getting dog-eared.'

Tom Welle, Advertising Director, Potomac Electric Power Company